Ontologies with Python

Programming OWL 2.0 Ontologies with Python and Owlready2

Lamy Jean-Baptiste

Apress®

Ontologies with Python

Lamy Jean-Baptiste
Université Sorbonne Paris Nord, LIMICS, Sorbonne Université,
INSERM, UMR 1142, Bobigny, France

ISBN-13 (pbk): 978-1-4842-6551-2 ISBN-13 (electronic): 978-1-4842-6552-9
https://doi.org/10.1007/978-1-4842-6552-9

Managing Director, Apress Media LLC: Welmoed Spahr
Acquisitions Editor: Spandana Chatterjee
Development Editor: Matthew Moodie
Coordinating Editor: Divya Modi

Cover designed by eStudioCalamar

Cover image designed by Pixabay

Distributed to the book trade worldwide by Springer Science+Business Media New York, 1 New York Plaza, Suite 4600, New York, NY 10004-1562, USA. Phone 1-800-SPRINGER, fax (201) 348-4505, e-mail orders-ny@springer-sbm.com, or visit www.springeronline.com. Apress Media, LLC is a California LLC and the sole member (owner) is Springer Science + Business Media Finance Inc (SSBM Finance Inc). SSBM Finance Inc is a **Delaware** corporation.

For information on translations, please e-mail booktranslations@springernature.com; for reprint, paperback, or audio rights, please e-mail bookpermissions@springernature.com.

Apress titles may be purchased in bulk for academic, corporate, or promotional use. eBook versions and licenses are also available for most titles. For more information, reference our Print and eBook Bulk Sales web page at http://www.apress.com/bulk-sales.

Any source code or other supplementary material referenced by the author in this book is available to readers on GitHub via the book's product page, located at www.apress.com/978-1-4842-6551-2. For more detailed information, please visit http://www.apress.com/source-code.

Printed on acid-free paper

Table of Contents

About the Author

Lamy Jean-Baptiste is a senior lecturer at Sorbonne Paris Nord University and a member of the LIMICS, a research lab focused on biomedical informatics. He is also the developer of the Owlready2 Python module that allows access to OWL ontologies. He has developed many research prototypes, and one of them (VCM iconic medical language) has been patented in the United States, with three licenses sold to industrial partners.

Jean-Baptiste speaks regularly at artificial intelligence and medical informatics conferences, has written over 50 journal papers, and is a moderator on the Owlready forum on Nabbles. He was awarded the best paper award at MEDINFO 2019, the largest international conference in medical informatics.

About the Technical Reviewers

Tee Diang is a software engineer with a strong background in Python and Java. She studied computer science with a focus on artificial intelligence, game development, and system engineering—from CPUs and the Internet itself to Python's rich history of libraries and standards to DevOps cloud infrastructure. Her most recent projects exemplify her ability to captivate users with her work.

Jeff grew up in the San Francisco Bay Area, surrounded by the burgeoning technology scene. Jeff has 10 years of experience working on development. He currently works at Apple. Jeff writes clean, consistent code. Outside of the work, he enjoys working on open source projects like broaden.io to help people to broaden their skills, broaden their education, and broaden their knowledge.

Acknowledgments

I would like to thank Moushin Gaouar, Appoh Kouame, and Adrien Basse for being among the first to test Owlready, as well as my friends and/or colleagues Rosy Tsopra, Gaoussou Camara, Antoine Gellman, Patricia Nadjar, Antoine Saab, David Perlmutter, Arnaud Rosier, Karima Sedki, Fadi Badra, Jordon Ritchie, Brandon Welch, Lina Soualmia, and Marie-Christine Jaulent for discussions on ontologies, long or short, and sometimes even before the existence of Owlready.

I also thank the ANSM (Agence Nationale de Sécurité du Médicament et des produits de santé, French drug agency) for having funded the VIIIP project (Integrated Visualization of Information on Therapeutic Innovation), during which Owlready was born (at the time under the name "Ontopy").

Finally, I thank all members of the Owlready forum on Nabble (`http://owlready.8326.n8.nabble.com/`) for their requests and their advice, which greatly influenced the content of this book.

CHAPTER 1

Introduction

For the past ten years, formal ontologies have become widely used in computer science to structure data and knowledge. In parallel, the Python programming language has become more and more widespread in teaching, business, and research. However, until recently, there were very few tools and resources dedicated to the use of ontologies in Python. In fact, most books or tutorials on ontologies are quite theoretical and do not address programming, or they are limited to more complex languages like Java.

This problem is particularly important in the biomedical field, where ontologies and Python are widely used. Too often, in my daily life as a teacher and researcher in medical informatics at Sorbonne Paris Nord University, I have seen students and engineers build ontologies that have subsequently not been used. The files remained on a USB key, because it was not easy to integrate ontologies with existing software.

This book exists to fill this gap. It shows how to use Python to easily access ontologies and publish them as dynamic websites, to build new ontologies, perform automatic reasoning, link entities to medical terminologies, or do some research in DBpedia… using Owlready, a Python module I develop since 2013 for "ontology-oriented programming". And, in this book, we will not be afraid to implement ontology-based programs: you will see more source codes than mathematical formulas!

L. Jean-Baptiste, *Ontologies with Python*, https://doi.org/10.1007/978-1-4842-6552-9_1

1.1 Who is this book for?

This book is for anyone who wants to manipulate and build ontologies in Python, or to discover the world of ontologies from a practical point of view, and especially for computer scientists and semantic web application developers, bioinformaticians, scientists in the field of artificial intelligence, students in these disciplines... or simply for the curious!

To read this book, it is recommended to know about object-oriented programming, in Python or in another object-oriented language (Java, C++, etc.). On the other hand, it is not necessary to know the Python language or to master formal ontologies, Chapters 2 and 3 containing reminders.

1.2 Why ontologies?

The concept of ontology comes from the philosophy and works of Plato. In computer science, an ontology is "a formal description of all the entities of a domain and the relations existing between these entities". This definition may seem complicated! It is in fact to describe knowledge in such a way that it can be exploited by a machine, and with a concern for completeness and "universality". Ontologies are part of the so-called "symbolic" artificial intelligence, which consists of structuring knowledge to make it accessible to a computer, as opposed to machine learning (such as neural networks, deep learning, etc.).

The following figure shows a very simple example of ontology in the field of ecology, represented diagrammatically (NB: "Pike" and "Roach" are two fish species):

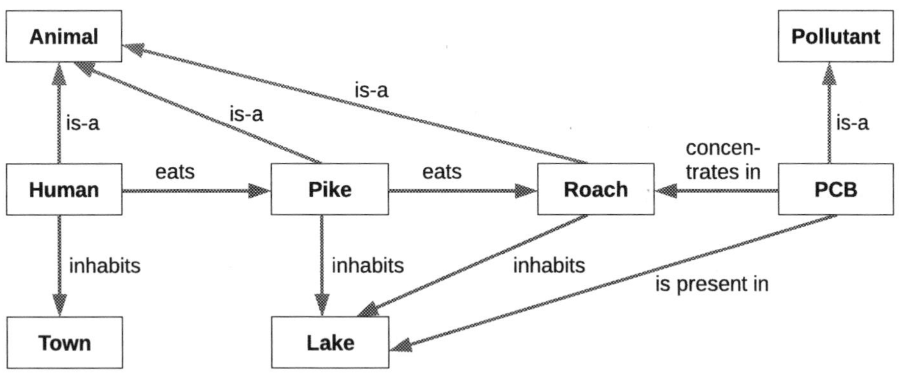

Here, we have eight entities, represented in the rectangles, and relationships between these entities. Several categories of relationship are present:

- Hierarchical "is-a" relations: They link an entity to a more general entity. For example, a human is an animal, pike is an animal, PCB is a pollutant, and so on. In programming, the term "inheritance" is also used to name these relationships.
- Geographical relationships ("lives", "present in"): They indicate the location of an entity, linking an entity to a place. For example, pike are located in lakes.
- Various transversal relationships ("eat", "concentrate in"): For example, the human eats pike.

By consulting this diagram, you will easily deduce that a human is likely to be intoxicated by PCB. The advantage of an ontology is to make this reasoning accessible not only to humans but also to machines: with the help of a software called reasoner, a computer will be able to reproduce this reasoning and to deduce that humans risk to be intoxicated by the PCB.

For this, ontologies rely on description logics (see Appendix A). The OWL language (Web Ontology Language, standardized by the W3C, World Wide Web Consortium) is one of the most used to formalize ontologies. OWL supports a large number of different description logics. The OWL language can be translated into RDF (Resource Description Framework), itself usually expressed in XML (Extensible Markup Language).

Ontologies have two main purposes:

- Automatic reasoning: Since the set of concepts, relations, and their properties is described in a formal way, it becomes possible to automatically perform logical inferences.
- Reuse of knowledge: All ontologies share the same namespace and can be linked together, leading to the *semantic web*.

In addition, there are many tools designed for ontologies, such as the Protégé editor or the HermiT and Pellet reasoners. Working with ontologies allows you to use all of these tools, although for a given project you may not need the full potential of ontologies.

1.3 Why Python?

The programming language most often used to handle ontologies is Java. However, Java is a complex language and, moreover, it is little used in some areas, such as the biomedical field.

On the contrary, the language that rises today is Python, especially in the biomedical field (indeed, several examples of this book will be from biology or medicine). Compared to other programming languages, the main advantage of Python is that it optimizes the programmer's time: Python allows the programmer to develop his/her program faster than with most other languages. More than 15 years ago, that's what convinced me to choose Python, when I realized that I needed only one day to perform in Python a task that would have required three days in Java!

Nowadays, Python is very often used as a glue to link other components, such as databases, websites, text files... or ontologies, as we will see in this book.

1.4 Why Owlready?

Owlready allows "ontology-oriented programming", that is, object-oriented programming in which objects and classes are the entities of an ontology. Ontology-oriented programming is an approach that is both simpler and more powerful than the usual Application Programming Interface (API) in Java, as proposed by OWLAPI and JENA, in which the entities of the ontology do not behave like objects and classes of the programming language.

Owlready provides the best of three worlds:

- **The expressiveness** of formal ontologies, that is to say, the capability to represent complex knowledge in detail, to relate them together, and to reason about this knowledge
- **The access speed** of a relational database, with its fast storage and search capabilities
- **The agility** of object-oriented programming languages such as Python, with the ability to execute "imperative" lines of code giving "orders" to the computer, which is not possible with an ontology or a database alone

Owlready includes a graph database with an OWL semantic level. This database is called *quadstore* because it stores quadruplets in RDF format, that is to say, RDF triples of the form (subject, property, object) to which is added an ontology identifier (see Chapter 11 for a more detailed explanation of RDF and Owlready's quadstore structure).

This quadstore stores all information from loaded ontologies in a compact format. It can be placed in RAM or on disk, in the form of an SQLite3 database file. Then, Owlready loads the ontology entities on demand into Python when they are used, and removes them from RAM automatically when they are no longer needed. In addition, if these entities are modified in Python, Owlready automatically updates the quadstore.

The following diagram shows the Owlready general architecture:

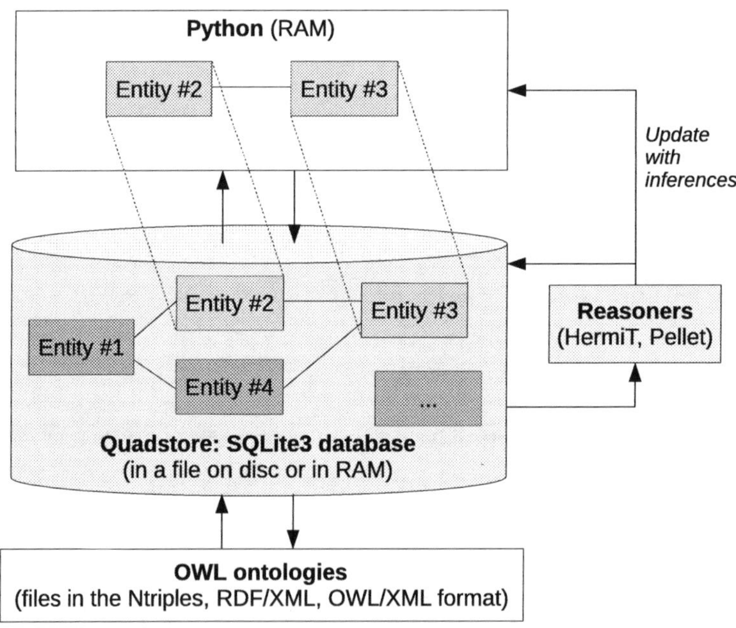

This architecture makes it possible to load voluminous ontologies (several tens or hundreds of gigabytes) while very quickly accessing specific entities, for example, with a textual search. It also allows a level of semantics corresponding to OWL ontologies (unlike many graph databases that are limited to an RDF level). However, Owlready can also be used as a simple object database, a graph database, or an Object-Relational Mapper (ORM), without taking advantage of the benefits that the expressiveness of ontologies can bring.

Owlready is released as free software (GNU LGPL license). This book covers Owlready version 2-0.25 (`owlready2` module). For its installation, you can refer to section 2.11. If you use Owlready in an academic context, please cite the following article:

> Lamy JB. ***Owlready: Ontology-oriented programming in Python with automatic classification and high level constructs for biomedical ontologies***. Artificial Intelligence In Medicine 2017;80:11-28 `http://www.lesfleursdunormal.fr/_downloads/article_owlready_aim_2017.pdf`

1.5 Book outline

The first two chapters contain reminders: Chapter 2 introduces Python, and Chapter 3 is an introduction to OWL ontologies. You can move quickly on these chapters if you already master these notions.

Then Chapters 4, 5, and 6 explain how to manipulate and create ontologies in Python with Owlready. These chapters present the basic features of Owlready.

The following chapters describe more specific features. Chapter 7 is concerned with automatic reasoning, Chapter 8 with annotations and textual search, and Chapter 9 with the management of medical terminologies.

Finally, the last two chapters describe advanced features. Chapter 10 shows how to integrate Python methods into classes of an OWL ontology, and Chapter 11 shows how to access Owlready's RDF quadstore directly.

The source code for this book is available on GitHub via the book's product page, located at `www.apress.com/978-1-4842-6551-2`.

1.6 Summary

In this introductory chapter, we presented formal ontologies, Python, and Owlready, and we drew an outline of the book content.

CHAPTER 2

The Python language: Adopt a snake!

Python is a versatile and easy-to-learn programming language. It has been in existence for almost 30 years, but it remained quite confidential for many years and is now a big success—to the point of being one of the most widely taught programming languages today. The main advantage of Python is its simplicity and time saving for the user: with Python, I achieve in one day what I would program in three days in Java and a week in C. Python allows a significant gain of productivity.

Python is an open source software, and it is available for free. It runs on virtually all existing operating systems (Linux PC, Windows PC, Mac, Android, etc.). There are historically two versions of Python: version 2.x (no longer supported but still used by old programs) and version 3.x (currently supported and recommended). Owlready requires version 3.x, so we'll use this one in this book. However, the differences between the two versions are minimal.

In this chapter, we will quickly introduce the basics of the Python language and its syntax. However, if you have no programming skill yet, we advise you to first consult a book entirely devoted to learning Python. On the contrary, if you already know the Python language, you can go directly to section 2.11 for installing Owlready.

L. Jean-Baptiste, *Ontologies with Python*, https://doi.org/10.1007/978-1-4842-6552-9_2

2.1 Installing Python

Under Linux, almost all distributions offer packages for Python (often these packages will even be already installed). You can check that they are present in the package manager of your distribution and install the package python3 if necessary. Also, install the python3-pip and python3-idle packages if your distribution distinguishes them from the main python3 package.

On Windows, it is necessary to install Python. You can download it from the following address:

`http://python.org/download/`

On Mac OS, Python is probably already installed; you can verify it by running the command "python3 -v" in a terminal. Otherwise, please install it from the preceding website.

2.2 Starting Python

To program in Python, you can either use an integrated development environment (IDE) or use a text editor and a terminal. If you're new to Python, the first option is probably the simplest; we suggest the IDLE environment that is usually installed with Python 3.

Python is an interpreted language, so it can be used in two different modes:

- **The "shell" mode**, in which the computer interprets one by one the lines of code entered by the programmer, as they are entered. This mode is convenient for performing quick tests. The default "Shell" window opened by IDLE corresponds to this mode (see the following example). The ">>>" sign at the beginning of the line is Python's command prompt: the interpreter prompts you to enter a new line of code.

Attention, in "shell" mode, the lines of code entered are not saved and will be lost when closing the terminal or IDLE!

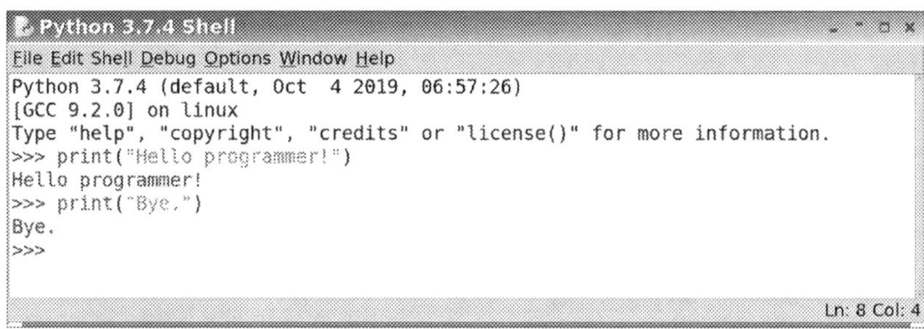

- **The "program" mode**, in which the user writes a multiline program, and then the computer executes the entire program. This mode allows you to perform complex programs. With IDLE, you can create a new program with the File ➤ New file menu. A new window will appear, in which you will write the program (see the following example). The file will then be saved (with the extension .py) and can be executed with the Run ➤ Run module menu (or by pressing the F5 key).

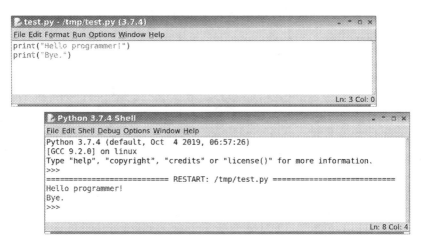

```
test.py - /tmp/test.py (3.7.4)
File Edit Format Run Options Window Help
print("Hello programmer!")
print("Bye.")
                                                    Ln: 3 Col: 0
```

```
Python 3.7.4 Shell
File Edit Shell Debug Options Window Help
Python 3.7.4 (default, Oct  4 2019, 06:57:26)
[GCC 9.2.0] on linux
Type "help", "copyright", "credits" or "license()" for more information.
>>>
========================= RESTART: /tmp/test.py =========================
Hello programmer!
Bye.
>>>
                                                    Ln: 8 Col: 4
```

On Linux, you may prefer to use a text editor to enter programs (e.g., Emacs, Vi) and a terminal to execute them:

- To have a "shell" mode, execute the command "python3" in the terminal:

  ```
  [Bash prompt]#  python3
  Python 3.7.1 (default, Oct 22 2018, 10:41:28)
  [GCC 8.2.1 20180831] on linux
  Type "help", "copyright", credits or "license" for more
  information.
  >>>
  ```

  To quit Python, press Ctrl+D.

- To run a program, run the command "python3 file_name.py" in the terminal (obviously replacing file_name.py with the name of the file where you saved your program, with the path if necessary).

By convention, in this book, we will write short examples of Python code in the manner of the "shell" mode: the Python code is preceded by the command prompt ">>>", while the eventual output displayed by these lines is displayed without this prefix, for example:

```
>>> print("Hello again!")
Hello again!
```

To execute this example, the ">>>" prompt should never be entered (neither in "shell" mode nor in "program" mode). Only the code following the prompt must be entered. When the command occupies multiple lines, Python adds "..." in "shell" mode, as in the following example:

```
>>> print(
... "Still here ?")
Still here ?
```

This is an "end of command" prompt. As before, the "..." should not be entered.

Longer code examples will be presented as programs, as follows:

```
# File file_name.py
print("It's me again!")
print("See you soon.")
```

The first line just indicates the filename; it does not have to be entered in the program.

Finally, in the lines of code, the ↲ character will be used at the end of a line to indicate a line break due to the limited width of the pages of this book. In this case, you do not have to go back to the line when you are programming, for example:

```
>>> x = "This is a very long text here, isn't it?"↲
+ "Indeed, it is."
```

2.3 Syntax

2.3.1 Comments

In Python, anything following the hash character "#" is a comment and is not taken into account by the Python interpreter. Comments are used to give guidance to programmers who will read the program, but ignored by the machine. Here is an example:

```
>>> # This text is a comment, and thus it is ignored by Python!
```

2.3.2 Writing on screen

The print() function is used to write on the screen (in the shell, or on the standard output in the "program" mode); we have already met it previously. It is possible to display several values separated by commas:

```
>>> print("My age is", 40)
My age is 40
```

The print() function can be omitted in the "shell" mode, but it is mandatory in the "program" mode.

```
>>> print(2 + 2)
4
>>> 2 + 2
4
```

2.3.3 Help

Python has a large number of predefined functions. In "shell" mode, the help() function is used to get help on a function, for example, for the print() function:

```
>>> help(print)
```

Then, in the "shell" mode, you may exit the man page by pressing the "Q" key on the keyboard.

2.3.4 Variables

A variable is a name to which a value is associated. Often, the value will only be known when the program is executed (e.g., when it is the result of a calculation).

The name of a variable must start with a letter or an underscore "_", and it can contain letters, numbers, and underscores. Python 3 accepts accented characters in variable names, but spaces are forbidden.

In Python, variables do not need to be declared, and they are not typed. The same variable can therefore contain any type of data, and the type of its value can change during the program. The operator "=" is used to define (or redefine) the value of a variable; it can be read "takes the value of" (be careful, this is not the usual meaning of "=" in mathematics).

```
>>> age = 39
>>> print(age)
39
```

In computation, the names of the variables are replaced by their values:

```
>>> age + 1
40
```

The "=" operator can also be used to redefine the value of a variable. For example, to increase the value of the variable age by 1, we will do:

```
>>> age = age + 1
>>> age
40
```

2.3.5 Indentation

Indentation corresponds to the spaces to the left of the lines of code. Unlike most other programming languages where indentation is just a convention, in Python indentation is significant. Therefore, a bad indentation is a syntax error in Python! In particular, we should not add space on the left outside conditions and loops (which we will see later). The following example shows an indentation error:

```
>>>          age
  File "<stdin>", line 1
    age
    ^

IndentationError: unexpected indent
```

In addition, it is recommended that you do not mix spaces and tabs when indenting Python programs.

2.4 Main datatypes

Python can manipulate various datatypes: integers (abbreviated as *int*), real numbers (often called *float*), Unicode character strings (abbreviated as *str*), and booleans (true or false value, abbreviated as *bool*). The datatype of a variable does not have to be declared and may change during the execution of the program. Here are examples of various datatypes:

```
>>> age        = 31 # Integer
>>> weight     = 64.5 # Floating-point number
>>> name       = "Jean-Baptiste Lamy" # Character string
>>> teacher    = True  # Boolean
>>> student    = False # Boolean
```

2.4.1 Integer (int) and floating-point numbers (float)

Integers are numbers without a decimal part. There are no limits to integer values in Python.

Real numbers are usually represented by floating-point numbers in computer science (they are called "float" because the position of the comma is said to be floating: there can be many digits before the decimal part and few after or vice versa). A dot is used to indicate the decimal part, as in the following example:

```
>>> poids = 64.4
```

In Python, floats actually have a precision equivalent to "double" numbers found in many other programming languages (including C, C++, and Java).

Be careful, 10.0 is a float, while 10 is an integer.

The following table summarizes the main algebraic operations on numbers:

Algebraic operations	Examples
Addition	`>>> 2 + 2` `4`
Subtraction	`>>> 4 - 2` `2`
Multiplication	`>>> 3 * 4` `12`
Division	`>>> 10 / 3` `3.3333333333333`
Integer division	`>>> 10 // 3` `3`
Power	`>>> 3 ** 2` `9`

2.4.2 Booleans (bool)

Booleans can take two values, which are written True (true, integer value 1) and False (false, integer value 0) in Python.

2.4.3 Character strings (str)

Character strings are texts or portions of text. There is no limit on the number of characters (zero, one, or more). Strings are always enclosed in quotation marks (single or double; it is better to use double quotes because the single quotation mark is the same character as the apostrophe). In Python 3, all strings are Unicode and can thus include any character from any language.

```
>>> name = "Jean-Baptiste Lamy"
>>> empty_string = ""
```

To insert special characters in strings, use escape codes starting with a backslash. Here are the most common:

Special characters	Escape codes
Line break	\n
Tab	\t
Backslash	\\
Simple quote	\'
Double quote	\"

In particular, on Windows, backslashes in filenames and paths must be doubled, for example, "`C:\\directory\\file.py`".

Python also allows long character strings, which can span multiple lines and include quotation marks. A long string starts with three quotation marks and also ends with three quotation marks, as in the following example:

```
>>> long_string = """This character string is long
... and may contain line breaks and
... quotation marks " without problems.
... Backslashs \\ must still be doubled, though."""
```

Single quotes can also be used for long character strings.

In Python, everything is an object, including strings. They thus have methods, which we can call with the pointed notation "object.method (parameters,...)". The following table summarizes the main operations and methods on strings.

String operations	Examples

Get the length of a string (= the number of characters)	`>>> s = "Goodbye"`
	`>>> len(s)`
	`7`

Get a character in a string (be careful, the first character is zero and not one; negative numbers are counted from the end)	`>>> s[0]`
	`"G" # First character`
	`>>> s[-1]`
	`"e" # Last character`

Get a part of the string	`>>> s[0:4]` `"Good"`

Find if a string is included in another	`>>> s.find("bye")`
	`4 # Found in position 4`
	`# (return -1 if not found)`

(*continued*)

String operations	Examples

Search from the end of the string (R stands for right)	`>>> s.rfind("o")`
	`2 # Found in position 2`
	`# (return -1 if not found)`

Split a string according to a separator	`>>> "alpha;beta;gamma".↲`
	`split(";")`
	`["alpha", "beta", "gamma"]`

Cut a string according to white spaces (spaces, line breaks, and tabs)	`>>> "alpha beta gamma".↲`
	`split()`
	`["alpha", "beta", "gamma"]`

Replace a part of a string by another string	`>>> "Come here!".↲`
	`replace("here", "there")`
	`"Come there!"`

Concatenate two strings (= put them end to end); be careful you have to add a space if you want one	`>>> "JB" + "LAMY"` `"JBLAMY"`

Format a string with values	`>>> last_name = "LAMY"`
	`>>> first_name = "JB"`
	`>>> "Hello %s!" %↲`
	`first_name`
	`"Hello JB!"`
	`>>> "Hello %s %s!" %↲`
	`(first_name, last_name)`
	`"Hello JB LAMY!"`
	`>>> rate = 90`
	`>>> "Success rate: %s %%"↲`
	`% rate`
	`"Success rate: 90 %"`

2.4.4 Lists (list)

Lists contain zero, one, or more elements (they are similar to arrays in other programming languages, but their size can vary). The elements can be of different types (integers, strings, etc.). The lists are created with square brackets; the elements are given inside the square brackets and separated by commas, for example:

```
>>> my_list    = [0, "Lamy", True]
>>> empty_list = [ ]
```

In a list of n elements, the elements are numbered from zero to $n - 1$. By convention, the lists often receive a plural variable name, for example, "animals" for a list of animals.

Python lists are also objects. The following table summarizes the main operations and methods available on lists.

List operations	Examples

Create a list	`>>> animals = ["elephant",`
	`...            "giraffe",`
	`...            "rhinoceros",`
	`...            "gazelle"]`

Get the length of a list (= the number of elements)	`>>> len(animals)` `4`

Get an element from the list (be careful, lists are numbered from zero and not one)	`>>> animals[0]`
	`"elephant" # First`
	`>>> animals[-1]`
	`"gazelle" # Last`

(continued)

List operations	Examples
Get a part of the list	`>>> animals[0:2]` `["elephant", "giraffe"]`
Add an element at the end	`>>> animals.append("lion")`
Add an element to a given position (0: first position, etc.)	`>>> animals.insert(0, "lynx")`
Concatenate two lists	`>>> [1, 2] + [3, 4, 5]` `[1, 2, 3, 4, 5]`
Remove a given element	`>>> animals.↲` `remove("gazelle")`
Remove the element at a given position	`>>> del animals[-2]`
Find if an element is present in a list	`>>> "lion" in animals` `True`
Sort a list (ascending/alphabetical order by default)	`>>> animals.sort()`

Get the highest element from a list, or the lowest	`>>> max([2, 1, 4, 3])`
	`4`
	`>>> min([2, 1, 4, 3])`
	`1`

2.4.5 Tuples (tuple)

Tuples are very similar to lists, the difference being that they are not modifiable. Tuples are written in parentheses, instead of square brackets:

```
>>> triple               = (1, 2, 3)
>>> pair                 = (1, 2)
>>> single_element_tuple = (1,) # Do not forget the comma here!
```

2.4.6 Dictionaries (dict and defaultdict)

A dictionary (or associative array, hashtable, or hashmap) maps keys to values. For example, a dictionary can match a word with its definition (hence the dictionary name). A dictionary is created with braces, in which are placed zero, one, or more "key: value" pairs, separated by ",". For example (remember that the "..." at the beginning of the lines are part of the Python prompt and should not be entered by the programmer):

```
>>> my_dict = {
...     "fruit"  : "a plant food with a sweet taste",
...     "apple"  : "a fleshy fruit with a red or green skin",
...     "orange" : "a juicy fruit with an orange skin",
... }
```

In the previous example, the keys are "fruit", "apple", and "orange", and the values are the definitions. Each key has one and only one value.

The keys of a dictionary must be immutable (i.e., nonmodifiable). Therefore, we cannot use a list as a key (a tuple is commonly used instead).

Python dictionaries are also objects. The following table summarizes the main operations and methods on dictionaries.

Dict operations	Examples
Get the number of keys (or values) in the dictionary	`>>> len(my_dict)` `3`
Get the value associated with a key	`>>> my_dict["apple"]` `"a fleshy fruit with a red or green skin"`
Add or modify the value for a given key	`>>> my_dict["clef"] = "value"`
Delete a key (and its associated value)	`>>> del my_dict["clef"]`

(*continued*)

Dict operations	Examples
Search if a key is present in the dictionary	`>>> "apple" in my_dict` `True`

Recover all the keys	`>>> for key in my_dict: ...`
	or
	`>>> keys = list(my_dict.↲`
	`keys())`

Recover all the values	`>>> for value in my_dict.↲`
	`values(): ...`
	or
	`>>> values = list(my_dict.↲`
	`values())`

Collect all (keys, values) pairs (as tuples)	`>>> for key, value in↲`
	`my_dict.items(): ...`
	or
	`>>> pairs = list(my_dict.↲`
	`items())`

Python also offers a default dictionary, called `defaultdict`, which is often useful. It is defined in the `collections` module (we will see modules later; in the following example, the first line corresponds to the import of the module; see 2.10.1). When you get a value from a default dictionary and the key is not present in the dictionary, it is automatically added with a default value. When it is created, the `defaultdict` takes a parameter that is the default datatype (it can be a datatype, a function, or a class, which we will see later).

The following example creates a `defaultdict` with the int type. The default value is the integer 0.

```
>>> from collections import defaultdict
>>> d = defaultdict(int)
>>> d["new_key"]
0
>>> d["new_key"] = d["new_key"] + 1
>>> d["new_key"]
1
>>> d["new_key"] = d["new_key"] + 1
>>> d["new_key"]
2
```

Here is a second example that creates a `defaultdict` with the list type. The default value is therefore an empty list. A `defaultdict` of list is commonly used when each key may be mapped to several values (i.e., a list of values).

```
>>> from collections import defaultdict
>>> d = defaultdict(list)
>>> d["new_key"]
[]
>>> d["new_key"].append("a")
>>> d["new_key"]
['a']
>>> d["new_key"].append("b")
>>> d["new_key"]
['a', 'b']
```

2.4.7 Sets (set)

Sets are very close to lists from a functionality point of view, and to dictionaries from an implementation point of view. Unlike lists, elements are not ordered, and there cannot be a duplicate. Sets are written in braces, like dictionaries, but with elements instead of "key: value" pairs:

```
>>> my_set = {1, 2, 1, 3}
>>> len(my_set)
3
```

Note that the duplicate (the second 1) has been removed.

The empty set must be created with the `set()` function, to avoid confusion with an empty dictionary (which is noted as `{}`):

```
>>> empty_set = set()
```

The `add()` method allows you to add an element to a set (it replaces the `append()` method of lists) and the `remove()` method to remove an element.

Classical set operations (union, intersection, etc.) are available via methods and operators ("&" for the intersection, "|" for the union). Immutable sets (`frozenset`) are used as keys in dictionaries, instead of sets. They are to sets what tuples are to lists.

2.4.8 Files (open)

Files are open with the `open()` function:

```
>>> my_file = open("path/filename.ext", "r")
```

The second parameter is the "mode"; it can be one of the following values:

- "r" to read a text file (default value)
- "w" to write a text file

- "rb" to read a binary file
- "wb" to write a binary file

Opening a file for writing automatically creates the file if it does not exist and overwrites it otherwise. Python handles the conversion of line breaks (Unix/Windows/Mac) and the encoding of text files (UTF-8 by default).

File operations	Examples
Read the whole content of the file, as a string	`>>> content = my_file.read()`
Write to a file	`>>> my_file.write("content")`
Close the file (automatically called when the file object is destroyed by Python)	`>>> my_file.close()`

2.4.9 Conversion between datatypes

It is sometimes necessary to convert from one type of data to another. The `int()`, `float()`, `str()`, `list()`, `tuple()`, `set()`, and `frozenset()` functions allow converting a value to an integer, float, string, list, tuple, set, or immutable set, respectively.

Convert to	Syntax
Integer	`int(x)`
Float	`float(x)`
Boolean	`bool(x)`
List	`list(x)`

(continued)

Convert to	Syntax
Tuple	`tuple(x)`
Set	`set(x)`
Immutable set	`frozenset(x)`
Dictionary	`dict(x)` `# x is of the form [(key1, value1), (key2, value2)...]`
String	`str(x)  # String for displaying to the user` `repr(x) # String for displaying to the programmer`

The following example converts the integer 8 to a string:

```
>>> str(8)
'8'
```

2.5 Conditions (if)

The conditions allow executing commands only in certain situations, which will be determined at the execution of the program. The general Python syntax for conditions is as follows:

```
if condition1:
    instruction executed if condition1 is true
    instruction executed if condition1 is true...
elif condition2:
    instruction executed if condition1 is false
    and condition2 is true...
```

```
else:
    instruction executed if condition1
    and condition2 are false...
continuation of the program
(executed whether the conditions are true or false)
```

`elif` is the contraction of `else` and `if`. The "elif" and "else" parts are optional, and several "elif" parts may be present. **The indentation (i.e., the white space at the beginning of the line) is important because it indicates where the condition ends.** The number of spaces is the choice of the programmer but must remain constant, and it is recommended to avoid mixing space characters and tabs.

The condition can use the standard comparison operators:

- < (less than)
- > (greater than)
- <= (less than or equal to)
- >= (greater than or equal to)
- == (equal to, not to be confused with the simple "=" used for defining variables)
- != (different from)
- `is` (test the identity between two objects)

Logical operators "and", "or", and "not" can be used to combine several conditions together, as in the following example:

```
>>> if (age > 18) and (age < 65):
...     print("You are an adult.")
```

When there is only one instruction to execute, it is possible to put everything on a single line:

```
>>> if age >= 65: print("You are an elderly person.")
```

Conditions can be nested, using multiple levels of indentation:

```
>>> if age == 0:
...     print("You are a newborn.")
...     if weight > 10.0:
...         print("I think there is an error in the weight!")
```

2.6 Loops (for)

A loop makes it possible to execute the same commands several times. In Python, loops traverse a list and execute a series of instructions for each element of the list (this is a type of loop often called "for each" in other programming languages). The current element is placed in a variable of your choice. The general syntax of the for loop is as follows:

```
for variable in my_list:
    if conditions1: continue # Move to the next item in the
    list
    if conditions2: break    # Stop the loop
    repeated instructions...
else:
    instructions executed only if the loop went all the way
    (i.e. no break was encountered)
continuation of the program (executed once)
```

The continue instruction interrupts the current iteration and immediately moves to the next element. The break instruction interrupts the loop and exits immediately from the loop. Finally, the else part is executed only if the loop has gone to the end (i.e., it has not been interrupted by break). Of course, the presence of continue, break, and else is not mandatory in a given loop.

The iterated list can be a variable containing a list, but also a string of characters (the loop then iterates over each character of the string), a set (the loop iterates over the elements of the set, in an arbitrary order), a dictionary (the loop iterates over the keys of the dictionary), and so on. It can also be a list of index generated with the range() function:

```
>>> range(4)
```

Be careful, the range() function of Python has nothing to do with the "range" of an OWL property, which we will see later!

Here is an example of a loop. It considers a list of animal names and displays one animal per line:

```
>>> animals = ["elephant", "zebra", "rhinoceros", "dolphin"]
>>> for animal in animals:
...      print(animal)
elephant
zebra
rhinoceros
dolphin
```

If you want to also display the number of each animal in the list, we can use range():

```
>>> for i in range(len(animals)):
...      print(i, animals[i])
0 elephant
1 zebra
2 rhinoceros
3 dolphin
```

Loops can also be integrated in the definition of a list: they are *comprehension lists*. Here is an example:

```
>>> integers      = [1, 2, 3]
>>> even_integers = [2 * i for i in integers]
>>> even_integers
[2, 4, 6]
```

This comprehension list is identical to the list created by the following loop:

```
>>> even_integers2 = []
>>> for i in integers:
...     even_integers2.append(2 * i)
>>> even_integers2
[2, 4, 6]
```

Similarly, Python proposes comprehension sets and dictionaries, for example:

```
>>> twofold = { i: 2 * i for i in integers }
>>> twofold
{1: 2, 2: 4, 3: 6}
>>> twofold[2]
4
```

When one wishes to loop on several lists, two cases can appear:

- The lists are not paired. In this case, we will use nested loops, as in the following example:

  ```
  >>> animals = ["elephant", "zebra", "rhinoceros",↲
  "dolphin"]
  >>> environments = ["savanna", "forest", "river"]
  >>> for animal in animals:
  ...     for environment in environments:
  ```

```
...         print("a", animal, "in the", environment)
a elephant in the savanna
a elephant in the forest
a elephant in the river
a zebra in the savanna
a zebra in the forest
a zebra in the river
a rhinoceros in the savanna
a rhinoceros in the forest
a rhinoceros in the river
a dolphin in the savanna
a dolphin in the forest
a dolphin in the river
```

- The lists are paired, two by two (or three by three, etc., that is to say that the first element of list 1 is associated with the first element of list 2, the second element of list 1 with the second element in list 2, etc.). The `zip()` function allows you to loop on two (or more) paired lists. In the following example, we have a list of animals and a list of environments paired, that is, animal #1 goes with environment #1, animal #2 with environment #2, and so on:

```
>>> animals = ["elephant", "zebra", "rhinoceros",↲
"dolphin"]
>>> environments = ["savanna", "forest", "savanna",↲
"river"]
>>> for animal, environment in zip(animals,↲
environments):
...      print("a", animal, "live in the", environment)
a elephant live in the savanna
```

```
a zebra live in the forest
a rhinoceros live in the savanna
a dolphin live in the river
```

2.7 Generators

A generator makes it possible to browse a series of elements (in the manner of a list); however, it does not store in memory all the elements like a list: the generator produces the elements one by one, and these must be immediately processed (e.g., using a loop). The generator therefore allows a gain in performance, especially when working on large volumes of data. This is why a number of Owlready methods return generators and not lists.

Generators can also be converted into lists with the `list()` function, for example, for display, as follows:

```
>>> print(list(my_generator))
```

On the contrary, to loop on a generator, it is best not to use `list()` to improve performance, as follows:

```
>>> for x in my_generator: print(x)
```

2.8 Functions (def)

Functions are used to define a group of instructions (or "subroutine"), with a view to executing it several times at different places of the main program. This group of instructions can receive parameters: these parameters will be passed to the call of the function and will be available inside the function as local variables. The functions are created with the `def` statement whose general syntax is:

```
def function_name(parameter1, parameter2 = default_value,...):
    function body
    return return_value
```

Functions can receive multiple parameters, and each can have a default value.

The `return` statement indicates the return value of the function, and interrupts it.

Then, the function can be called with parentheses (parentheses are mandatory, even if there are no parameters):

```
returned_value = function_name(parameter1_value, parameter2_
value)
returned_value = my_function_with_no_parameter()
```

Here is a simple example of a function:

```
>>> def twofold(x):
...         return x * 2
>>> twofold(3)
6
>>> twofold("bla")
'blabla'
```

Note that the function parameters are not typed. That's why in the previous example we were able to use our `twofold()` function on both an integer and a string.

When calling the function, the parameters can be named, which allows passing them in any order:

```
returned_value = function_name(parameter2 = parameter2_value,
                               parameter1 = parameter1_value)
```

A function can also have a variable number of parameters:

```
def my_function(*args, **kargs):
    function body
    return returned_value
```

args (*arguments*) will receive a tuple with the values of non-named parameters, and kargs (keyword arguments) a dictionary with named parameters. Here is an example:

```
>>> def function_with_variable_parameters(*args, **kargs):
...     print(args, kargs)
>>> function_with_variable_parameters(1, 2, 3, extra_param = 4)
(1, 2, 3) { "extra_param": 4 }
```

This syntax can also be used when calling a function:

```
>>> kargs = { "parameter1": 1, "parameter2": 2 }
>>> function(**kargs)
# equivalent to function(parameter1 = 1, parameter2 = 2)
```

2.9 Classes (`class`)

2.9.1 Classes and instances

Classes are the basis of object-oriented programming. A class represents a template for creating objects, for example, we may have a class for creating animals or books. A class can also be seen as a general category of objects, for example, a "book" is a general category, and many different books exist with different titles, authors, and so on.

By convention, class names always start with a capital letter (e.g., "Book"). The class defines the available properties for each object of this class (e.g., for the class Book: title, author, and price) and the methods that can be applied to each object (e.g., for the class Book: format a book citation).

The class will then create objects of the class, called "instances", for example, "The Lord of the Rings" and "Nine Princes in Amber" will be two instances of the same "Book" class. The class therefore makes it possible to "factorize" the part common to the instances: the property definitions and the methods, while the values of the properties are specific to each instance.

In Python, classes are created with the `class` statement. The methods are created inside classes with the `def` statement (as for functions); the first parameter represents the object on which the method is applied (it is called `self` by convention; it is equivalent to the keyword `this` in Java or C++ but appears explicitly in the method parameters). Attributes are not typed, just like variables. They are defined by giving them a value, with the syntax "`self.attribute_name = value`".

The general syntax of the `class` statement is:

```
class my_class(parent_class1, parent_class2,...):
    class_attribute_name = value

    def __init__(self, parameters...): # constructor
        self.object_attribute_name = value

    def method1(self, parameters...):
        method_body
        return returned_value
    def method2(self, parameters...):
        method_body
        return returned_value
```

When a class is empty (it does not contain any method), it is necessary to add a `pass` statement, to indicate it to Python:

```
class my_empty_class(parent_class1, parent_class2,...):
    pass
```

In the body of methods, the "`self`" active object must always be specified when one wants to obtain or modify its attributes (`self.attribute`) or to call its methods (`self.method(parameters...)`).

`__init__()` is a special method called a "constructor". If present, the constructor is automatically called when a new instance is created. The constructor can receive parameters, whose values will be given when the instance is created.

Here is an example of a definition of the "Book" class:

```
>>> class Book(object):
...     def __init__(self, title, author, price):
...         self.title  = title
...         self.author = author
...         self.price  = price
...     def format_citation(self):
...         return '%s' by %s (price: %s€) % (self.title,↲
                self.author, self.price)
```

In the previous definition, we defined the Book class from the `object` class, which is the most general class in Python.

Then, to create an instance of a class, the class is called in the manner of a function. Any parameters will be passed to the `__init__()` constructor.

```
my_object = my_class(constructor_parameters...)
```

The dotted notation is used to access the attributes and methods of the object:

```
print(my_object.attribute)
my_object.attribute = value
my_object.method(parameters...)
```

The `self` parameter is **never** given when calling the method on an instance. The previous call is equivalent to

```
my_object_class.method(my_object, parameters...)
```

For example, we can create one or more instances of the Book class, obtain their property values or modify them, and call their methods:

```
>>> ldr = Book("The Lord of the Rings", "JRR Tolkien", 24)
>>> npa = Book("Nine Princes in Amber", "R Zelazny", 12)
>>> npa.author
'R Zelazny'
>>> npa.price = 10
>>> npa.format_citation()
"'Nine Princes in Amber' by R Zelazny (price: 10€)"
```

2.9.2 Inheritance

Inheritance is a fundamental mechanism in object-oriented programming. This mechanism allows you to create new classes that share a similar blueprint to a given class, that is to say, to define subcategories within a class. For example, comics are a particular subcategory of books: the Comic class is a subclass that inherits from Book. The general class (here, Book) is called the "superclass" or "parent class", and the more specific class (here, Comic) is called the "subclass" or the "child class".

The child class inherits all the attributes and methods of its parent class(es): just like the instances of the Book class, those of the Comic class have a title, an author, and a price (attributes), and it is possible to format a citation (method). However, the child class may have additional attributes and methods. For example, a comic book is characterized by its author (or scriptwriter) but also by its illustrator: we can therefore add an "illustrator" attribute to the Comic class. Inheritance makes it possible to "factorize" the source code and to simplify it by avoiding repeating the attributes and methods common to the parent class and its children classes.

In addition, it is possible to redefine the methods of the parent class in the child class. For example, the constructor of the Comic class can be redefined to accept an additional "`illustrator`" parameter, and the format_citation() method can be redefined to display the illustrator name. When redefining a method, it is possible to delegate to the parent class method by calling the parent class using the keyword super(), as in the following example:

```
class my_child_class(my_parent_class1, my_parent_class2,...):
    def my_method(self, parameters...):
        parent_returned_value = super().my_method
        (parameters...)
        additional child class method body
        return child_return_value
```

The following example defines the Comic class, inheriting from the Book class:

```
>>> class Comic(Book):
...     def __init__(self, title, author, illustrator, price):
...         super().__init__(title, author, price)
...         self.illustrator = illustrator
...     def format_citation(self):
...         return "'%s' written by %s and illustrated by %s↲
(price: %s€)" % (self.title, self.author, self.illustrator,↲
self.price)
```

The constructor method __init__() and the format_citation() method have been redefined in the Comic child class. The new constructor definition supports the illustrator attribute and delegates to the parent class method for managing the title, author, and price attributes.

The following example creates an instance of Comic:

```
>>> re = Comic("Return to the Earth", "Yves Ferry",↲
"Manu Larcenet", 10)
>>> re.format_citation()
"'Return to the Earth' written by Yves Ferry and illustrated by↲
Manu Larcenet (price: 10€)"
```

Note that we can call the `format_citation()` method without knowing if the object on which we call it is a Book or a Comic. Python will automatically choose the right method, depending on the class of the object. This mechanism is called *polymorphism.*

The following example goes through the three instances we created and displays their citation. The `x` variable sometimes contains a Book and sometimes a Comic, and the `format_citation()` method is called without knowing the exact class of the object `x`.

```
>>> for x in [ldr, npa, re]:
...     print(x.format_citation())
"'The Lord of the Rings' by JRR Tolkien (price: 24€)"
"'Nine Princes in Amber' by R Zelazny (price: 10€)"
"'Return to the Earth' written by Yves Ferry and illustrated↲
by Manu Larcenet (price: 10€)"
```

Python also allows multiple inheritance: several parent classes can be given when defining a child class, separated by commas.

2.9.3 Special method names

In Python, method names with two underscores at the beginning and end are special methods. Here are the main ones:

- `__init__(self, parameters...)`: Constructor
- `__del__(self)`: Destructor
- `__repr__(self)`: Returns a string for displaying to the programmer
- `__str__(self)`: Returns a string for displaying to the final user

2.9.4 Functions and operators for object-oriented programming

The following three attributes and functions can be used to analyze the relationships between objects and/or classes:

- `object.__class__` returns the class or the type of an object, for example:

```
>>> ldr.__class__
<class 'Book'>
>>> "blabla".__class__
<class 'str'>
```

- `isinstance(object, Class)` tests whether the given object belongs to the given class (including child classes, grandchild, *etc.*), for example:

```
>>> isinstance(ldr, Book)
True
>>> isinstance(ldr, Comic)
False
>>> isinstance(re, Book)
True
>>> isinstance(re, Comic)
True
```

- `issubclass(Class, parent_class)` tests whether the given class inherits from `parent_class`, for example:

```
>>> issubclass(Comic, Book)
True
>>> issubclass(Book, Comic)
False
```

The is operator allows testing whether two objects are the same:

```
>>> ldr is ldr
True
>>> ldr is npa
False
```

Finally, the following functions are used to manipulate the attributes of an object when the name of the attribute is not known at the time of writing the program, but is available during execution in a variable (as a string):

- hasattr(object, attribute_name) tests whether the object has an attribute named attribute_name.
- getattr(object, attribute_name) returns the value of the attribute named attribute_name for the object.
- setattr(object, attribute_name, value) defines the value of the attribute named attribute_name for the object.
- delattr(object, attribute_name) deletes the attribute named attribute_name from the object.

```
>>> attribute_name = "author"
>>> hasattr(ldr, attribute_name)
True
>>> getattr(ldr, attribute_name)
'JRR Tolkien'
```

These methods are particularly useful for introspection, that is, for manipulating objects in a generic way, without knowing their class or their attributes.

2.10 Python modules

Python modules define additional functions and classes in a specific domain (such as mathematics, bioinformatics, 3D graphic, etc.). Owlready2 is an example of Python module. The functions and classes contained in these modules are not available by default in Python; it is mandatory to import the corresponding modules before accessing and using them.

2.10.1 Importing a module

There are two ways for importing a module in Python:

1. Importation of the module with its name. With this method, it is necessary to mention the name of the module followed by a "." in front of each of the functions and classes of the module. Here is an example with the `math` module:

```
>>> import math
>>> math.cos(0.0)
1.0
```

2. Import the contents of the module. With this method, the functions and classes of the module can be used directly, without having to mention the name of the module at each call. On the other hand, if several modules define functions or classes having the same name, this could be problematic: in this case, the last import will overwrite the previous one. Here is another example with the `math` module:

```
>>> from math import *
>>> cos(0.0)
1.0
```

The Python language includes a large number of "standard" modules, which are installed with Python itself. The official Python documentation describes each of these modules; it is available online at the following address:

`https://docs.python.org/3/py-modindex.html`

Other modules can be installed from PyPI (Python Package Index), available at

`https://pypi.org/`

2.10.2 Installing additional modules

The "pip3" tool allows downloading, installing, and updating automatically Python 3 modules over the Internet from PyPI. This tool can be used on the shell command line (under Unix/Mac) or in the MS-DOS command prompt (on Windows). The following command line installs a Python module (or update it, if it is already installed):

```
pip3 install -U name_of_the_module_to_install
```

It is preferable to install the modules as "root" (or superuser, under Linux/Mac) or "administrator" (under Windows), so that they are available to all users. However, this is not an obligation: if you do not have the necessary rights for a global installation, you can install the modules only for the current user, with the "`--user`" parameter. The following command line installs a module for the current user:

```
pip3 install -U --user name_of_the_module_to_install
```

2.11 Installing Owlready2

Owlready version 2 can be installed from the Internet with the "pip3" tool; the corresponding module is called "owlready2" (be careful not to forget the version number 2).

In addition, Owlready offers a version optimized in Cython, a language derived from Python compiling in code C. In order to benefit from this optimized version, it is necessary to install beforehand the "cython" module. However, if the installation of Cython went wrong, or if you do not have a C compiler (especially on Windows), you can install Owlready without Cython, at the price of (slightly) reduced performances when loading ontologies.

Finally, the following Python modules will also be used in the rest of the book: "Flask", "MyGene", and "RDFlib".

2.11.1 Installing Owlready2 from terminal

The following commands can be used to install Owlready2 and the other modules in a terminal (Bash terminal under Linux/Mac, DOS command-line interface under Windows):

```
pip3 install -U cython
pip3 install -U owlready2 Flask mygene rdflib
```

If you do not have root or administrator privileges, use the following commands to install the modules for the active user:

```
pip3 install -U --user cython
pip3 install -U --user owlready2 Flask mygene rdflib
```

2.11.2 Installing Owlready2 from IDLE or Spyder (or any Python shell)

You can use the following Python commands to install Owlready2 from any Python 3.7.x console, including those found in the integrated development environment, including IDLE or Spyder3:

```
>>> import pip.__main__
>>> pip.__main__._main(["install", "-U", "--user", "cython"])
```

```
>>> pip.__main__._main(["install", "-U", "--user", "owlready2",
"rdflib")
>>> pip.__main__._main(["install", "-U", "--user",
"Flask", "mygene")
```

2.11.3 Manual installation of Owlready2

In case of troubles, Owlready2 can also be installed manually in five steps:

1. Download the compressed sources from PyPI: `https://pypi.org/project/Owlready2/#files`.

2. Decompress the compressed sources, for example, under "C:\" under Windows.

3. The source directory is named "Owlready2-0.xx" where "xx" is the version number (e.g., "Owlready2-0.25"). Rename this directory as "owlready2", for example, "C:\owlready2".

4. Add the directory containing the source directory ("C:\" in our example) in your PYTHONPATH; this can be done in Python as follows (NB: do not forget to double any backslash!):

   ```
   >>> import sys
   >>> sys.path.append("C:\\")
   ```

5. You can now import Owlready2!

   ```
   >>> import owlready2
   ```

2.12 Summary

In this chapter, we have seen how to perform basic programming in Python, including the language syntax, control structures such as conditions and loops, and object-oriented programming. We also reviewed the main Python datatypes, such as character strings or lists. Finally, we have seen how to install Python modules and in particular Owlready and the other modules needed for the examples in the rest of this book.

CHAPTER 3

OWL ontologies

The term "ontology" comes from philosophy and corresponds to the "science of being". This term was then used in computer science to designate a formal definition of all the objects in a domain and the relationships existing between these objects. It is thus a "formal ontology". An ontology therefore aims to structure and formalize objects in a domain, as independent as possible of the intended application: the ontology can thus be reused for other applications in the same domain.

Concretely, formal ontologies can be used to achieve two objectives:

- Perform automatic reasoning: Formal ontologies allow logical deductions to be made, using a reasoner. For example, an ontology of animals can deduce that a white and black striped animal is actually a zebra. Automatic reasoning will be more particularly on the subject of Chapter 7 of this book.
- Link knowledge from different sources: Formal ontologies use Internet addresses (called IRI, Internationalized Resource Identifier) to identify different entities (or objects). Therefore, all ontologies share the same namespace: any ontology can refer to any other. In addition, ontologies allow the definition of equivalence relationships: thus, if the same thing has

L. Jean-Baptiste, *Ontologies with Python*, https://doi.org/10.1007/978-1-4842-6552-9_3

been declared as two distinct entities in two different ontologies by two different people, a third person can add an equivalence relationship between those entities so that they become one.

These two objectives are complementary, because linking knowledge can make new reasoning possible.

In this chapter, we will explain what a formal ontology is, without going into the theoretical aspects. We will emphasize the similarities and differences between ontologies and the object model used in programming, and we will construct a simple example of ontology which we will then use again to illustrate the examples in the following chapters.

3.1 An ontology… what does it look like?

From a theoretical point of view, an ontology contains axioms. Description logics are used to formalize the definitions of entities and represent them in the form of logical axioms. Appendix A briefly describes these logics. However, it doesn't matter if you don't understand description logics and the associated formulas—I myself started using formal ontologies long before I knew or understood these formulas! This will not prevent you from programming your first ontologies in the rest of this book or even using the ontologies effectively.

From a practical point of view, an ontology makes it possible to define a model, in the manner of classes and instances of programming languages like Python (see 2.9), but with a higher level of expressiveness, that is to say, in much more detail. Ontology and object-oriented programming therefore share many elements in common, but often use different terms to refer to identical or very similar things. The following table gives a correspondence between the vocabularies of the world of object-oriented programming and that of formal ontologies:

Object-oriented programming	Formal ontology
Object	Entity
Module	Ontology
Class	Class
Class inheritance	Class inheritance, also called "is-a" relation
— (no equivalent)	Property inheritance
Instance	Individual
Attribute or property	Property, role, or predicate
Value of an attribute for an instance	Relation
Class name	IRI
Datatype	Datatype
Method	— (no equivalent)
— (no equivalent)	Logical constructor Restriction Disjoint

The ontology-oriented programming, which we will see in the next chapter, will bring these two worlds together.

An ontology is therefore a set of entities, which can be classes, properties, or individuals. Compared to the object model of Python (or any other object-oriented programming language), we have three main differences:

- Properties are defined independently and outside the classes.

- Individuals can belong to one class, but also to several classes (this is multiple instantiation, which is similar to multiple inheritance, but for instances).
- The ontology is based on the Open-World assumption: that is, anything that is not expressly prohibited is considered possible. For example, if we define that the book "The Lord of the Rings" has as author "JRR Tolkien", the Open-World assumption leaves the possibility that other additional authors exist for this book. Since JRR Tolkien is the sole author, we must also indicate that "The Lord of the Rings" has no other authors than "JRR Tolkien" (typically using an OWL restriction).

Several languages exist for ontologies; OWL (Web Ontology Language) is by far the most widely used today. OWL ontologies can be saved in files in RDF/XML format (the most common format), but also in OWL/XML, N-Triples, Turtle, and other formats.

3.2 Creating ontologies manually with the Protégé editor

It is possible to create an ontology by hand with an ontology editor. By far the most used editor is Protégé. It is available free of charge at the following address: `https://protege.stanford.edu`. We will use it later to build our example ontology on bacteria.

3.3 Example: An ontology of bacteria

In order to illustrate the construction of an ontology and the possibilities it can offer, we will take as an example an ontology of bacteria. This ontology aims to describe bacteria and their physical and chemical characteristics. We will, however, limit ourselves to a few simple characteristics and a small number of species for obvious reasons of brevity. I apologize in advance to my biologist readers for the sometimes crude simplifications that we will have to carry out—the conception of a complete and exact ontology of bacteria would constitute a real research work in its own right!

We will only retain the following three characteristics for describing bacteria:

1. Their shape: Bacteria can be round or rod shaped (elongated shape).

2. Their grouping: Bacteria can be isolated from each other or grouped in pairs, in clusters, or in chains, which can be small or long chains.

3. Their Gram status: Gram + bacteria are colored by the Gram test, unlike Gram - bacteria.

Figure 3-1 shows a classification of bacteria according to these characteristics. Round bacteria are called "coccus", and rod ones are called "bacillus".

In addition, we will only retain the following three families of pathogenic bacteria:

1. Staphylococcus: Round shape, grouped in clusters, Gram +

2. Streptococcus: Round shape, grouped in small chains but never isolated, Gram +

3. Pseudomonas: Rod shape, grouped in pairs or isolated, Gram –

Thereafter, we will consider that a bacterium can have several groupings: indeed, the observation never relates to a single bacterium but on several. It is therefore common to observe several groupings for the same species of bacteria: for example, Staphylococci which group in clusters may occasionally be present singly or in pairs. However, Streptococci are never isolated but always grouped (in pairs, in clusters, and, of course, preferably in chains).

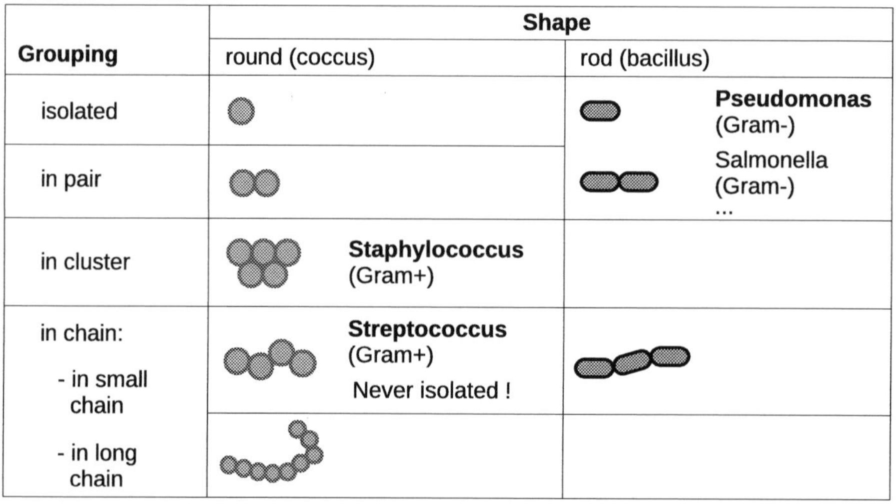

Grouping	**Shape**	
	round (coccus)	rod (bacillus)
isolated		**Pseudomonas** (Gram-) Salmonella (Gram-) ...
in pair		
in cluster	**Staphylococcus** (Gram+)	
in chain: - in small chain	**Streptococcus** (Gram+) Never isolated !	
- in long chain		

Figure 3-1. *Simple classification of bacteria according to three criteria*

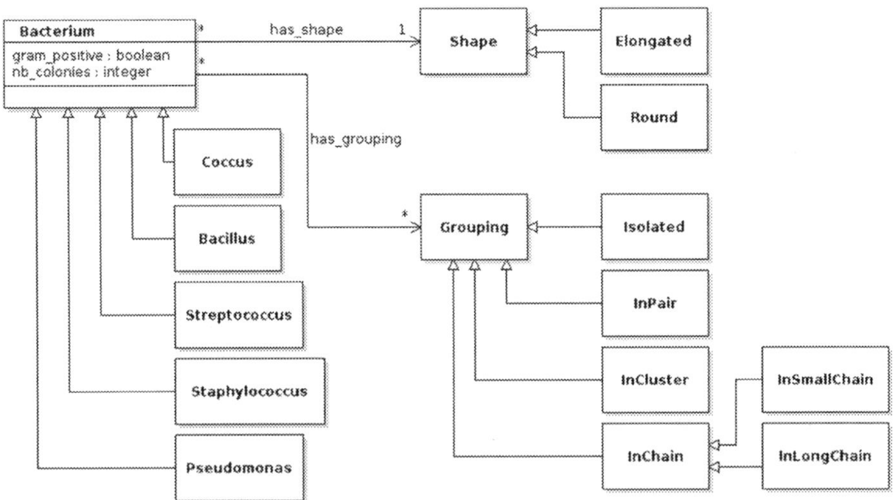

Figure 3-2. *UML class diagram of the bacteria ontology*

Figure 3-2 gives the class diagram in UML (Unified Modeling Language). Please note, however, that ontologies allow more information to be represented than what appears on the class diagram. For example, (practically) all Gram + bacteria of round form grouped in clusters are Staphylococci. For this species, it will therefore be possible to deduce the class of bacteria, its shape, grouping, and Gram status. On the contrary, Pseudomonas are not the only bacteria of rod shape, isolated, or in pairs. This is an important difference because it will impact automatic reasoning; however, a "classic" object model (like that of Python; see 2.9) does not allow taking it into account.

At the very beginning of this chapter, we defined an ontology as "as independent as possible from the intended application". For example, the ontology of bacteria could have multiple applications, such as:

- Create an encyclopedic website describing the properties of the different bacteria (see 4.12)
- Facilitate the entry or extraction of information on bacteria (see 5.14)

- Help identify an unknown bacterium (see 7.7)
- Enrich with information on bacteria already existing ontologies or resources, such as UMLS (see 9.10)
- Facilitate statistical studies in a hospital by allowing the grouping of similar bacteria (to answer questions such as "has the number of infections with anaerobic bacteria increased in the last month?")

Each of these applications could be achieved with a specific knowledge base. For example, the identification of bacteria could be done with a knowledge base composed of rules like the following one:

IF shape = round AND grouping = in cluster AND gram = '+'

THEN staphylococcus

However, an ontology is capable of achieving **all** these applications from the same source of knowledge, which greatly facilitates the maintenance and reuse of this knowledge.

In the following sections, we will build a (small) formal ontology in OWL from this classification of bacteria, using the Protégé editor.

3.4 Creating a new ontology

When you launch the Protégé editor, it automatically creates a new empty ontology. The editor includes several tabs; by default, the Active Ontology tab is displayed.

In this tab, we will define the IRI of our ontology. The IRI is the "name" of the ontology, and this name takes the form of an Internet address. Please note, however, the IRI must be in the form of an Internet address, but the ontology does not need to be available on the Internet at this address! It is thus usual to create ontologies whose IRI begins with "`http://www.semanticweb.org/`" or "`http://www.test.org/`", without holding the rights to these Internet domain names.

We will call our bacteria ontology:

```
http://lesfleursdunormal.fr/static/_
downloads/bacteria.owl
```

(NB: This Internet address points to my personal site, on which you can actually download the full ontology). You can enter this IRI in the "Ontology IRI" field of Protégé, as shown in the following screenshot:

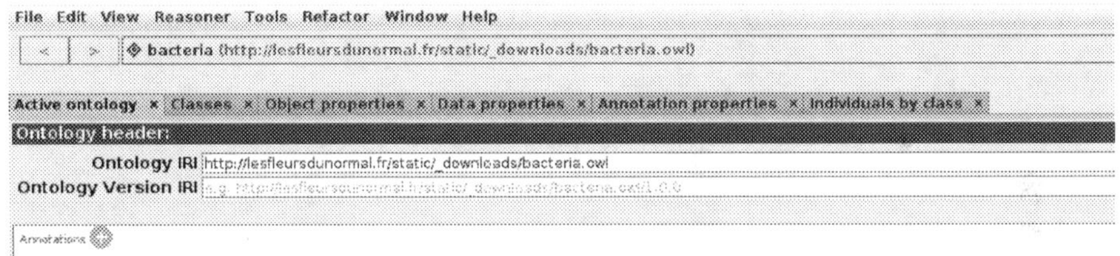

You can then save the ontology in RDF/XML format, in a file that you will call "bacteria.owl". Do not forget thereafter to regularly save the ontology during its edition.

3.4.1 Classes

In Protégé, the "Classes" tab allows you to navigate through existing classes and to create new classes. The buttons and allow you to create a new daughter or sister class of the selected class, respectively. Using these buttons, we can create a class hierarchy corresponding to our previous UML model, as in the following screenshot:

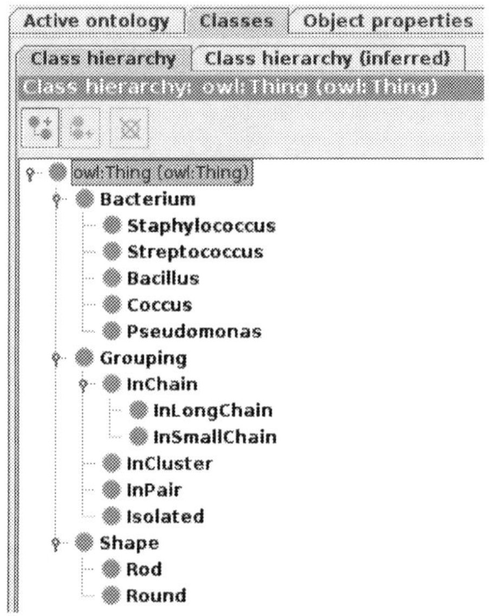

In ontologies, inheritance is also called "is-a relationship": for example, we can say that a Pseudomonas *is a* Bacterium.

3.4.2 Disjoints

An important difference between an ontology and an object model is as follows: in an ontology, an individual can belong to *several* classes. Therefore, a given shape could very well be *both* round and rod! The Open-World assumption allows this type of interpretation: anything that is not formally prohibited is considered possible.

In our ontology of bacteria, we want to prohibit this: a given shape is either round or rod, but cannot be both at the same time. For this, we must declare the two classes Round and Rod as *disjoint*. Two disjoint classes cannot have individuals in common.

The disjoint classes are declared in the "Description" panel of the "Classes" tab. We will select the Rod class and then click the "+" button to the right of the "Disjoint with" section and choose the Round class in the "Class hierarchy" tab of the dialog box. You should get the following result:

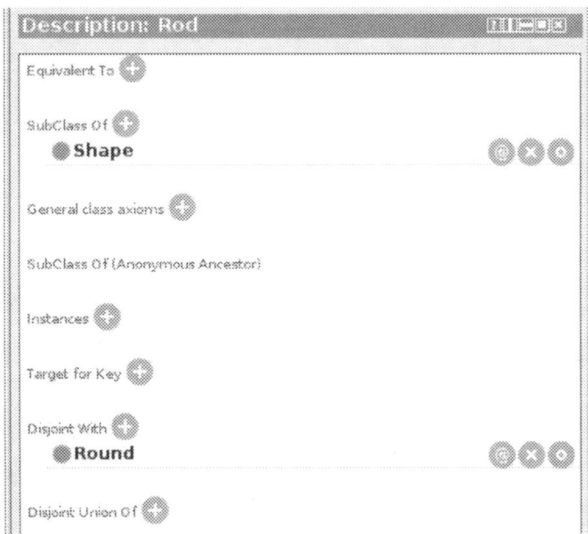

The two classes are now disjoint. Note that it is not necessary to declare the second class (Round) disjoint from the first (Rod): this is automatically deduced from the previous declaration.

In the same way, the InSmallChain class must be declared disjoint from the InLongChain class.

The Isolated, InPair, InCluster, and InChain classes must be declared as *pairwise disjoint*: that is to say that any pair made up of two classes from this list are disjoint. To do this, simply select one of the classes (e.g., Isolated), click the "+" button to the right of "Disjoint with", and select the other three classes simultaneously (by pressing the control key, not by clicking three times the "+" button!). The result should be as follows:

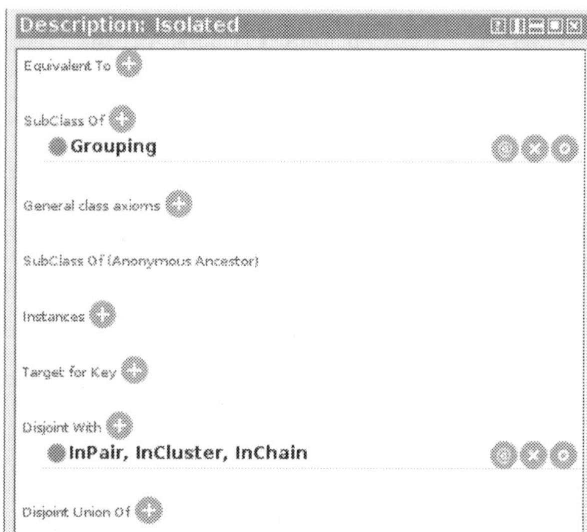

Attention, concerning the subclasses of Grouping, the disjoint does not mean that a given bacterium cannot be observed with two different groupings (e.g., Isolated or InPair, like Pseudomonas). The disjoint only means that a given grouping cannot be both Isolated and InPair, but it does not prohibit a bacterium from having two distinct groupings, one of the class Isolated and the other of the class InPair.

In the same way, the classes Bacteria, Shape, and Grouping must be declared disjoint: for example, a geometric shape cannot be the same thing as a bacterium! It may seem obvious to a human, but remember that it is not to a machine. Ontologies seek to formalize knowledge comprehensively, including the most obvious piece of knowledge.

3.4.3 Partitions

We have defined two classes of shapes, Round and Rod, which are now disjoint. However, we have not excluded the existence of other shapes, for example, triangular. Again, the Open-World assumption makes such interpretations possible. However, there are only two possible shapes for a bacterium: Round or Rod. We must declare that all Shape is either Round or Rod: it is a partition (we will say that the classes Round and Rod constitute a partition of the class Shape).

To do this, we select the Shape class, and, in the "Description" panel, we click the "+" to the right of "SubClass Of". This "+" button allows you to add superclasses to the class; these can be named classes, but also OWL logical constructors, like here. In the dialog box that appears, we select the "Class expression editor" tab, and we enter the constructor "Round or Rod". You should obtain the following result:

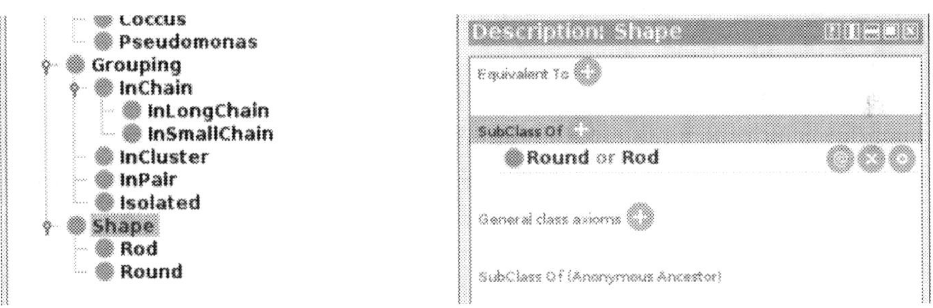

This constructor "or" allows two classes to be linked with a logical OR (also called a *union*, when we think in set logic). It means that the Shape class is a subclass of the union of the Rod and Round classes. Consequently, any shape is now either round or rod, and there are therefore no other possible shapes.

In the same way, we must partition InChain (SubClass Of "InSmallChain or InLongChain") and Grouping (SubClass Of "Isolated or InPair or InCluster or InChain").

3.4.4 Data properties

We will now deal with the properties. In ontologies, unlike object-oriented programming, properties are defined independently of classes. OWL considers three categories of properties: data properties whose values are data (numbers, texts, dates, Booleans, etc.), object properties whose values are entities (i.e., ontology individuals), and annotation properties which do not intervene in semantics or reasoning and can therefore mix data and entities without restriction.

In Protégé, the "Data Properties" tab allows you to create data properties. OWL supports inheritance between properties, in addition to inheritance between classes; however, we will not use it here. Using the and buttons, which work similarly to those for classes, we will create two new data properties called "gram_positive" and "nb_colonies". This last property will not be really useful to describe bacteria, but it will serve as an example of numeric data property.

You should arrive at the following result:

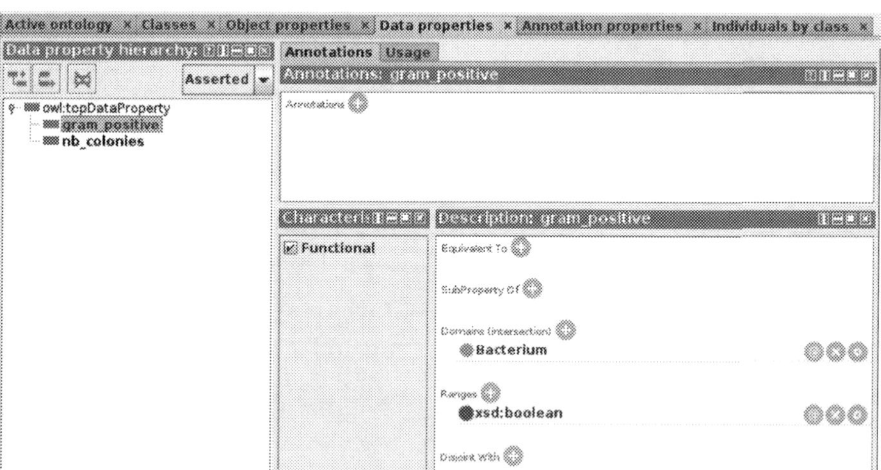

Each data property can be configured by specifying:

- Its *domain* ("Domains (intersection)" in Protégé): This is the class for which the property is defined.
- Its *range* ("Ranges"): This is the associated datatype. It can be an integer or a real number, Boolean, character string, date, and so on. Please note: to work with Python and Owlready afterward, it is preferable to use the types integer for integer numbers and decimal for real numbers (refer to Table 4-1 for more information). Attention, the range of an OWL property has nothing to do with the Python `range()` function which allows you to create lists of numbers (see 2.6).
- Its *functional* status ("Functional" checkbox): When a property is functional, a given individual can have (at most) only one value for this property. On the contrary, if the property is not functional, a given individual can have several values.

Domain and range are optional. It is possible to define several domains and ranges; however, it is the **intersection** of the different domains/ranges that is considered and not their union, which is often not the desired result. For example, consider the property "has_shape" and two classes, Bacteria and Viruses, of which individuals can have a shape. If we define two domains, Bacteria and Virus, only individuals belonging to *both* the Bacteria class and the Viruses class can have a shape! If one wants to say that all Viruses and all Bacteria may have a shape, it is necessary to define the domain as being the *union* of classes, that is to say, "Bacterium or Virus".

Here, we will configure our two data properties as follows:

- gram_positive: Functional (check the box), domain: Bacteria, range: Boolean
- nb_colonies: Functional (check the box), domain: Bacteria, range: integer

3.4.5 Object properties

In Protégé, the "Object Properties" tab allows you to create object properties. Using the and buttons, we create four new object properties called "has_shape", "has_grouping", "is_shape_of", and "is_grouping_of", as in the following screenshot:

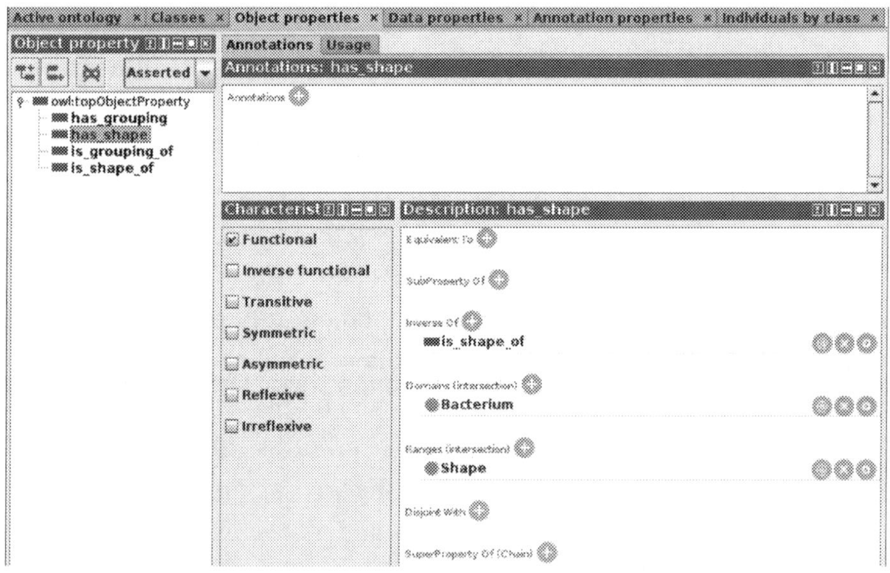

Each object property can be configured by specifying:

- Its *domain* ("Domains (intersection)" in Protégé): This is the class for which the property is defined.

- Its *range* ("Ranges (intersection)"): This is the class of associated objects.

  As before, if several domains or ranges are indicated, it is their intersection that is considered.

- Its *inverse property* ("Inverse Of"): The inverse property corresponds to existing relationships when the property is read backward; if a property exists between A and B, then its inverse property exists between B and A. For example, the property "is_shape_of" is the inverse of "has_shape": if a bacterium X has the shape A, then A is the shape of X. These inverse properties will be useful in Python to navigate using the relation has_shape/is_shape_of in both directions.

- Its *functional* status ("Functional" checkbox): When a property is functional, a given individual can have (at most) only one value for this property. On the contrary, if the property is not functional, a given individual can have several values.

- Its *inverse functional* status ("Inverse functional" checkbox): A property is inverse functional if the inverse property is functional. For example, the property is_father_of is inverse functional: a man A can be the father of several children B, C, D, and so on, but for each of these children, A is their only father.

- Its *transitive* status ("Transitive" checkbox): A property is transitive if it is possible to "chain" this property on several objects. For example, the property "is_larger_than" is transitive: if an individual A is larger than B and if B is himself larger than C, then we can deduce that A is larger than C.

- Its *symmetric* status ("Symmetric" checkbox): A property is symmetrical if it can be read indifferently in both directions (it is thus its own inverse). For example, the property "is_married_to" is symmetrical: if person A is married to person B, then B is married to A.
- Its *asymmetric* status ("Asymmetric" checkbox): A property is asymmetrical if it is never symmetrical. For example, the property "has_father" is asymmetric: if A has for father B, then it is not possible that B has for father A.
- Its *reflexive* status ("Reflexive" checkbox): A property is reflexive if it always applies between any object and itself. For example, the property "knows" is reflexive: each person X knows himself.
- Its *irreflexive* status ("Irreflexive" checkbox): A property is irreflexive if it is never reflexive. For example, the property "is_married_to" is irreflexive: one cannot be married to him/herself.

Here, we will configure our object properties as follows:

- has_shape: Functional (check the box), domain: Bacteria, range: Shape
- has_grouping: Nonfunctional (do not check the box), domain: Bacteria, range: Grouping
- is_shape_of: Nonfunctional, domain: Form, range: Bacterium, inverse: has_shape
- is_grouping of: Nonfunctional, domain: Grouping, range: Bacteria, inverse: has_grouping

Note that it is enough to define the inverse property of only one of the two properties of the couple: for example, here, we do not need to specify that has_shape has for inverse is_shape_of. This can be easily deduced from the inverse property of is_shape_of.

3.4.6 Restrictions

Now that we have created the properties, we can go back to the classes and add restrictions, based on these properties.

The restrictions are added in the "Classes" tab of Protégé, by clicking the "+" button to the right of "SubClass Of" in the "Description" section. "SubClass Of" allows you to add superclasses to the class; it can be an OWL named class created as before but also constructors, such as partitions (see 3.4.3) but also restrictions.

For example, the bacterium Pseudomonas has a Gram negative staining. This results in OWL by the following restriction: the Boolean property "gram_positive" must have the false value. This restriction is assimilated to a class: it is the class of bacteria having the false value for the "gram_positive" property. We can therefore define the Pseudomonas class as a subclass of this restriction class.

OWL offers several categories of restrictions. The following restrictions are used to model the relationships between two classes:

- Existential restriction (*some*): It represents the class of individuals who have at least one relation of a certain property with an individual belonging to a certain class.

  This restriction is written "property **some** class" in Protégé. For example, we have seen (Figure 3-1) that Pseudomonas all have a Rod shape. Rod is a class, which means that there might be several subtypes of the Rod shape (e.g., we could distinguish regular and irregular rod shapes). This restriction will therefore be written "has_shape some Rod".

- Cardinality restrictions (*exactly, min, max*): It represents the class of individuals who have a certain number of relations of a certain property with an individual belonging to a certain class. The number can be exact (*exactly*) or a minimum (*min*) or maximum (*max*) value.

  These restrictions are written "property **exactly** number class", "property **min** number class", or "property **max** number class" in Protégé. It is a more specific version of the existential restriction: an existential restriction is equivalent to a restriction of cardinality "min 1".

- Universal restriction (*only*): It represents the class of individuals who have only a relation of a certain property with one (or more) individuals belonging to a certain class (including its subclasses).

  This restriction is written "property **only** class" in Protégé. For example, the Pseudomonas is observed only with a Rod shape, which we will write "has_shape only Rod".

  Be careful not to confuse the universal restriction "has_shape only Rod" with the previous existential restriction, "has_shape some Rod". The existential restriction states that all Pseudomonas have at least one Rod shape, while the universal restriction states that all Pseudomonas have no other shape than

Rod. It is quite common to combine two similar restrictions, one universal and the other existential, with the same target class.

On the other hand, we will not use a universal restriction for grouping, because we have seen previously that bacteria can occasionally present other groups than their typical grouping.

The following restriction makes it possible to model a relation between a class and an individual or a datatype value:

- Value restriction (*value*, sometimes called *role-filler*): It represents the class of individuals who have a certain value for a certain property.

  This restriction is written "property **value** individual/datatype" in Protégé. For example, Pseudomonas is always associated with Gram negative staining. This restriction will be written "gram_positive value false".

To add restrictions in Protégé, after clicking the "+" button, you can:

- Either manually enter the restriction in the "Class expression editor" tab (tip: the tabulation key allows you to complete a partial entry, e.g., "Bact" for "Bacteria"),
- Or use the "Object restriction creator" or "Data restriction creator" tab (depending on the type of property) and choose the values from the drop-down lists.

To further describe the Pseudomonas class, we will add the following restrictions:

- "has_shape some Rod"
- "has_shape only Rod"
- "gram_positive value false"[1]

Note that we have used an existential and a universal restriction for the shape, since Rod is a class and not an individual or a data, and on the contrary a value restriction for the Gram coloring, because false is a datatype value.

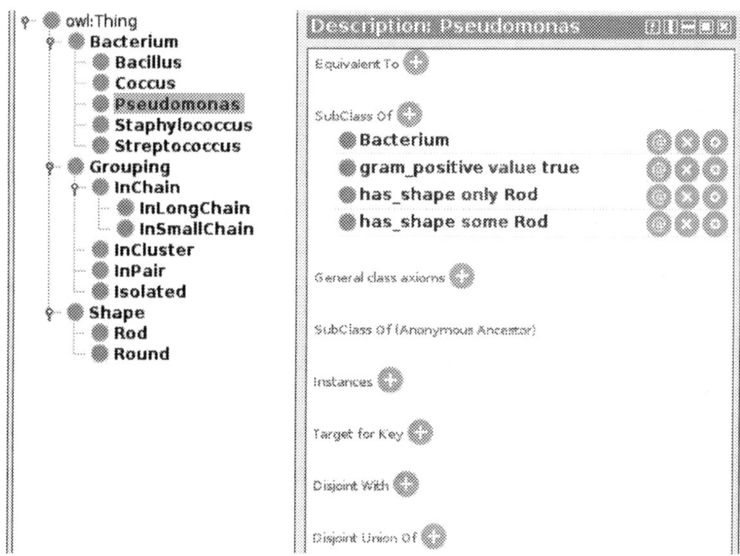

[1]Attention, in OWL, false and true are written without capital letters, while in Python they are written with (i.e., False and True; see 2.4.2).

3.4.7 Union, intersection, and complement

OWL also allows the use of logical operators as constructors. These operators have different names depending on whether they are considered from a logical point of view or from a set theory point of view; however, it is indeed the same thing. Three operators are available:

- **Logical AND** or intersection: These are individuals belonging to several classes at the same time.

  The intersection is written "class1 **and** class2" in Protégé. Of course, more classes can be included in the intersection, for example, "class1 **and** class2 **and** class3".

- **Logical OR** or union: These are individuals belonging to a class among several.

  The union is written "class1 **or** class2" in Protégé. Similarly, unions are not limited to two classes, for example, "class1 **or** class2 **or** class3". For example, the Pseudomonas can have two groupings: Isolated and InPair. We can therefore build the union of these two classes, which will be written "Isolated or InPair".

  Furthermore, we have already used the union previously, to express the partitions (see 3.4.3).

- **Logical NOT** or complement: These are individuals who do not belong to a given class. The complement is written "**not** class" in Protégé.

OWL also allows you to combine logical operators with restrictions and classes, by grouping the different elements in parentheses.

In order to refine the Pseudomonas class, we will add the following superclass:

- "has_grouping some (Isolated or InPair)"

This restriction states that all Pseudomonas have at least one Isolated or InPair grouping.

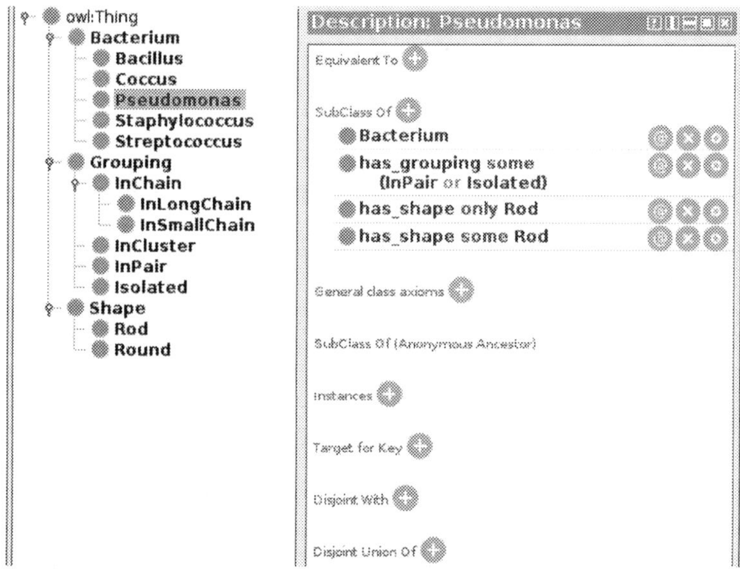

3.4.8 Definitions (equivalent-to relations)

In the previous two sections, we used restrictions and constructors to describe the properties of the class. However, this is not a definition in the formal sense, because we have not fully and uniquely described the class. For example, all Pseudomonas have a Rod shape, but not all bacteria with a Rod shape are Pseudomonas!

OWL allows you to give a class a formal equivalence definition, *via* an equivalence relation. Then, the defined classes allow reclassifying individuals during automatic reasoning (which we will see later in section 3.5 and in Chapter 7).

For example, the Coccus class is the class of bacteria with a Round shape (i.e., at least one Round shape and only Round shape). We can therefore define it as follows:

- Coccus: "Bacterium and (has_shape some Round)
 and (has_shape only Round)"

Note that, unlike the restrictions and constructors that we used previously as a superclass for Pseudomonas, equivalences must be defined "in one piece". We cannot divide the definition into three parts "Bacteria", "has_shape some Round", and "has_shape only Round" unless we change its meaning entirely!

To add the restriction in Protégé, click the "+" button to the right of "Equivalent To", then manually enter the restriction in the "Class expression editor" tab (again, you can use the tabulation key for completion).

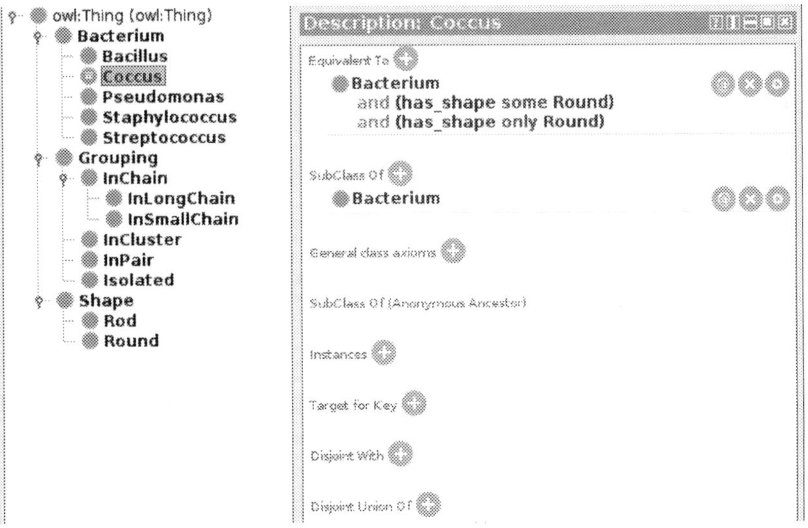

Protégé marks the defined classes with a different icon: a brown circle in which appears the symbol "≡" which means "equivalent to" in description logics.

Similarly, we will define the Bacillus, Staphylococcus, and Streptococcus classes as follows:

- Bacillus: "Bacterium and (has_shape some Rod)
  and (has_shape only Rod)"
- Staphylococcus: "Bacterium and (has_shape some Round)
  and (has_shape only Round)
  and (has_grouping some InCluster)
  and (gram_positive value true)"
- Streptococcus: "Bacterium and (has_shape some Round)
  and (has_shape only Round)
  and (has_grouping some InSmallChain)
  and (has_grouping only (not Isolated))
  and (gram_positive value true)"

For Streptococcus, the restriction "has_grouping only (not Isolated)" indicates that Streptococcus can only have groupings other than Isolated: it is never observed isolated.

3.4.9 Individuals

The "Individuals" tab of Protégé allows you to navigate through individuals and create new ones. In order to test our ontology, we will create a few individuals. To do this, select the class in the "Class hierarchy" panel and then click the button in the "Members list" panel (this panel lists the individuals belonging to the class). We will first select the Round class and create a shape that we will call "round1", as in the following screenshot:

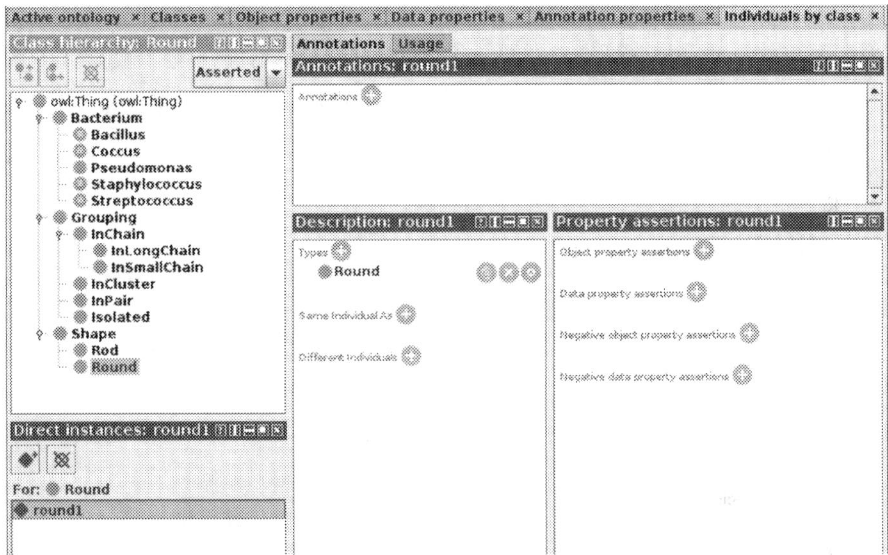

In the same way, we create an individual called "in_cluster1", belonging to the class "InCluster".

Then, we create an individual called "unknown_bacterium", belonging to the "Bacterium" class. Finally, in the "Property assertions" panel, we enter the relationships of this individual by clicking the "+" buttons to the right of "Object property assertions" and "Data property assertions". We will enter the following relationships:

- Object property:
  - has_shape: round1
  - has_grouping: in_cluster1

- Data property:
  - gram_positive: true
  - nb_colonies: 6

The following screenshot shows the expected result:

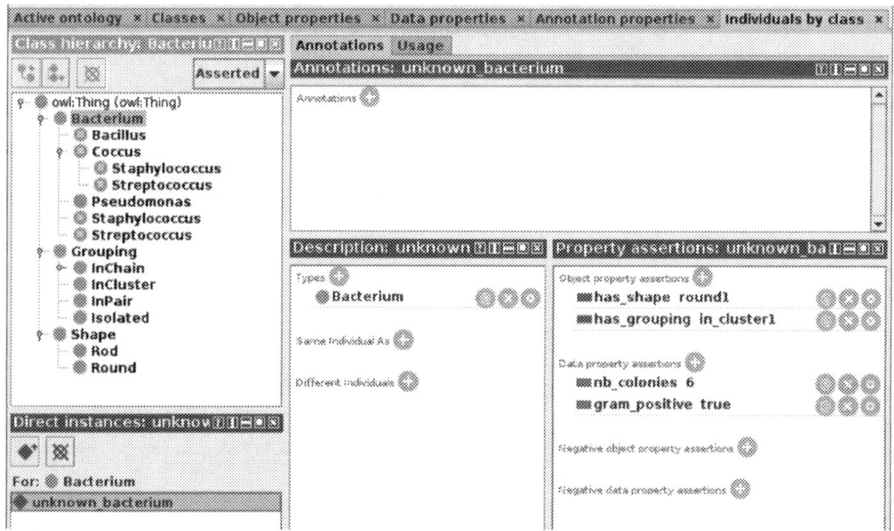

3.4.10 Other constructs

OWL and Protégé also offer other constructors, of less frequent use.

- The **set of individuals** (also called *one of*) allows creating a class restricted to a set of individuals. It is written between braces: "{individual1, individual2, ...}". It can also be used to transform an individual into a class (also called the *singleton* class because it has only one instance/individual), as follows: "{individual}".

- The **inverse** of a property is written "inverse (property)". For example, "inverse (has_shape)" is equivalent to "is_shape_of" in our ontology of bacteria. This constructor is especially useful when the ontology does not define named inverse properties.
- A property chain is written "property1 o property2" (the circle corresponds to the lowercase letter "o"). They are also called the property *composition*. They make it possible to "chain" several properties, for example, "is_shape_of o has_grouping" to pass directly from a shape to the groupings of bacteria having this shape.

3.5 Automatic reasoning

Now our bacteria ontology is ready!

To verify the absence of inconsistency in the ontology and test the automatic reasoning, we can use the "Reasoner ➤ Start reasoner" menu which will execute the automatic reasoner. Several reasoners are available; I recommend the use of HermiT.

Once the reasoning has been carried out, individuals are reclassified in Protégé. For example, the individual "unknown_bacterium" that we had created was of the class Bacteria. We can see that it has been reclassified into a new class: Staphylococcus (the new classes appear on a yellow background in Protégé). Indeed, this bacterium satisfies the conditions to be a Staphylococcus (round shape, grouped in clusters, Gram + status).

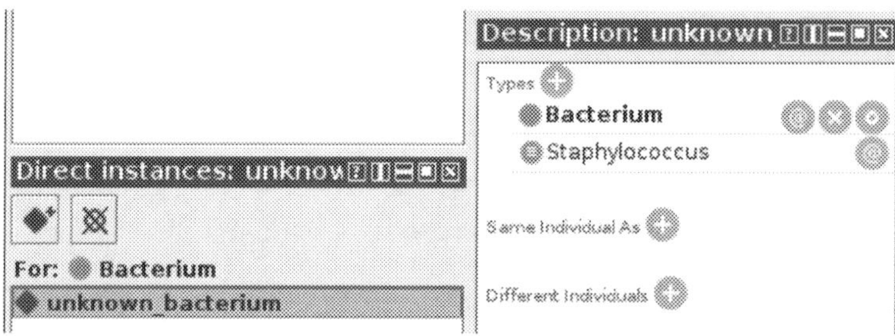

In addition, the reasoner also reorganized the classes. To observe this, we will return to the Classes tab and click "Class hierarchy (inferred)". The class tree has been changed. We can see, for example, that the Pseudomonas class has been reclassified as a subclass of the Bacillus class. Indeed, all the individuals of this class satisfy the definition of the Bacillus class, since Pseudomonas all have a Rod shape.

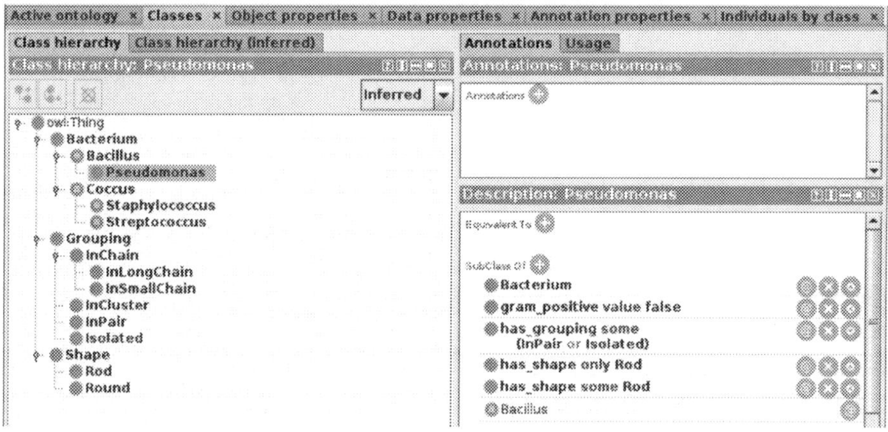

You may also try the following two experiences:

1. Create an individual of the Bacterium class, with a Rod shape, grouped in pairs and/or isolated, and a Gram negative status. This individual will be reclassified in the Bacillus class, but not in Pseudomonas. Indeed, we have not given a formal

definition of the Pseudomonas class; the reasoner cannot therefore deduce that such a bacterium is a Pseudomonas. The absence of definition was a desired choice when designing the ontology, because Pseudomonas are not the only bacteria with a rod shape, isolated or in pairs, and Gram negative (see Figure 3-1).

2. Create an individual of the Bacterium class, with a round shape, grouped in small chain, and having a Gram positive status. This individual will be reclassified in the Coccus class, but not in Streptococcus. However, this class does contain a definition! However, the individual we just created does not fully meet the definition of the Streptococcus class.

   In fact, in the definition, we indicated "has_grouping only (not Isolated)". In the individual, we indicated an InSmallChain grouping; however, the property "has_grouping" is not functional, and therefore several values are possible. The Open-World assumption implies that the reasoner cannot exclude the existence of another grouping, not mentioned in the ontology, which could be Isolated.

   Consequently, to be able to deduce that our individual is a Streptococcus, it would be necessary to indicate in the ontology that the individual has no other groupings than those explicitly mentioned or that he has no grouping of the class Isolated.

On the other hand, in the formal definitions, we also used universal constraints ("only") on the "has_shape" property. However, this does not prevent the classification of individuals in the Coccus, Bacillus, and Staphylococcus classes. Why? Because the property is functional and the Round and Rod classes are disjoint. Therefore, when a bacterium has a Rod shape, it is impossible for it to have a Round shape, and vice versa. On the contrary, the property "has_grouping" is not functional, and therefore this reasoning is no longer possible.

We will come back to this problem, and the solution will be provided in 7.3.

3.6 Modeling exercises

Here are some exercises to train you in ontology modeling:

1. In the bacteria ontology, add an individual of the Staphylococcus class having a rod shape. Run the reasoner; what do you observe?

2. Using the Protégé editor, extend the ontology of bacteria by adding the catalase test. This biological test helps to identify bacteria, and its result can be positive or negative. The catalase test is positive for Staphylococci and Pseudomonas, negative for Streptococci.

3. Using the Protégé editor, extend the bacteria ontology by adding the color of the bacteria. Staphylococci are white or golden (this is the

famous *Staphylococcus aureus*), Streptococci are translucent, and Pseudomonas are generally colored (that is to say, not white).

4. Using the Protégé editor, add a new class of bacteria: *Mycobacterium leprae* (Hansen's bacillus, which causes leprosy). This species of bacteria is Gram positive, rod shape, and isolated or grouped in pairs. The catalase test is not relevant for this bacterium because it is very difficult to grow in vitro. The color is yellow. Finally, all of these characteristics are sufficient to identify the bacteria.

5. In the Protégé editor, add an individual of the class Bacterium, rod shape, isolated, and yellow in color. Check that this individual is properly classified as *Mycobacterium leprae*.

6. In the ontology of bacteria, add a disjunction between the different subclasses of Bacteria (Staphylococci, Streptococci, Pseudomonas, etc.). Does this change the result of the reasoning on the unknown bacterium?

7. An OWL ontology was carried out to structure the drug interactions. This ontology is intended to automatically detect interactions within prescriptions prescribed by doctors, using a reasoner. Could the Open-World assumption pose a problem during the reasoning?

8. Using the Protégé editor, build an ontology describing the books, the authors, and the editors. You take inspiration from the object model presented in 2.9.

3.7 Summary

In this chapter, we have presented OWL ontologies and the use of the Protégé editor, through the example of a simple ontology of bacteria. We have seen the main OWL constructs and also some frequently encountered difficulties, such as those related to the Open-World assumption.

CHAPTER 4

Accessing ontologies in Python

In this chapter, we'll see how to access the contents of an ontology in Python using Owlready. We will use the ontology of bacteria that we created in Chapter 3, as well as Gene Ontology, an ontology widely used in bioinformatics.

4.1 Importing Owlready

Owlready (version 2) is imported in Python as follows:

```
>>> from owlready2 import *
```

Note that it is better to use the import of the contents of the module with "from owlready2 import *" rather than importing the module with "import owlready2" (see 2.10.1), because Owlready redefines some Python functions, such as the `issubclass()` function.

4.2 Loading an ontology

Owlready allows you to load an OWL ontology into Python and to access OWL entities as you would access "traditional" objects from a Python module.

L. Jean-Baptiste, *Ontologies with Python*, https://doi.org/10.1007/978-1-4842-6552-9_4

An ontology can be loaded in three different ways:

1. From its IRI (*Internationalized Resource Identifier*), that is, an Internet address:

   ```
   >>> onto = get_ontology("http://lesfleursdunormal.↲
   fr/static/_downloads/bacteria.owl").load()
   ```
   The ontology is then downloaded from the Internet and loaded.

2. From a local file containing a copy of the ontology, for example, under Linux/Unix/Mac:

   ```
   >>> onto = get_ontology("/home/jiba/owlready/↲
   bacteria.owl").load()
   ```

   or under Windows:

   ```
   >>> onto = get_ontology("C:\\owlready\\bacteria.↲
   owl").load()
   ```

   It is also possible to load the ontology from a local copy into the current directory:

   ```
   >>> onto = get_ontology("bacteria.owl").load()
   ```

   The ontology is then loaded from an already existing OWL file (you will obviously get an error if the file enclosed in quotation marks does not exist; of course, the filename in the preceding lines of code are just examples). Be careful, under Windows, do not forget to double the backslashes in filenames!

3. From a Python file object obtained with the `open()`, `urlopen()`, and other functions (see 2.4.8). This case is much rarer, but sometimes useful (we will use it to load DBpedia in 8.8.1). Here is an example:

```
>>> my_file = open("/path/to/file.owl")
>>> onto = get_ontology("http://lesfleursdunormal.↲
fr/static/_downloads/bacteria.owl")
>>> onto.load(fileobj = my_file)
```

Owlready currently supports the following file formats for reading:

- RDF/XML (most frequent file format for OWL ontologies)
- OWL/XML
- N-Triples

Owlready maintains a cache of loaded ontologies: if the same ontology is loaded a second time, the same ontology object will be returned without having to reread the corresponding file. To force the reloading of an ontology, we will use the optional `reload` parameter of the `load()` method:

```
>>> onto.load(reload = True)
```

The `base_iri` attribute of the ontology allows obtaining its IRI:

```
>>> onto.base_iri
'http://lesfleursdunormal.fr/static/_downloads/bacteria.owl#'
```

Note that Owlready automatically determined the separator, "#" or "/", to be placed after the IRI of the ontology and added it to the end (here, it is "#"). However, it is also possible to explicitly include the separator at the end of the IRI when calling `get_ontology()`.

4.3 Imported ontologies

The ontology's `imported_ontologies` attribute contains the list of other ontologies it imports:

```
>>> onto.imported_ontologies
[]
```

Here, our bacteria ontology does not import any other ontology (hence the preceding empty list). Imported ontologies are automatically loaded by Owlready, recursively.

4.4 Listing the content of the ontology

The ontology object has many methods for traversing the entities contained in the ontology, according to their type. The following table summarizes all of these methods:

Methods	**Entities traversed**
`individuals()`	All individuals
`classes()`	All classes
`properties()`	All properties
`object_properties()`	All object properties
`data_properties()`	All data properties
`annotation_properties()`	All annotation properties
`disjoints()`	All pairwise disjoints (including pairwise distinct individuals and disjoint/distinct pairs)
`disjoint_classes()`	All pairwise disjoint classes (including disjoint pairs of classes)

(*continued*)

Methods	Entities traversed
disjoint_properties()	All pairwise disjoint properties (including disjoint pairs of properties)
different_individuals()	All pairwise distinct individuals (including distinct pairs of individuals)
rules()	All SWRL rules
variables()	All SWRL variables
general_axioms()	All general axioms

These methods return generators (see 2.7); to display the content, use the `list()` Python function, which converts the generator into a list:

```
>>> onto.classes()
<generator object _GraphManager.classes at 0x7f5a000fae58>
```

```
>>> list(onto.classes())
[bacteria.Bacterium, bacteria.Shape, bacteria.Grouping,
bacteria.Round, bacteria.Rod, bacteria.Isolated, bacteria.
InPair, bacteria.InCluster, bacteria.InChain, bacteria.
InSmallChain, bacteria.InLongChain, bacteria.Pseudomonas,
bacteria.Coccus, bacteria.Bacillus, bacteria.Staphylococcus,
bacteria.Streptococcus]
```

However, it is best not to use `list()` when the generator is present in a loop, to improve performance:

```
>>> for c in onto.classes(): print(c.name)
Bacterium
Shape
Grouping
[...]
```

4.5 Accessing entities

When loading ontologies, Owlready analyzes the ontology file and automatically translates it as an RDF graph in the form of "subject - verb - object" triples (we will return in more detail on RDF in Chapter 11). This RDF graph is stored in a database in the SQLite3 format, which is by default in RAM (but the database can also be stored on the disk, as we will see in 4.7). Then, Python objects for accessing the entities contained in the ontology are created dynamically, on demand. Thus, if an ontology includes 100 classes but only 1 is used in Python, only this class will be created in Python, and the other 99 will remain at the RDF graph level in the database.

The `IRIS` pseudo-dictionary allows access to any entity from its IRI. For example, to access the individual "unknown_bacterium" whose complete IRI is the following:

`http://lesfleursdunormal.fr/static/_downloads/bacteria.owl#unknown_bacterium`

we will use

```
>>> IRIS["http://lesfleursdunormal.fr/static/_downloads/↲
bacteria.owl#unknown_bacterium"]
```

However, this notation is quite verbose. Owlready allows an easier access to the entities present in the ontology, with dotted notation ".", as if the ontology was a Python module containing classes and objects. For example, we can also access the individual "unknown_bacterium" as follows:

```
>>> onto.unknown_bacterium
```

When the dotted notation is used, Owlready takes the base IRI of the ontology (`onto.base_iri`, here "`http://lesfleursdunormal.fr/static/_downloads/bacteria.owl#`") and appends what appears after the dot (here, "unknown_bacterium") to obtain the IRI of the requested entity.

Some IRIs may contain characters not supported by Python in attribute names (e.g., spaces); in this case, the following alternative syntax can also be used:

```
>>> onto["unknown_bacterium"]
```

Finally, some ontologies define entities whose IRI does not start with the IRI of the ontology; in this case, it can be accessed via the `IRIS` pseudo-dictionary or via namespaces (see 4.8).

The `iri` attribute of the entity contains its full IRI and the `name` attribute the last part of the IRI (after the "#" character or the last "/"):

```
>>> onto.unknown_bacterium.iri
'http://lesfleursdunormal.fr/static/_downloads/↲
bacteria.owl#unknown_bacterium'
>>> onto.unknown_bacterium.name
'unknown_bacterium'
```

4.5.1 Individuals

Individuals can be manipulated as if they were "normal" Python objects. In particular, it is possible to test their membership in a given class with the `isinstance()` function, as for any Python object:

```
>>> isinstance(onto.unknown_bacterium, onto.Bacterium)
True
```

The `__class__` attribute allows obtaining the class of an object:

```
>>> onto.unknown_bacterium.__class__
bacteria.Bacterium
```

However, in ontologies, an object can belong to several classes simultaneously, which is not allowed in Python. In this case, Owlready automatically creates a "merge" class that inherits from all the individual's classes. In order to obtain the list of the classes of the individual, it is therefore preferable to use the is_a attribute (which also contains the restrictions and the logical constructors, if any):

```
>>> onto.unknown_bacterium.is_a
[bacteria.Bacterium]
```

Finally, the equivalent_to attribute contains the list of equivalent individuals (often called "same as" in OWL or in the Protégé editor).

```
>>> onto.unknown_bacterium.equivalent_to
[]
```

Here, the list is empty because our unknown bacterium has not been defined as equivalent to any other.

4.5.2 Relations

The relations of an individual can be obtained via the dotted notation pointed "individual.attribute", for example:

```
>>> onto.unknown_bacterium.gram_positive
True
>>> onto.unknown_bacterium.has_shape
bacteria.round1
>>> onto.unknown_bacterium.has_grouping
[bacteria.in_cluster1]
```

Relations return a list of values (as for the attribute "has_grouping" earlier) or a single value if the property is functional (as for the other two attributes earlier).

The `first()` method of lists of values can be used to retrieve the first result (defaulting to None when the list is empty).

```
>>> onto.unknown_bacterium.has_grouping.first()
bacteria.in_cluster1
```

In addition, Owlready automatically takes into account inverse properties when querying for relations. For example, we can ask which bacterium is associated with the grouping "in_cluster1":

```
>>> onto.in_cluster1.is_grouping_of
[bacteria.unknown_bacterium]
```

The relation "in_cluster1 is_grouping_of unknown_bacterium" does not appear in the ontology (we did not enter it in Protégé in Chapter 3). However, it is easily deduced from the relation "unknown_bacterium has_for_grouping in_cluster1" that we entered.

The values present in the ontology are automatically translated into Python datatypes (`int`, `float`, `str`, etc.), according to the correspondence given in Table 4-1.

When the property names are prefixed with "`INDIRECT_`", Owlready also returns the indirectly defined relations, taking into account:

1. Transitive, symmetrical, and reflexive properties
2. Inheritance relation between properties (i.e., subproperties)
3. The classes to which the individual belongs (existential or value restriction on the class)
4. Inheritance between classes (existential or value restriction on superclasses)
5. Equivalence relations (classes and equivalent properties and identical individuals)

Here is an example:

Table 4-1. *Correspondence between OWL and Python + Owlready datatypes. When multiple OWL datatypes correspond to the same Python type, the OWL datatype in bold is the one used by Owlready by default when saving ontologies*

OWL	Python + Owlready
XMLSchema#integer	int
XMLSchema#byte	
XMLSchema#short	
XMLSchema#int	
XMLSchema#long	
XMLSchema#unsignedByte	
XMLSchema#unsignedShort	
XMLSchema#unsignedInt	
XMLSchema#unsignedLong	
XMLSchema#negativeInteger	
XMLSchema#nonNegativeInteger	
XMLSchema#positiveInteger	
XMLSchema#boolean	bool
XMLSchema#decimal	float
XMLSchema#double	
XMLSchema#float	
owl#real	
XMLSchema#string	str

(*continued*)

Table 4-1. (*continued*)

OWL	Python + Owlready
XMLSchema#normalizedString	owlready2.normstr
XMLSchema#anyURI	
XMLSchema#Name	
PlainLiteral	str (if no language is specified) owlready2.locstr (if a language is specified, see 8.2)
XMLSchema#dateTime	datetime.datetime
XMLSchema#date	datetime.date
XMLSchema#time	datetime.time

```
>>> onto.unknown_bacterium.INDIRECT_has_grouping
[bacteria.in_cluster1]
```

The `get_properties()` method returns a generator listing all the properties for which the individual has at least one relation, for example:

```
>>> list(onto.unknown_bacterium.get_properties())
[bacteria.has_shape, bacteria.has_grouping,
bacteria.gram_positive, bacteria.nb_colonies]
```

Finally, the `get_inverse_properties()` method does the same with inverse properties and returns pairs of the form "(subject, property)", for example:

```
>>> list(onto.round1.get_inverse_properties())
[(bacteria.unknown_bacterium, bacteria.has_shape)]
```

4.5.3 Classes

Classes can be obtained in the same way as other entities:

```
>>> onto.Bacterium
```

The ontology classes are real Python classes and can be used as such. For example, the `issubclass()` function tests whether a class is a descendant (subclass, sub-subclass, *etc.*) of another:

```
>>> issubclass(onto.Coccus, onto.Bacterium)
True
```

The `__bases__` attribute is used to obtain the list of parent classes. However, as for individuals, it is best to use the `is_a` attribute (which also contains the restrictions and the logical constructors):

```
>>> onto.Coccus.is_a
[bacteria.Bacterium]
```

The `subclasses()` method gets the list of child classes (note that `subclasses()` returns a generator, hence the use of `list()`):

```
>>> list(onto.Bacterium.subclasses())
[bacteria.Pseudomonas, bacteria.Coccus, bacteria.Bacillus]
```

The `ancestors()` and `descendants()` methods are used to obtain the set of ancestor classes (parents, grandparents, *etc.*) and descendant classes (children, grandchildren, *etc.*), respectively.

```
>>> onto.Bacterium.descendants()
{bacteria.Bacterium, bacteria.Pseudomonas, bacteria.Streptococcus,
bacteria.Staphylococcus, bacteria.Bacillus, bacteria.Coccus}
```

By default, the starting class is included in the results (this is why we find bacteria.Bacterium in the previous result). The optional argument include_self removes the starting class. It is used as follows:

```
>>> onto.Bacterium.descendants(include_self = False)
{bacteria.Pseudomonas, bacteria.Streptococcus,
bacteria.Staphylococcus, bacteria.Bacillus, bacteria.Coccus}
```

The instances() method is used to obtain the list of individuals belonging to a class (including instances of child and descendant classes):

```
>>> onto.Bacterium.instances()
[bacteria.unknown_bacterium]
```

The direct_instances() method works in the same way but is limited to direct instances.

The equivalent_to attribute contains the list of equivalent classes:

```
>>> onto.Streptococcus.equivalent_to
[bacteria.Bacterium
& bacteria.has_shape.some(bacteria.Round)
& bacteria.has_shape.only(bacteria.Round)
& bacteria.has_grouping.some(bacteria.InSmallChain)
& bacteria.has_grouping.only(Not(bacteria.Isolated))
& bacteria.gram_positive.value(True)]
```

We obtain the formal definition that we entered in Chapter 3 with the different OWL constructors; we will see how to manipulate these in Chapter 6.

As before, it is possible to prefix by "INDIRECT_" to obtain the indirect equivalences (e.g., if A is equivalent to B and B is equivalent to C, we will obtain that A is equivalent to both B and C).

```
>>> onto.Streptococcus.INDIRECT_equivalent_to
```

Finally, disjoints() and constructs() methods return generators listing all disjoints and constructors referencing the class, respectively.

4.5.4 Existential restrictions

Owlready allows you to access existential restrictions (those of type some and value) as if they were "class properties", using the dotted notation "Class.property", for example, on the class Streptococcus:

```
>>> onto.Streptococcus.gram_positive
True
>>> onto.Streptococcus.has_grouping
[bacteria.InSmallChain]
```

Owlready also provides detailed access to all the constructors used in the definition of a class (see 6.2).

4.5.5 Properties

Superproperties, subproperties, ancestors, descendants, and equivalent properties can be obtained in the same way as for classes.

The `domain` and `range` attributes are used to obtain the domain and range of the property. Be careful, these attributes each return a list. When multiple values are present, OWL considers that the domain or the range is the *intersection* of the different values.

```
>>> onto.has_grouping.domain
[bacteria.Bacterium]
>>> onto.has_grouping.range
[bacteria.Grouping]
```

The `range_iri` attribute is used to get the range of the property as a list of IRIs, which is useful for distinguishing the different types of data supported by OWL (e.g., XMLSchema#decimal, XMLSchema#double, and XMLSchema#float, while the range attribute is the Python `float` type for all three in Owlready, Python having only one type of floating number).

The python_name attribute is used to change the name under which a property is accessible with the dotted notation. This allows you to use a name more "in the spirit" of Python. Indeed, the OWL properties are often called "has_...", whereas in Python the attribute names rarely start like this. Similarly, in Python, we prefer to put a plural "s" at the end of an attribute containing a list of values. For example, we can change the name of the property "has_grouping" to "groupings" as follows:

```
>>> onto.has_grouping.python_name = "groupings"
>>> onto.unknown_bacterium.groupings
[bacteria.in_cluster1]
```

Note that the name of the property is only changed when using the dotted notation in Python. On the other hand, the object property remains accessible as an onto.has_grouping, and its IRI does not change. It is possible to return to the previous name as follows:

```
>>> onto.has_grouping.python_name = onto.has_grouping.name
```

The get_relations() method returns a generator listing all (subject, object) pairs for the property, for example:

```
>>> for subject, object in onto.has_grouping.get_relations():
...     print(subject, "has for grouping" , object)
bacteria.unknown_bacterium  has for grouping  bacteria.in_cluster1
```

It is also possible to obtain the value of a property for a given individual with the alternative syntax "property[individual]". Unlike the usual syntax "individual.property", this alternative syntax always returns a list of values (even in the case of a functional property), which may be useful in some situations:

```
>>> prop = onto.gram_positive
>>> prop[onto.unknown_bacterium]
[True]
```

This syntax can also be useful if the property name contains invalid characters in Python (e.g., ".") or if the ontology includes several properties with different IRIs but ending with the same name. The following example shows how to access a property with an invalid name in Python:

```
onto["my.propertyindividual"]
```

4.6 Searching for entities

The `search()` method of the ontology object makes it possible to search for entities from their IRI and/or their relations. When searching, the following keywords are usable and combinable with each other:

- `iri` to search by IRI
- `type` to search for individuals of a given class
- `subclass_of` to search for descendant classes of a given class
- `is_a` to search for both individuals and descendant classes of a given class
- any property name to search by relation

In addition, in strings, "*" can be used as a wildcard. The following example searches for all entities whose IRI contains "Coccus":

```
>>> onto.search(iri = "*Coccus*")
[bacteria.Coccus]
```

By default, the search is case-sensitive. The `_case_sensitive` parameter is used to change this behavior, for example:

```
>>> onto.search(iri = "*Coccus*", _case_sensitive = False)
[bacteria.Coccus, bacteria.Staphylococcus, bacteria.
Streptococcus]
```

This time, we find more results, because "Staphylococcus" and "Streptococcus" do contain "coccus", but with a lowercase "c" and not an uppercase one.

The result returned by search() looks like a Python list and can be used as a list. However, it is not a classic list; we can check it with the __class__ attribute:

```
>>> r = onto.search(iri = "*Coccus*", _case_sensitive = False)
>>> r.__class__
<class 'owlready2.triplelite._SearchList'>
```

It is a special list, called a "lazy" list, whose elements are only determined at the very last moment. For example, in the following code, the first line creates the "lazy" list, but the search is not performed yet. It will only be done at the very last moment, when we ask to access the contents of the list (e.g., with print() for the display).

```
>>> r = onto.search(iri = "*Coccus*", _case_sensitive = False)
>>> print(r) # The search is only performed here
[bacteria.Coccus, bacteria.Staphylococcus, bacteria.
Streptococcus]
```

The search() method can accept multiple parameters. The following example searches for all individuals belonging to the Bacterium class with a positive Gram (= having the gram_positive relationship to True):

```
>>> onto.search(type = onto.Bacterium, gram_positive = True)
[bacteria.unknown_bacterium]
```

The string "*" can be used as a "wildcard", that is to say, to search for the existence of a relation, whatever the associated value (including nontextual values: numbers, objects, etc.). The following example searches for all bacteria for which Gram status is known (whatever it is):

```
>>> onto.search(type = onto.Bacterium, gram_positive = "*")
[bacteria.unknown_bacterium]
```

A list of several values can also be used as an argument to search(). In this case, only the entities having a relationship with each of the elements of the list are returned. Here is an example (you will have to create the individuals isolated1 and by_two1 in the ontology to test this example):

```
>>> onto.search(type = onto.Bacterium,↲
has_grouping = [onto.isolated1, onto.by_two1])
```

It is also possible to search for individuals having no relation, using the None value. For example, we can search for bacteria that have no shape as follows:

```
>>> onto.search(type = onto.Bacterium, has_shape = None)
```

To search in all ontologies (in case several have been loaded), it is possible to search the default "world", default_world, as follows:

```
>>> default_world.search(iri = "*Coccus*")
```

Searches with search() can also be nested. In this case, Owlready automatically combines the searches to make a single optimized SQL query in the quadstore. The following example searches for all bacteria with an InChain grouping (including InSmallChain and InFilament). For this, we nest two calls to search(): one to find InChain groupings and another to find the associated bacteria.

```
>>> onto.search(type = onto.Bacterium,↲
has_grouping = onto.search(type = onto.InChain))
```

Finally, the search_one() method works in the same way as search() but returns only one result, instead of a list.

To perform more complex searches, it is possible to use the SPARQL query language by combining Owlready with RDFlib (see section 11.3).

4.7 Huge ontologies and disk cache

Gene Ontology (GO) is a widely used ontology in bioinformatics that is quite voluminous (nearly 200 MB). The loading of GO, using the following command, takes several tens of seconds or even a few minutes, depending on the power of the computer and the download time of the OWL file:

```
>>> go = get_ontology("http://purl.obolibrary.org/obo/go.owl").↲
load()
```

By default, Owlready stores the quadstore containing the ontology in RDF format in RAM. At the end of the execution of the Python program, the quadstore is lost, and the OWL file must be reloaded at each new execution. In order to avoid these long reloads, it is possible to place the quadstore on the disk, using the `default_world.set_backend()` method. Then, `default_world.save()` will save it, for example:

```
>>> default_world.set_backend(filename = "quadstore.sqlite3")
>>> go = get_ontology("http://purl.obolibrary.org/obo/go.owl").↲
load()
>>> default_world.save()
```

Here, we used a relative file path for the quadstore; we could have used an absolute path (e.g., "`/home/jiba/owlready/quadstore.sqlite3`" on Linux/Mac or "`C:\\quadstore.sqlite3`" on Windows).

To load the ontologies from the quadstore, during a new execution of Python, it is enough to redefine the quadstore file and to load the ontology, by using the same three lines as before (the line `default_world.save()` can be ignored or kept; it will have no effect because there is no change to save). The loading is then immediate, because the ontology is recovered directly from the quadstore, without any operation for downloading or parsing the OWL file.

Attention, if several ontologies are loaded in memory (e.g., the ontology of preceding bacteria and GO), all the ontologies are stored in the same quadstore and thus saved in the same file.

Finally, the `default_world.save()` method is used to save the changes made in the quadstore (this method corresponds to the "commit" operation on the database, so it has a cost of almost zero performance if there are no changes to record, even for very large ontologies). If the changes are not saved, they will be lost at the end of the program execution.

4.8 Namespaces

Some ontologies define entities in a namespace that is not their own. This is the case with GO: the GO IRI is "`http://purl.obolibrary.org/obo/go.owl`", but GO entities have IRIs that start with "`http://purl.obolibrary.org/obo/`" (without the "go.owl" suffix). Consequently, it is not possible to use the go ontology object to access the entities with the dotted notation:

```
>>> go.GO_0035065
None
```

Indeed, the preceding line corresponds to the IRI "`http://purl.obolibrary.org/obo/go.owl#GO_0035065`", while the expected IRI of the concept is "`http://purl.obolibrary.org/obo/GO_0035065`" (so without the "go.owl" suffix).

To access GO entities, it is possible to use the IRIS global pseudo-dictionary (see 4.5). Another option is to create a namespace for the "`http://purl.obolibrary.org/obo/`" IRI, as follows:

```
>>> obo = get_namespace("http://purl.obolibrary.org/obo/")
```

The obo namespace can then be used to access the entities with the dotted notation:

```
>>> obo.GO_0035065
obo.GO_0035065
>>> obo.GO_0035065.label
['regulation of histone acetylation']
```

4.9 Modifying entity rendering as text

By default, Owlready displays the name of the entity, preceded by a period and the last piece of the IRI (without the extension ".owl", if present). However, when the names of the entities are arbitrary identifiers, this display is not satisfactory, as in the following example:

```
>>> obo.GO_0035065
obo.GO_0035065
```

The global function set_render_func() allows redefining the way in which Owlready renders entities. In the following example, we use the "label" annotation property to render or, failing that, the name of the entity (i.e., its identifier):

```
>>> def my_rendering(entity):
...     return entity.label.first() or entity.name
>>> set_render_func(my_rendering)
>>> obo.GO_0035065
regulation of histone acetylation
```

In GO, almost all entities are classes (and not individuals; this is a fairly common practice in biomedical ontologies). As seen previously (in 4.5.4), it is possible to access the existential restrictions of these classes with the dotted notation, as in the following example (where RO_0002211 is the name GO for the "regulates" property):

```
>>> obo.GO_0035065.RO_0002211
[histone acetylation]
```

However, it is sometimes laborious to use property names when these are arbitrary codes, as before. The next three lines allow you to use the property labels instead of their name (after replacing the spaces with underscores):

```
>>> for prop in go.properties():
...     if prop.label:
...         prop.python_name = prop.label.first().replace(" " ,
            "_")
```

This makes it easier to query the ontology:

```
>>> obo.GO_0035065.regulates
[histone acetylation]
```

Be careful, however, because GO does not guarantee the conservation of labels from one version to another! This tip is therefore to be avoided in programs designed to last.

As before, it is possible to prefix the property name with "INDIRECT_" to also obtain the restrictions defined indirectly, for example, those which are inherited from superclasses:

```
>>> obo.GO_0035065.INDIRECT_regulates
[cellular component organization,
 metabolic process,
 protein metabolic process,
 protein acetylation,
 histone acetylation,
 ...]
```

4.10 Local directory of ontologies

Owlready can also work with one or more directories containing local copies. Local copies will be used as a priority, instead of downloading ontologies from the Internet. The local directories must be filled in the global variable onto_path, in the following way under Unix/Linux/Mac:

```
>>> onto_path.append("/home/jiba/owlready")
>>> onto = get_ontology("http://lesfleursdunormal.fr/static/↲
_downloads/bacteria.owl#").load()
```

or under Windows:

```
>>> onto_path.append("C:\\owlready")
>>> onto = get_ontology("http://lesfleursdunormal.fr/static/↲
_downloads/bacteria.owl#").load()
```

The global variable onto_path contains a list of local ontology directories; it is empty by default. Before downloading an ontology from the Internet, Owlready checks whether a local copy is not available in one of the directories in onto_path. In the previous example, if a "bacteria.owl" file is present in the cache directory ("/home/jiba/owlready" in the Linux/Unix/Mac example or "C:\\owlready" in the Windows example), this file will be used. Otherwise, the ontology will be downloaded from the Internet.

onto_path works similarly to the sys.path list which allows Python to find Python modules and packages or to the equivalent CLASSPATH environment variable in Java.

In addition, the optional parameter only_local allows you to prohibit the loading of an ontology from the Internet, as in the following example:

```
>>> onto = get_ontology("http://lesfleursdunormal.fr/static/↲
_downloads/bacteria.owl#").load(only_local = True)
```

Local ontology directories are particularly useful if you want to use different versions of ontologies found on the Internet, for example, older versions or in "exotic" formats. In particular, some ontologies available online are in formats that Owlready cannot read. Using a local directory, it is possible to provide Owlready with versions of these ontologies previously translated into RDF/XML or N-Triples (e.g., manually via Protégé).

4.11 Reloading an ontology in the quadstore

When using local files (local ontology directory as before or loading an ontology from a local OWL file) and a quadstore stored on the disk, the question of updating ontologies in the quadstore arise. When the local OWL file is modified, the ontology must be updated in the quadstore. This can be done with the `reload` option of the `load()` method seen previously, but also with the `reload_if_newer` option which reloads the ontology only if the OWL file is newer than the version stored in the quadstore:

```
>>> go = get_ontology("http://purl.obolibrary.org/obo/↲
go.owl#").load(reload_if_newer = True)
```

Please note reloading the ontology from the OWL file overwrites the version stored in the quadstore. You must therefore avoid simultaneously modifying the OWL file of the ontology and its version stored in the quadstore!

4.12 Example: creating a dynamic website from an ontology

In this example, we are going to generate a dynamic website to present the classes and individuals of an ontology. For this, we will use Owlready as well as Flask, a Python module which allows you to easily create websites. Flask allows you to associate a URL path on a website with a Python function; when this path is requested, the function is called, and it must return the corresponding HTML page. The path is defined by adding `@app.route('/path')` on the line preceding the function (it is a Python function decorator). The paths can contain parameters (indicated between angle brackets `<...>` in the path) which will be passed as arguments to the Python function.

The following function shows a simple example of a web page with Flask:

```
from flask import Flask, url_for

app = Flask(__name__)

@app.route('/path/<parameter>')
def generate_web_page(parameter):
    html  = "<html><body>"
    html += "The value of the parameter is: %s % parameter"
    html += "</body></html>"
    return html
```

The full program of our website is as follows:

```
# File dynamic_website.py
from owlready2 import *
onto = get_ontology("bacteria.owl").load()

from flask import Flask, url_for
app = Flask(__name__)
```

```
@app.route('/')
def ontology_page():
    html  = """<html><body>"""
    html += """<h2>'%s' ontology</h2>""" % onto.base_iri
    html += """<h3>Root classes</h3>"""
    for Class in Thing.subclasses():
        html += """<p><a href="%s">%s</a></p>""" %↲
(url_for("class_page", iri = Class.iri), Class.name)

    html += """</body></html>"""
    return html

@app.route('/class/<path:iri>')
def class_page(iri):
    Class = IRIS[iri]
    html = """<html><body><h2>'%s' class</h2>""" % Class.name

    html += """<h3>superclasses</h3>"""
    for SuperClass in Class.is_a:
        if isinstance(SuperClass, ThingClass):
            html += """<p><a href="%s">%s</a></p>""" %↲
(url_for("class_page", iri = SuperClass.iri), SuperClass.name)
        else:
            html += """<p>%s</p>""" % SuperClass

    html += """<h3>equivalent classes</h3>"""
    for EquivClass in Class.equivalent_to:
        html += """<p>%s</p>""" % EquivClass

    html += """<h3>Subclasses</h3>"""
    for SubClass in Class.subclasses():
        html += """<p><a href="%s">%s</a></p>""" %↲
(url_for("class_page", iri = SubClass.iri), SubClass.name)
```

```
    html += """<h3>Individuals</h3>"""
    for individual in Class.instances():
        html += """<p><a href="%s">%s</a></p>""" %↲
(url_for("individual_page", iri = individual.iri),↲
individual.name)

    html += """</body></html>"""
    return html

@app.route('/individual/<path:iri>')
def individual_page(iri):
    individual = IRIS[iri]
    html = """<html><body><h2>'%s' individual</h2>""" %↲
    individual.name

    html += """<h3>Classes</h3>"""
    for Class in individual.is_a:
        html += """<p><a href="%s">%s</a></p>""" %↲
(url_for("class_page", iri = Class.iri), Class.name)

    html += """<h3>Relations</h3>"""
    if isinstance(individual, onto.Bacterium):
        html += """<p>shape = %s</p>""" % individual.has_shape
        html += """<p>grouping = %s</p>""" % individual.has_grouping
        if   individual.gram_positive == True:
            html += """<p>Gram +</p>"""
        elif individual.gram_positive == False:
            html += """<p>Gram -</p>"""

    html += """</body></html>"""
    return html

import werkzeug.serving
werkzeug.serving.run_simple("localhost", 5000, app)
```

In this program, we have defined three functions, each associated with a URL path and corresponding to three different types of pages on the website:

- The "ontology" page (path "/" which corresponds to the root of the website) displays the IRI of the ontology and lists the root classes (i.e., direct subclasses of Thing). For each class, we display its name in an Internet link which points to the corresponding class page. The URLs of these links are obtained with the `url_for()` function from Flask, which returns the URL for a given web page from the name of the corresponding function and any parameters.
- The "class" page (path "/class/IRI_of_the_class") displays the name of the requested class and lists its superclasses, its equivalent classes, its subclasses, and its individuals. For superclasses, we display the name of the superclass with a link as previously when it is an entity (i.e., an instance of ThingClass) or simply the class (without links) when it is an OWL logical constructor (e.g., a restriction).
- The individual page (path "/individual/IRI_of_individual") displays the name of the requested individual and lists its classes. If it is a bacterium, we also display its shape, its grouping, and its Gram status.

The last two lines are used to launch the website with the Werkzeug server (a Python module installed by Flask). Once the program has been executed, the website can be consulted at the address "`http://127.0.0.1:5000`" in your browser. The following screenshots show the "ontology" and "class" pages of the dynamic website:

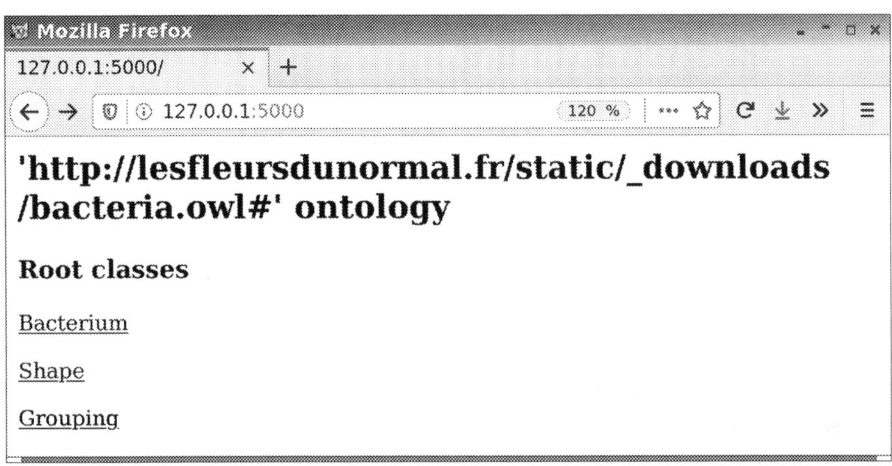
Mozilla Firefox
127.0.0.1:5000/
127.0.0.1:5000
120 %
'http://lesfleursdunormal.fr/static/_downloads/bacteria.owl#' ontology
Root classes
Bacterium
Shape
Grouping

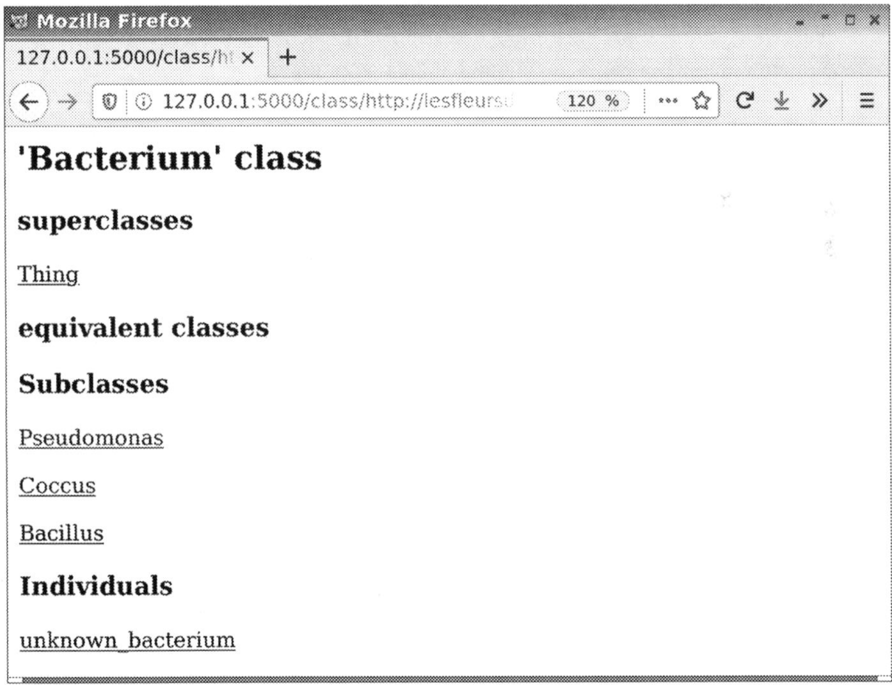
Mozilla Firefox
127.0.0.1:5000/class/ht
127.0.0.1:5000/class/http://lesfleurs
120 %
'Bacterium' class
superclasses
Thing
equivalent classes
Subclasses
Pseudomonas
Coccus
Bacillus
Individuals
unknown_bacterium

4.13 Summary

In this chapter, you have learned how to use Owlready for accessing and reading OWL ontologies in Python. We have used the bacteria ontology designed in the previous chapter, but also a much larger and complex resource, Gene Ontology. Finally, we have seen how to use ontology in Flask-based dynamic websites.

CHAPTER 5

Creating and modifying ontologies in Python

In this chapter, we will see how to create a *de novo* ontology in Python and how to modify or enrich an already existing ontology. Almost all of the objects, attributes, and lists of Owlready seen in the previous chapter can be modified: when the value of these is modified, Owlready automatically updates the corresponding RDF triples in the quadstore (however, do not forget to save it if it is stored on the disk; see 4.7).

5.1 Creating an empty ontology

The `get_ontology()` function allows you to create an empty ontology from its IRI (it is preferable to indicate the separator, "#" or "/", at the end of the IRI, because Owlready cannot guess it since the ontology is empty!):

```
>>> from owlready2 import *
>>> onto = get_ontology("http://test.org/onto.owl#")
```

Note that, contrary to what we did in Chapter 4, we did not call the `load()` method. This was in charge of loading the ontology; if `load()` is not called, the ontology therefore remains empty.

L. Jean-Baptiste, *Ontologies with Python*, https://doi.org/10.1007/978-1-4842-6552-9_5

Subsequently, when creating OWL entities or RDF triples, it is important to indicate in which ontology they are placed. In fact, unlike the Python classes that belong to the module in which they are created, OWL entities do not "belong" specifically to an ontology: a class can be defined in an ontology A and then enriched in an ontology B, for example, with new parent classes.

Owlready uses the syntax "with ontology: ..." to indicate the ontology that will receive the new RDF triples:

```
with onto:
    <Python code>
```

All RDF triples created in the code block "<Python code>" placed inside the `with...:` block will be added to the ontology `onto`.

5.2 Creating classes

To create an OWL class, simply create a Python class that inherits from `Thing`. For example, we can create the Bacterium, Shape, and Grouping classes as follows:

```
>>> with onto:
...     class Bacterium(Thing): pass
...     class Shape(Thing): pass
...     class Grouping(Thing): pass
```

Note that, since these classes are empty (that is to say that they have no method), we must use the keyword `pass` (see 2.9).

In order to observe what is happening inside the Owlready quadstore, we can use the function `set_log_level()` which modifies the level of logging. By setting the level to its maximum (9), Owlready indicates the RDF triples added, deleted, or modified in the quadstore. Here is an example:

```
>>> set_log_level(9)
>>> with onto:
...     class TestClass(Thing): pass
* Owlready2 * ADD TRIPLE http://test.org/onto.owl#TestClass↲
    http://www.w3.org/1999/02/22-rdf-syntax-ns#type↲
    http://www.w3.org/2002/07/owl#Class
* Owlready2 * ADD TRIPLE http://test.org/onto.owl#TestClass↲
    http://www.w3.org/2000/01/rdf-schema#subClassOf↲
    http://www.w3.org/2002/07/owl#Thing
```

Here, the creation of the TestClass class triggered the addition of two RDF triples: the first indicates that TestClass is an OWL class, and the second indicates that TestClass inherits from Thing.

To stop logging, we will simply do:

```
>>> set_log_level(0)
```

We can also create new OWL classes by inheriting from a class that itself inherits from `Thing`, for example, the Shape or the Grouping classes:

```
>>> with onto:
...     class Rod(Shape): pass
...     class Isolated(Grouping): pass
...     class InPair(Grouping): pass
```

The IRI of the created classes is obtained by concatenating the base IRI of the ontology with the name of the class:

```
>>> Bacterium.iri
'http://test.org/onto.owl#Bacterium'
```

The parent class can also come from another ontology, such as the Bacterium class from the ontology of bacteria (which must be previously loaded, here in the ontology `onto_chap3` variable, from an OWL file "bacteria.owl" located in the current directory; make sure that you are running the example in the working directory used in Chapter 3):

```
>>> onto_chap3 = get_ontology("bacteria.owl").load()
>>> with onto:
...     class MyBacteriumClass(onto_chap3.Bacterium): pass
```

Multiple inheritance is possible and can be used as in Python. The following example creates the Ribozyme class, which inherits both RNA and enzyme (a ribozyme being an RNA that behaves like an enzyme):

```
>>> with onto:
...     class RNA(Thing): pass
...     class Enzyme(Thing): pass
...     class Ribozyme(RNA, Enzyme): pass
```

5.2.1 Creating classes dynamically

The Python `types` module allows you to create classes dynamically, when the name of the class is not known at the time of writing the program, but is available in a variable at runtime. Here is an example:

```
>>> import types
>>> class_name = "MyClass"
>>> SuperClasses = [Thing]
>>> with onto:
...     NewClass = types.new_class(class_name, tuple↲
        (SuperClasses))
```

Please note the `new_class()` function expects a tuple with the parent classes, not a list! This is why in the example we used the `tuple()` function to transform the list into a tuple.

5.3 Creating properties

In Owlready, properties are assimilated to classes, because OWL properties behave similarly to classes (with in particular inheritance support). In fact, OWL properties are actually "classes of relationship". Properties are created by defining a class that inherits from `DataProperty`, `ObjectProperty`, or `AnnotationProperty`. In addition, the classes `FunctionalProperty`, `InverseFunctionalProperty`, `TransitiveProperty`, `SymmetricProperty`, `AsymmetricProperty`, `ReflexiveProperty`, and `IrreflexiveProperty` can be used as additional superclasses (using multiple inheritance) in order to create functional, inverse functional, transitive, and other properties.

The `domain` and `range` class attributes are used to query or define the domain and the range of the property, in the form of a list.

The following example creates the functional functional property has_shape:

```
>>> with onto:
...     class has_shape(ObjectProperty, FunctionalProperty):
...         domain = [Bacterium]
...         range  = [Shape]
```

For `DataProperty`, the possible ranges appear in the right column of Table 4-1.

In addition, Owlready offers a simplified notation "domain >> range" which is used in place of the parent property (NB: the type of property, `DataProperty` or `ObjectProperty`, is automatically deduced from the range), for example:

```
>>> with onto:
...     class has_grouping(Bacterium >> Grouping):
...         pass
...     class has_shape(Bacterium >> Shape, FunctionalProperty):
...         pass
```

```
...     class gram_positive(Bacterium >> bool, FunctionalProperty):
...         pass
```

OWL also allows you to create subproperties, that is, properties that inherit from another property, as follows:

```
>>> with onto:
...     class has_rare_shape(has_shape): pass
```

5.4 Creating individuals

Individuals are created like any other instance in Python, by calling the class:

```
>>> my_bacterium = Bacterium()
```

The new individual is, by default, displayed in the format "ontology_name.individual name", where ontology_name is the ontology filename (without the .owl extension) and individual name is the class name in lowercase plus a number:

```
>>> my_bacterium
onto.bacterium1
```

Owlready automatically assigns a new IRI to the individual, created by taking the IRI of the ontology (that of the block with ...: or by default the one associated with the class) and adding the name of the class in lowercase followed by a number starting at 1:

```
>>> my_bacterium.iri
'http://test.org/onto.owl#bacterium1'
```

Be careful not to confuse the name of the Python variable that contains the individual locally (here, "my_bacterium") with the name of the entity (here, "bacterium1"). When accessing the individual from the ontology, you must use the name of the entity and not the name of the variable, for example, `onto.bacterium1`. On the other hand, when accessing the individual directly in Python, you must use his variable name, because it is a Python variable, for example, `my_bacterium`.

```
>>> my_bacterium is onto.bacterium1
True
```

It is possible to specify the name of the individual by passing it as the first argument to the constructor of the class:

```
>>> my_bacterium = Bacterium("my_bacterium")
>>> my_bacterium
onto.my_bacterium
```

It is also possible to provide the value of one or more relations when creating the individual, using named arguments:

```
>>> my_bacterium = Bacterium("my_bacterium",
...                          gram_positive = True,
...                          has_shape = Rod(),
...                          has_grouping = [Isolated()] )
```

Here, we have created a new instance of the Rod class for the value of the property has_shape and a new instance of the `Isolated` class for the property has_grouping. For the latter, we have given as value a list because the property is not functional.

Finally, Owlready also allows you to create anonymous individuals (represented by anonymous nodes in the RDF graph). These are created by passing 0 (zero) instead of the individual's name (the number obtained is arbitrary, and you may therefore have another one):

```
>>> anonymous_bacterium = Bacterium(0)
>>> anonymous_bacterium
_:52
```

5.5 Modifying entities: relations and existential restrictions

Relationships between individuals and existential restrictions can be modified like any other attribute in Python. For example, it is possible to modify an individual's relationships as follows:

```
>>> my_bacterium.gram_positive = True
```

If it is a property of type ObjectProperty, a new instance of the expected class can be created (here, the Rod class):

```
>>> my_bacterium.has_shape = Rod()
>>> my_bacterium.has_shape
onto.rod1
```

When the property is functional, Owlready expects a single value (as in the preceding two lines). Otherwise, Owlready expects a list of values. However, the lists used by Owlready are not "ordinary" Python lists, as we can see by looking at the class of these lists and comparing it to plain Python lists:

```
>>> my_bacterium.has_grouping.__class__
<class 'owlready2.prop.IndividualValueList'>

>>> [].__class__
<class 'list'>
```

Owlready's lists are "CallbackList" which are able to detect the addition or deletion of elements in the list, in order to automatically update the quadstore. It is therefore possible to directly modify these lists, for example, with the append(), insert(), or remove() methods:

```
>>> my_bacterium.has_grouping = [Isolated()]
>>> my_bacterium.has_grouping.append(InPair())
```

Notice that Owlready automatically transforms any list assigned to a relation into a CallbackList (such as the list "`[Isolated()]`" in the preceding example).

As seen in the previous chapter (section 4.5.4), existential restrictions and value restrictions ("some" and "value" restrictions) are accessible in Owlready as class properties. It works in reading but also in writing.

For example, we can change the Gram status of the Pseudomonas class as follows:

```
>>> onto_chap3.Pseudomonas.gram_positive = True
```

And restore it as follows:

```
>>> onto_chap3.Pseudomonas.gram_positive = False
```

We will also return to class properties in more detail in 6.3. Beyond existential restrictions, Owlready allows you to create any kind of OWL constructors, which we will see later (in 6.1).

5.6 Creating entities within a namespace

By default, Owlready creates entities in the ontology namespace, that is, the entity's IRI begins with the ontology's IRI. However, it is sometimes necessary to create entities whose IRI does not start with that of ontology. To do this, you need to create a namespace and then use that namespace in the `with` block. Contrary to what we had done previously in 4.8, the namespace must here be created from the ontology, so that the RDF triples are added in the given ontology. The following example defines in the ontology `onto` a class whose IRI is "`http://purl.obolibrary.org/obo/OBOBacterium`":

```
>>> obo = onto.get_namespace("http://purl.obolibrary.org/obo/")
>>> with obo:
...     class OBOBacterium(Thing): pass
>>> OBOBacterium.iri
'http://purl.obolibrary.org/obo/OBOBacterium'
```

The same method can be used for individuals:

```
>>> with obo:
...     my_bacterium = OBOBacterium("my_bacterium")
>>> my_bacterium.iri
'http://purl.obolibrary.org/obo/my_bacterium'
```

5.7 Renaming entities (refactoring)

The name and iri attributes of any entity can be modified to change the entity's IRI (an operation sometimes known as refactoring). Modifying the name attribute allows you to change the name of the entity while keeping it in the same namespace, while modifying the iri attribute allows you to change both the namespace and the name.

```
>>> my_bacterium.iri = "http://test.org/other_onto.↲
owl#bacterium1"
```

Attention, renaming the entity changes its name in the ontology, but not the name of the Python variables! After the preceding line, the individual is still available in the Python variable my_bacterium. However, it is no longer available as onto.my_bacterium but can be retrieved by creating the corresponding namespace:

```
>>> get_namespace("http://test.org/other_onto.owl").bacterium1
```

Also be careful, renaming an entity does not move it to another ontology.

5.8 Multiple definitions and forward declarations

When several entities are defined with the same IRI, Owlready does not create a new entity but returns the already existing entity. This is updated if necessary, for example, with the new relationships, the parent class (for individuals) and/or inheritances (for classes). In the following example, only one individual of the class Bacterium is created, because `bacterium_a` and `bacterium_b` have the same IRI. However, the second creation adds the relation "gram_positive" with the value `False`.

```
>>> with onto:
...     bacterium_a = Bacterium("the_bacterium")
...     bacterium_b = Bacterium("the_bacterium",
...                             gram_positive = False)
>>> bacterium_a is bacterium_b
True
```

In this way, it is possible to make forward declarations for classes or individuals. In the following example, the Bacterium class is first created, and then it is used in the has_shape property domain. The definition of the class Bacterium is then continued to add the existential restriction "to have at least one shape".

```
>>> with onto:
...     class Bacterium(Thing): pass
...     class Shape(Thing): pass
...     class has_shape(Bacterium >> Shape): pass
...     class Bacterium(Thing):
...         has_shape = Shape
```

Here, the definition of the property has_shape uses the class Bacterium, and the (complete) definition of the class Bacterium requires the property has_shape. It would therefore be impossible to achieve this example without a forward declaration.

5.9 Destroying entities

The global function `destroy_entity()` allows destroying an entity (class, individual, property, etc.).

```
>>> temporary_bacterium = Bacterium()
>>> destroy_entity(temporary_bacterium)
```

5.10 Destroying an ontology

The `destroy()` method allows you to permanently delete an ontology. This method frees up the place occupied by the ontology in the quadstore.

```
>>> onto_temp = get_ontology("http://tmp.org/onto.owl")
>>> onto_temp.destroy()
```

5.11 Saving an ontology

The `save()` method allows saving an ontology on disk:

```
onto.save(file)
```

where file can be a filename or a Python file object. If the file is not specified, Owlready saves the ontology in the corresponding directory in `onto_path` (see section 4.10).

The optional format attribute specifies the format of the ontology file. Currently, Owlready supports two file formats for writing: RDF/XML (format = rdfxml) and N-Triples (format = ntriples). By default, the RDF/XML format is used. For example, you can save an ontology in N-Triples as follows:

```
>>> onto.save("file.owl", format = "ntriples")
```

5.12 Importing ontologies

To import an ontology, simply add it to the imported_ontologies list of the destination ontology:

```
>>> onto.imported_ontologies.append(another_onto)
```

To remove the import, simply remove the ontology from the list with remove():

```
>>> onto.imported_ontologies.remove(another_onto)
```

5.13 Synchronization

When a multithreaded program uses Owlready to create or modify ontologies, several threads may want to write to the quadstore at the same time, which can cause database corruption. Note that even if each thread writes to a different ontology, the problem remains the same, because all the ontologies actually share the same quadstore. In the case of a multithreaded program, it is therefore necessary to synchronize the writes (on the contrary, the readings do not need to be synchronized).

In particular, web servers generated with Flask are generally multithreaded (by default, Flask uses the Werkzeug server which starts the server in multithreaded mode). In the previous chapter, we did not have a synchronization problem because the server only read the ontology, but did not modify it.

Owlready manages synchronization automatically, as follows. Owlready automatically locks the write database at the entry of a with ontology: ... block and unlocks it at the exit of the block. Similarly, the following functions and methods are also automatically synchronized: `get_ontology()`, `ontology.load()`, `ontology.destroy()`, and `sync_reasoner()` (which we will see in the next chapter).

In conclusion, as long as you use the syntax "with ontology: ...", you (practically) don't have to worry about synchronization! We will see an example of synchronization in the dynamic multithreaded website of section 7.7.

5.14 Example: populating an ontology from a CSV file

Populating an ontology consists of creating a large number of individuals (or possibly classes). This is often done from external resources, such as spreadsheet files (e.g., LibreOffice Calc, Excel, etc.). These spreadsheet files can be saved in CSV format which is easily readable in Python.

The Python `csv` module makes it easy to read and write CSV files in Python. It contains two classes, `csv.reader` and `csv.writer`, for reading and writing respectively. Each takes an open Python file object as a parameter. The `next()` function allows you to get the next line from a `reader`.

In the next two sections, we will see an example of populating the ontology of bacteria with individuals, then with classes.

5.14.1 Populating with individuals

The following figure shows a simple example of a CSV file describing individuals of the class Bacteria. This file is named "population_individuals.csv"; here is what it looks like:

	A	B	C	D	E
1	ID	gram_positive	shape	grouping	nb_colonies
2	bact1	True	Round	InCluster	2
3	bact2	False	Rod	InChain	5
4	bact3	True	Rod	Isolated	4
5	bact3			InPair	
6					

When a bacterium has several groupings, it can be described on several lines (e.g., the bacterium "bact3" in the previous figure).

The following program is used to populate the ontology with individuals created from the data in the CSV file:

```
# File population_individuals.py
from owlready2 import *
import csv

onto = get_ontology("bacteria.owl").load()

onto_individuals = get_ontology("http://lesfleursdunormal.fr/↲
static/_downloads/bacteria_individuals.owl")
onto_individuals.imported_ontologies.append(onto)

f = open("population_individuals.csv")
reader = csv.reader(f)
next(reader)

with onto_individuals:
    for row in reader:
```

```
        id, gram_positive, shape, grouping, nb_colonies = row
        individual = onto.Bacterium(id)

        if gram_positive:
            if gram_positive == "True": gram_positive = True
            else:                       gram_positive = False
            individual.gram_positive = gram_positive

        if nb_colonies:
            individual.nb_colonies = int(nb_colonies)

        if shape:
            shape_class = onto[shape]
            shape = shape_class()
            individual.has_shape = shape

        if grouping:
            grouping_class = onto[grouping]
            grouping = grouping_class()
            individual.has_grouping.append(grouping)

onto_individuals.save("bacteria_individuals.owl")
```

The program includes the following steps:

1. Import the owlready and csv Python modules.
2. Load the bacteria ontology.
3. Create a new ontology to store individuals, named "bacteria_individuals.owl". Indeed, when content is generated automatically, it is preferable to store it in a separate ontology in order to be able to distinguish it from the content produced by hand in Protégé. This new ontology imports the previous "bacteria.owl" ontology.

4. Open the CSV file for reading, and skip the first line with the `next()` function. Indeed, the first line contains the column headers ("id", "gram_positive", etc.) but does not describe a bacterium.

5. Start a "with: ..." block, indicating that all the RDF triples created will be saved in the new ontology.

6. For each row remaining in the CSV file:

   (a) Retrieve the identifier, the Gram status, the form, the grouping, and the number of colonies in the current row.

   (b) Create the individual of the Bacterium class with the desired identifier. Note that if an individual has already been created with the same identifier, the already existing one is returned.

   (c) For the "gram_positive" and "nb_colonies" properties:

      i. Check that the value is not missing in the CSV file.

      ii. Convert the value to the desired format. Indeed, all the values extracted from the CSV file are character strings. Here, we convert the values to boolean (for Gram status) and to integer (for number of colonies).

      iii. Assign a value to the individual.

(d) For the "shape" and "grouping" properties, the steps are similar. We retrieve the corresponding class in the ontology of bacteria (with the syntax "ontology[name of the entity]"), and we create a new instance. Then we assign the value to the individual. For the "grouping" property, the value in Owlready is a list because the property is not functional, so we add the new value to this list.

7. Save the new ontology.

Subsequently, if the CSV file is modified, it is easy to delete the "bacteria_individuals.owl" ontology and recreate it by running the program again.

5.14.2 Populating with classes

Ontologies can also be populating from a CSV file describing classes instead of individuals. In fact, in the biomedical field, the entities considered can almost always be subdivided: for example, the species of bacteria into subspecies and then in strains, drugs according to the dosage, brand or batch number of the manufacturer, diseases according to severity, chronicity, and so on. In this case, it is frequent to use only classes to model a domain.

The following figure shows a simple example of a CSV file describing subclasses of bacteria:

	A	B	C	D	E
1	ID	parent	gram_positive	shape	grouping
2	Enterococcus	Coccus	False	Round	InSmallChain
3	BacillusAnthracis	Bacterium	True	Rod	InLongChain
4	Bifidobacterium	Bacterium	True	Rod	Isolated
5	Bifidobacterium				InPair
6					

This file is named "population_classes.csv". This file is similar to the previous CSV file for individuals, but it has a new column "parent", used for inheritance. In addition, the column "nb_colonies" has been removed, because the number of colonies can be counted for a given observation, but not for a species of bacteria. When a class has several parents and/or several groupings, it can be described on several lines (like the class Bifidobacterium in the previous figure).

The following program populates the ontology with classes created from the data in the CSV file:

```
# File population_classes.py
from owlready2 import *
import csv, types

onto = get_ontology("bacteria.owl").load()

onto_classes = get_ontology("http://lesfleursdunormal.fr/↲
static/_downloads/bacteria_classes.owl")
onto_classes.imported_ontologies.append(onto)

f = open("population_classes.csv")
reader = csv.reader(f)
next(reader)

with onto_classes:
    for row in reader:
        id, parent, gram_positive, shape, grouping = row

        if parent: parent = onto[parent]
        else:      parent = Thing

        Class = types.new_class(id, (parent,))
```

```
        if gram_positive:
            if gram_positive == "True": gram_positive = True
            else:                       gram_positive = False
            Class.gram_positive = gram_positive

        if shape:
            shape_class = onto[shape]
            Class.has_shape = shape_class

        if grouping:
            grouping_class = onto[grouping]
            Class.has_grouping.append(grouping_class)

onto_classes.save("bacteria_classes.owl")
```

This program follows the same structure as the previous one, with three differences:

- The name of the parent class is present in the "parent" row. The class itself is obtained from the ontology, and it defaults to `Thing`.
- The new class is created using the `types` Python module to dynamically create a class whose name is available in a variable (see section 5.2.1). If a class with the same name has already been created previously, the same class is returned (after being updated if a new parent class has been specified).
- For the shape and grouping properties, we use the class directly without creating an instance. The properties of the new class are therefore defined as existential restrictions, which are used as class properties in Owlready (see sections 4.5.4 and 5.5).

We made the choice not to use a formal definition in the classes (using "equivalent_to", as we did for the Pseudomonas class in Chapter 3). We could have made a different choice and created definitions using equivalence relations and constructors (we will do this in the next chapter; see 6.6).

To check that the program is working properly, we can open the ontology created in Python in the Protégé editor, as shown in the following image:

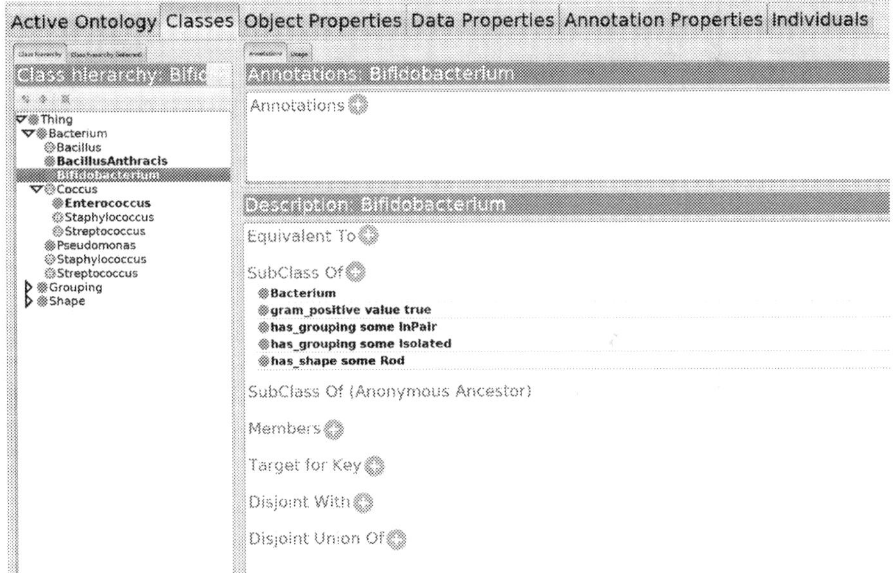

5.15 Summary

In this chapter, you have learned how to modify existing ontologies in Python and to create new ontologies from scratch. We also discussed the problem of synchronization in a multithreaded program. Finally, we have seen how to populate an ontology from simple CSV files, accessible with any spreadsheet software.

CHAPTER 6

Constructs, restrictions, and class properties

In this chapter, we will see how to handle all the OWL constructors in Python with Owlready. We will also see the different "shortcuts" that Owlready offers to facilitate the use of constructors and in particular restrictions.

6.1 Creating constructs

OWL constructors allow you to define logical constructions from classes, individuals, and properties (see sections 3.4.6 and 3.4.7).

In Owlready, restrictions are created with the syntax "property.restriction_type(value)", using the same keywords for restriction types as in Protected:

- `property.some(Class)` for an existential restriction
- `property.only(Class)` for a universal restriction
- `property.value(individual or data)` for a value restriction (also called *role-filler*)

L. Jean-Baptiste, *Ontologies with Python*, https://doi.org/10.1007/978-1-4842-6552-9_6

- `property.exactly(cardinality, Class)` for an exact cardinality restriction
- `property.min(cardinality, Class)` and `property.max(cardinality, Class)` for minimal and maximal cardinality restrictions, respectively

The logical operators NOT (complement), AND (intersection), and OR (union) are obtained as follows:

- `Not(Class)`
- `And([Class1, Class2,...])` or `Class1 & Class2 & ...`
- `Or([Class1, Class2,...])` or `Class1 | Class2 | ...`

A set of individuals is obtained as follows:

- `OneOf([individual1, individual2,...])`

The inverse of a property is obtained as follows:

- `Inverse(Property)`

A property chain (also called composition) is obtained as follows:

- `PropertyChain([Property1, Property2,...])`

In the previous definitions, the classes can be entities, but also other constructors. Constructors can therefore be nested within each other.

Constructors can be used in the `is_a` and `equivalent_to` attributes of classes. For example, we can create the Coccus class (which groups round bacteria; see 3.3), entirely in Python, as follows:

```
>>> from owlready2 import *
>>> onto = get_ontology("bacteria.owl").load()
>>> with onto:
...     class Coccus(onto.Bacterium):
...         equivalent_to = [
```

```
...           onto.Bacterium & onto.has_shape.some(onto.Round)
...                & onto.has_shape.only(onto.Round)
...           ]
```

Similarly, we can define the Pseudomonas class with four restrictions:

```
>>> with onto:
...       class Pseudomonas(onto.Bacterium):
...           is_a = [
...             onto.has_shape.some(onto.Rod),
...             onto.has_shape.only(onto.Rod),
...             onto.has_grouping.some(onto.Isolated |↲
                onto.InPair),
...             onto.gram_positive.value(False)
...           ]
```

Owlready will automatically complete the `is_a` list of the class created with the class (or classes) declared as the parent class in Python (here, the `Bacterium` class). We can verify that as follows:

```
>>> Pseudomonas.is_a
[bacteria.Bacterium,
 bacteria.has_shape.some(bacteria.Rod),
 bacteria.has_shape.only(bacteria.Rod),
 bacteria.has_grouping.some(bacteria.Isolated | bacteria.InPair),
 bacteria.gram_positive.value(False)]
```

6.2 Accessing construct parameters

The following attributes provide access to the information contained in the main constructors (for the full list of constructors and their attributes, refer to C.6 in the reference manual, Appendix C):

- Logical operators AND and OR (intersection and union, class `And` and `Or`, respectively):
  - Attribute `Classes`: The list of classes to which the intersection or union relates
- Restrictions (class `Restriction`):
  - Attribute `property`: The property to which the restriction relates
  - Attribute `type`: The type of restriction (a value chosen among the constants `SOME`, `ONLY`, `VALUE`, `MAX`, `MIN`, and `EXACTLY`)
  - Attribute `value`: The value to which the restriction relates (a class for types `SOME`, `ONLY`, `MAX`, `MIN`, and `EXACTLY`, an individual or a value for type `VALUE`)
  - Attribute `cardinality`: The number of relationships concerned (only available for `MAX`, `MIN`, and `EXACTLY` restrictions)

For example, if we take the class Streptococcus and its equivalent definition, we can analyze it as follows in Python:

```
>>> onto.Streptococcus.equivalent_to[0]
bacteria.Bacterium
& bacteria.has_shape.some(bacteria.Round)
& bacteria.has_shape.only(bacteria.Round)
& bacteria.has_grouping.some(bacteria.InSmallChain)
```

```
& bacteria.has_grouping.only(Not(bacteria.Isolated))
& bacteria.gram_positive.value(True)
>>> onto.Streptococcus.equivalent_to[0].Classes[1]
bacteria.has_shape.some(bacteria.Round)
>>> onto.Streptococcus.equivalent_to[0].Classes[1].property
bacteria.has_shape
>>> onto.Streptococcus.equivalent_to[0].Classes[1].type == SOME
True
>>> onto.Streptococcus.equivalent_to[0].Classes[1].value
bacteria.Round
```

If we do not know the category of constructors used, the isinstance() Python function allows us to test it, for example:

```
>>> constructor = onto.Streptococcus.equivalent_to[0]
>>> if   isinstance(constructor, And):
...     print("And", constructor.Classes)
... elif isinstance(constructor, Or):
...     print("Or", constructor.Classes)
... elif isinstance(constructor, Restriction):
...     print("Restriction", constructor.property,↲
        constructor.type, constructor.value)
And [bacteria.Bacterium,
     bacteria.has_shape.some(bacteria.Round),
     bacteria.has_shape.only(bacteria.Round),
     bacteria.has_grouping.some(bacteria.InSmallChain),
     bacteria.has_grouping.only(Not(bacteria.Isolated)),
     bacteria.gram_positive.value(True)]
```

In addition, the attributes listed here are all modifiable: Owlready automatically updates the quadstore when the attributes are modified. For example, we can change the restriction on the Gram status of the Streptococcus class as follows:

```
>>> onto.Streptococcus.equivalent_to[0].Classes[-1].value = False
```

6.3 Restrictions as class properties

Owlready provides access to all of the OWL constructors, as we saw in the two previous sections. However, the creation of constructors or the access to the information contained in them is often complex and tedious. This is why Owlready also offers several "shortcuts" to facilitate the use of constructors. We have already seen an example of a shortcut for accessing existential restrictions as if they were class properties in 4.5.4.

Indeed, restrictions are often used to represent relationships between classes. The relationships between two classes are more complex than the relationships between two individuals: between two individuals, either the relationship exists (which corresponds to a triple in the quadstore), or it does not exist. On the contrary, a class brings together several individuals, which leads to several scenarios:

- All the individuals of the first class are in relation with at least one individual of the second class: it is the existential restriction ("some" in Protégé).
- All individuals of the first class are in relation with only individuals of the second class: this is the universal restriction ("only" in Protégé).
- Each individual of the first class is in relation to each individual of the second class: OWL does not directly allow this type of relationship between classes

to be created. However, it is possible to obtain an equivalent result by *reifying* the property, that is to say, by transforming it into a class associated with two properties.

Owlready allows translating the relations between two classes into class properties, and *vice versa*. This allows you to easily create or read constructors corresponding to the following forms:

- (Property some Class)
- (Property value individual)
- (Property only (Class or ...))
- (Property only ({ individual,... }))
- (Property only (Class or ... or { individual,... }))

The special annotation "`class_property_type`" indicates which type of restriction is used for a given property. The possible values are

- `["some"]`: When this value is used, class properties correspond to existential restrictions ("some"). This is the default value for a property if the annotation "`class_property_type`" is not specified.
- `["only"]`: When this value is used, class properties correspond to universal restrictions ("only").
- `["some, only"]`: When this value is used, class properties correspond to both existential and universal restrictions.
- `["relation"]`: This value leads to creating direct relationships between classes, using an RDF triple. Please note these direct relationships are not valid in OWL, and they will not be taken into account by the

reasoners. However, many RDF graph databases use direct relationships between classes; this value makes it possible to read or produce such databases. These RDF databases are devoid of formal semantics and therefore are not OWL ontologies.

We can use these class properties to more easily define classes of bacteria in the ontology of bacteria from Chapter 3. We will start by modifying three properties, gram_positive, has_shape, and has_grouping, in order to specify the type of class property associated with each. We have chosen to keep the same modeling choices as in Chapter 3: we will use existential restrictions for gram_positive and has_grouping and both existential and universal restrictions for has_shape:

```
>>> with onto:
...     onto.gram_positive.class_property_type = ["some"]
...     onto.has_shape.class_property_type = ["some, only"]
...     onto.has_grouping.class_property_type = ["some"]
```

Then, we can create a new Pseudomonas class, called Pseudomonas2, in a simpler way than before (see 6.1), by simply defining the values of the class properties:

```
>>> with onto:
...     class Pseudomonas2(onto.Bacterium): pass
...     Pseudomonas2.gram_positive = False
...     Pseudomonas2.has_shape = onto.Rod
...     Pseudomonas2.has_grouping = [onto.Isolated | onto.InPair]
```

The following syntax is equivalent, but simpler. It consists in defining the class properties in the body of the class (see 2.9 for the syntax of the class statement in Python and the use of class properties):

```
>>> with onto:
...     class Pseudomonas3(onto.Bacterium):
```

```
...         gram_positive = False
...         has_shape = onto.Rod
...         has_grouping = [onto.Isolated | onto.InPair]
```

We can then verify that the restrictions have been created as expected:

```
>>> Pseudomonas3.is_a
[bacteria.Bacterium,
 bacteria.has_shape.some(bacteria.Rod),
 bacteria.has_shape.only(bacteria.Rod),
 bacteria.has_grouping.some(bacteria.Isolated | bacteria.InPair),
 bacteria.gram_positive.value(False)]
```

The Pseudomonas3 class obtained is identical to that defined here using the constructor (see 6.1).

We can also create new classes of bacteria using class properties:

```
>>> with onto:
...     class Listeria(onto.Bacterium):
...         gram_positive = True
...         has_shape     = onto.Rod
...         has_grouping  = [onto.InLongChain]
>>> Listeria.is_a
[bacteria.Bacterium,
 bacteria.has_shape.some(bacteria.Rod),
 bacteria.has_shape.only(bacteria.Rod),
 bacteria.has_grouping.some(bacteria.InLongChain),
 bacteria.gram_positive.value(True)]
```

Classes and their class properties can be changed; Owlready will automatically update the restrictions in the quadstore. In the following example, we add a grouping to the Listeria class:

```
>>> Listeria.has_grouping.append(onto.Isolated)
>>> Listeria.is_a
```

```
[bacteria.Bacterium,
 bacteria.has_shape.some(bacteria.Rod),
 bacteria.has_shape.only(bacteria.Rod),
 bacteria.has_grouping.some(bacteria.InLongChain),
 bacteria.has_grouping.some(bacteria.Isolated),
 bacteria.gram_positive.value(True)]
```

Class properties also work for "reading", that is, to analyze the constructors of a class, even if they were not created via Owlready class properties. For example, if we create the `Listeria2` class like this, using constructors:

```
>>> with onto:
...     class Listeria2(onto.Bacterium):
...         is_a = [onto.has_shape.some(onto.Rod),
...                 onto.has_shape.only(onto.Rod),
...                 onto.has_grouping.some(onto.InLongChain),
...                 onto.gram_positive.value(True)]
```

We can still use class properties to analyze constructors (or modify them):

```
>>> Listeria2.has_grouping
[bacteria.InLongChain]
```

This explains why we were able to use the class properties in Chapter 4 to access an external ontology.

The following table summarizes the types of class properties supported by Owlready and the constructors it generates. In this table, `C`, `C1`, and `C2` are classes, `i1` and `i2` are individuals, and `p` is a property.

p.class_property_type	**Translation of** <<C.p = [C1, C2,..., i1, i2,...]>>
["some"]	C subclassof: p some C1 C subclassof: p some C2 ... C subclassof: p value i1 C subclassof: p value i2 ...
["only"]	C subclassof: p only (C1 or C2... or {i1, i2...})
["some, only"]	C subclassof: p some C1 C subclassof: p some C2 ... C subclassof: p value i1 C subclassof: p value i2 ... C subclassof: p only (C1 or C2... or {i1, i2...})
["relation"]	Assert the following RDF triples: (C, p, C1) (C, p, C2) ... (C, p, i1) (C, p, i2) ...

6.4 Defined classes

Owlready also allows you to use class properties to create defined classes, with definitions of the following form:

- Parent_class1 and Parent_class2 ...
  and (Property some Class) ...
  and (Property value individual) ...
  and (Property only (Class ... or { individual,... }))

To do this, Owlready uses the special boolean annotation "`defined_class`" to indicate that a class is defined. If this annotation is `True` for a class, Owlready will generate a definition from the class properties instead of the restrictions seen in the previous section. The default value is `False` for this annotation.

The following example creates a new defined class of Bacterium:

```
>>> with onto:
...     class Corynebacterium(onto.Bacterium):
...         defined_class = True
...         gram_positive = False
...         has_shape = onto.Rod
...         has_grouping = [onto.InCluster]
```

Note the first line of the class body, "`defined_class = True`", which indicates that it is a defined class.

We can verify that the definition has been created:

```
>>> Corynebacterium.equivalent_to
[bacteria.Bacterium
& bacteria.gram_positive.value(False)
& bacteria.has_shape.some(bacteria.Rod)
& bacteria.has_shape.only(bacteria.Rod)
& bacteria.has_grouping.some(bacteria.InCluster)]
```

On the other hand, Owlready did not create a simple restriction (that is to say, apart from those present in the definition):

```
>>> Corynebacterium.is_a
[bacteria.Bacterium]
```

As before, the class properties can be modified, and Owlready will update the definition automatically. Similarly, the properties of the class also allow access to the information present in the definition, even if it was not created with Owlready.

When creating the definition, Owlready combines the different values of the class properties into a single definition. Generally, if `C`, `P1`, `P2`, `S1`, `S2`, `O1`, and `O2` are classes, `s` is a property that uses existential restrictions, `o` is a property that uses universal restrictions, and `s1`, `s2`, `o1`, and `o2` are individuals, when we define:

```
C.is_a = [P1, P2,...]
C.s = [S1, S2,..., s1, s2,...]
C.o = [O1, O2,..., o1, o2,...]
```

Owlready will generate the following definition:

```
C equivalent_to P1 and P2...
            and (s some S1) and (s some S2)...
            and (s value s1) and (s value s2)...
            and (o only (O1 or O2... or {o1, o2...}))
```

6.5 Example: creating the ontology of bacteria in Python

The following program, given by way of illustration, makes it possible to recreate the ontology of bacteria of Chapter 3 from scratch, entirely in Python, using constructors. Creating an ontology in Python may seem more laborious than with Protégé, but it also has advantages: in particular, it is possible to copy and paste definitions, which allows you to quickly create similar classes.

```
# File create_onto.py
from owlready2 import *

onto = get_ontology("http://lesfleursdunormal.fr/static/↲
_downloads/bacteria.owl#")

with onto:
    class Shape(Thing): pass
    class Round(Shape): pass
    class Rod(Shape): pass

    AllDisjoint([Round, Rod])

    class Grouping(Thing): pass
    class Isolated(Grouping): pass
    class InPair(Grouping): pass
    class InCluster(Grouping): pass
    class InChain(Grouping): pass
    class InSmallChain(InChain): pass
    class InLongChain(InChain): pass

    AllDisjoint([Isolated, InPair, InCluster, InChain])
    AllDisjoint([InSmallChain, InLongChain])

    class Bacterium(Thing): pass
    AllDisjoint([Bacterium, Shape, Grouping])

    class gram_positive(Bacterium >> bool, FunctionalProperty):
        pass
    class nb_colonies(Bacterium >> int, FunctionalProperty):
        pass
```

```
class has_shape(Bacterium >> Shape, FunctionalProperty):
    pass
class has_grouping(Bacterium >> Grouping): pass

class is_shape_of(Shape >> Bacterium):
    inverse = has_shape
class is_grouping_of(Grouping >> Bacterium):
    inverse = has_grouping

class Pseudomonas(Bacterium):
    is_a = [ has_shape.some(Rod),
             has_shape.only(Rod),
             has_grouping.some(Isolated | InPair),
             gram_positive.value(False) ]

class Coccus(Bacterium):
    equivalent_to = [ Bacterium
                    & has_shape.some(Round)
                    & has_shape.only(Round) ]

class Bacillus(Bacterium):
    equivalent_to = [ Bacterium
                    & has_shape.some(Rod)
                    & has_shape.only(Rod) ]

class Staphylococcus(Coccus):
    equivalent_to = [ Bacterium
                    & has_shape.some(Round)
                    & has_shape.only(Round)
                    & has_grouping.some(InCluster)
                    & gram_positive.value(True) ]

class Streptococcus(Coccus):
    equivalent_to = [ Bacterium
```

```
                              & has_shape.some(Round)
                              & has_shape.only(Round)
                              & has_grouping.some(InSmallChain)
                              & has_grouping.only( Not(Isolated) )
                              & gram_positive.value(True) ]

    unknown_bacterium = Bacterium(
        "unknown_bacterium",
        has_shape = Round(),
        has_grouping = [ InCluster("in_cluster1") ],
        gram_positive = True,
        nb_colonies = 6
    )
onto.save("bacteria.owl")
```

6.6 Example: populating an ontology with defined classes

In this example, we will continue the population of the ontology of bacteria. This time, we will populate the ontology with classes (as in 5.14.2), but using definitions with equivalence relations. We will reuse the same CSV file as before (called "population_classes.csv"):

	A	B	C	D	E
1	ID	parent	gram_positive	shape	grouping
2	Enterococcus	Coccus	False	Round	InSmallChain
3	BacillusAnthracis	Bacterium	True	Rod	InLongChain
4	Bifidobacterium	Bacterium	True	Rod	Isolated
5	Bifidobacterium				InPair
6					

We can populate the ontology in two ways: either by using class properties (which is the simplest option) or by using constructors (which is more complicated, but may be necessary if you want to create definitions more complex than those generated by Owlready).

6.6.1 Populating using class properties

The following program uses class properties to populate the ontology of bacteria with defined classes, from the data in the preceding CSV file:

```
# File population_defined_classes1.py
from owlready2 import *
import csv, types

onto = get_ontology("bacteria.owl").load()

onto.gram_positive.class_property_type = ["some"]
onto.has_shape.class_property_type = ["some", "only"]
onto.has_grouping.class_property_type = ["some"]

onto_classes = get_ontology("http://lesfleursdunormal.fr/↲
static/_downloads/bacteria_defined_classes.owl")
onto_classes.imported_ontologies.append(onto)

f = open("population_classes.csv")
reader = csv.reader(f)
next(reader)

with onto_classes:
    for row in reader:
        id, parent, gram_positive, shape, grouping = row

        if parent: parent = onto[parent]
        else:      parent = Thing
```

```
        Class = types.new_class(id, (parent,))
        Class.defined_class = True

        if gram_positive:
            if gram_positive == "True": gram_positive = True
            else:                       gram_positive = False
            Class.gram_positive = gram_positive

        if shape:
            shape_class = onto[shape]
            Class.has_shape = shape_class

        if grouping:
            grouping_class = onto[grouping]
            Class.has_grouping.append(grouping_class)

onto_classes.save("bacteria_defined_classes.owl")
```

This program is very similar to the one we saw in the previous chapter to create undefined classes (see 5.14.2). It only differs in two points:

- At the start of the program, for each of the three properties, we indicated the type of the associated class properties.
- When we create a class, we indicate that it is a defined class (with “Class.defined_class = True”).

To verify the proper functioning of the program after its execution, we can open the ontology created in Python in the Protégé editor, as shown in the following screenshot:

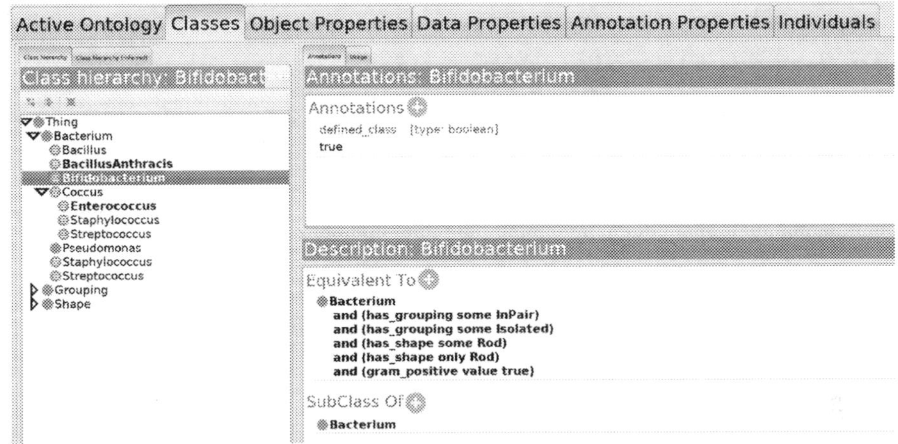

6.6.2 Populating using constructs

The following program also populates the ontology of bacteria with defined classes, from data in the CSV file. Unlike the previous one, it does not use class properties but directly creates constructors. This second program is more complex than the previous one, which shows the interest of Owlready's class properties!

```
# File population_defined_classes2.py
from owlready2 import *
import csv, types

onto = get_ontology("bacteria.owl").load()

onto_classes = get_ontology("http://lesfleursdunormal.fr/↲
static/_downloads/bacteria_defined_classes.owl")
onto_classes.imported_ontologies.append(onto)

f = open("population_classes.csv")
reader = csv.reader(f)
next(reader)
```

```
id_2_parents       = defaultdict(list)
id_2_gram_positive = {}
id_2_shape         = {}
id_2_groupings     = defaultdict(list)

for row in reader:
    id, parent, gram_positive, shape, grouping = row

    if parent:
        id_2_parents[id].append(onto[parent])

    if gram_positive:
        if gram_positive == "True": gram_positive = True
        else:                       gram_positive = False
        id_2_gram_positive[id] = gram_positive

    if shape:
        shape_class = onto[shape]
        id_2_shape[id] = shape_class

    if grouping:
        grouping_class = onto[grouping]
        id_2_groupings[id].append(grouping_class)

with onto_classes:
    for id in id_2_parents:
        if id_2_parents[id]:
            Class = types.new_class(id,↲
            tuple(id_2_parents[id]))
        else:
            Class = types.new_class(id, (Thing,))

        conditions = []
```

```
        if id in id_2_gram_positive:
            conditions.append(onto.gram_positive.value(↲
                                id_2_gram_positive[id]))

        if id in id_2_shape:
            conditions.append(onto.has_shape.some↲
            (id_2_shape[id]))
            conditions.append(onto.has_shape.only↲
            (id_2_shape[id]))

        for grouping in id_2_groupings[id]:
            conditions.append(onto.has_grouping.some(grouping))

        if   len(conditions) == 1:
            Class.equivalent_to.append(conditions[0])
        elif len(conditions) > 1:
            Class.equivalent_to.append( And(conditions) )

onto_classes.save("bacteria_defined_classes.owl")
```

The program has two parts. The first part reads the entire CSV file and stores all the data in dictionaries, and the second creates the classes and the equivalence relationships. Indeed, the equivalence relations must be defined "in one piece" (as we saw in 3.4.8). It is therefore necessary to have all the information on a class to be able to create its definition. However, in our CSV file, a class can be defined on several lines (e.g., here, the class Bifidobacterium). In this case, we cannot create the definition after only reading the first line.

The first part uses standard dictionaries and `defaultdict`, that is, dictionaries with a default value (see 2.4.6), to simplify the program. This dictionary automatically creates the missing entries and initializes them with the value of an empty list.

The second part of the program goes through all the class identifiers in the `id_2_parents` dictionary. For each identifier, we create a class inheriting from the parent classes or, failing that, from `Thing`. Next, we create a list of conditions called `conditions`, initially empty. Then we look at the values available in the dictionaries for the properties `gram_positive`, `has_shape`, and `has_grouping`, and we add in the list conditions the corresponding restrictions:

- For the `gram_positive` property, we used a value restriction because it is a data property.
- For the `has_form` property, we used two restrictions, an existential restriction and a universal restriction, in the manner of what we had done in Chapter 3.
- For the `has_grouping` property, we used a single, existential, restriction in order to leave open the possibility of other groupings.

Finally, we add an equivalence relation in `Class.equivalent_to`. If the `conditions` list contains only one condition, we add this unique condition in `Class.equivalent_to`. If the `conditions` list contains conditions, we perform the intersection of these conditions with the operator `And()`, and then we add this intersection to `Class.equivalent_to`. This means that when several conditions are present, all of them must be satisfied.

The ontology created by this program is equivalent to that created by the previous program.

6.7 Summary

In this chapter, you have learned how to handle OWL constructs and class restrictions, a major feature in OWL. We also presented the various shortcuts Owlready proposes, such as class properties or defined classes. Finally, we have seen how to create defined classes from CSV files and how to create the ontology of bacteria of Chapter 3 entirely in Python. You are now able to create in Python almost everything that can be created in Protégé.

CHAPTER 7

Automatic reasoning

In this chapter, we will see how to use the HermiT and Pellet reasoners in Python, in order to check the consistency of an ontology and to perform automatic deductions and classification, on the basis of the logical constructors.

7.1 Disjoints

Owlready allows creating disjoints between classes with the class AllDisjoint. For example, we can declare the classes Isolated, InPair, InCluster, and InChain as pairwise disjoint, as follows:

```
>>> from owlready2 import *
>>> onto = get_ontology("bacteria.owl").load()

>>> AllDisjoint([onto.Isolated, onto.InPair, onto.InCluster,
... onto.InChain])
```

Note that Owlready, like Protégé, does not distinguish disjoints between two entities from pairwise disjoints between several entities, unlike OWL. Owlready will automatically choose the right OWL method according to the number of entities involved in the disjoint. In addition, AllDisjoint also works with a list of properties (disjoint properties) or a list of individuals (different individuals).

L. Jean-Baptiste, *Ontologies with Python*, https://doi.org/10.1007/978-1-4842-6552-9_7

It is possible to find all the disjoint to which a class belongs, with the disjoints() method. It returns a generator to list the AllDisjoints involving a given entity. Then, the entities attribute of an AllDisjoint makes it possible to obtain the list of entities declared as disjoint.

7.2 Reasoning with the Open-World assumption

The sync_reasoner() function allows you to run the reasoner and automatically apply the facts deduced to the quadstore. By default, the HermiT reasoner is used. The sync_reasoner_pellet() and sync_reasoner_hermit() functions are used to specify the reasoner; Pellet and HermiT work the same way in Owlready.

Note: HermiT and Pellet are Java programs, so you will need to install a Java virtual machine to use them. If you don't have Java, you may install it from www.java.com/ (for Windows and Mac OS) or from the packages of your Linux distribution (the packages are often named "jre" or "jdk" for Java Runtime Environment and Java Development Kit). On the other hand, the reasoners themselves are supplied with Owlready. If Java has been installed in a nonstandard directory (especially on Windows), it is possible to enter the path to Java as follows (replace the path with yours):

```
import owlready2
owlready2.JAVA_EXE = "C:\\Program Files\\Java\\jre8\\bin\\↲
java.exe"
```

For example, let's take the ontology of bacteria and start by checking the class to which the individual "unknown_bacterium" belongs:

```
>>> onto.unknown_bacterium.__class__
bacteria.Bacterium
```

We then run the reasoner:

```
>>> sync_reasoner()
* Owlready2 * Running HermiT...
    java [...]
* Owlready2 * HermiT took 0.5354642868041992 seconds
* Owlready * Reparenting bacteria.unknown_bacterium [...]
```

By default, Owlready displays the reasoner's command line and the reclassifications carried out (the `debug = 0` parameter makes it possible to avoid this display).

Here, we note that the individual "unknown_bacterium" has been reclassified in the Staphylococcus class, as it had been in Protégé:

```
>>> onto.unknown_bacterium.__class__
bacteria.Staphylococcus
```

The facts deduced by the reasoner are by default stored in the ontology "`http://inferrences/`". It is possible to place them in another ontology by using a "with: ..." block, as in the following example:

```
>>> onto_inferences = get_ontology("http://lesfleursdunormal.↲
fr/static/_downloads/bacteria_inferences.owl#")
>>> with onto_inferences:
...     sync_reasoner()
```

This ontology contains the inferences; it can then be saved (see 5.11):

```
>>> onto_inferences.save("bacteria_inferences.owl")
```

The inferences can thus be loaded from the ontology "bacteria_inferences.owl". This will avoid having to call the reasoner again, which saves time.

Owlready also allows you to restrict the reasoning to certain ontologies, by passing a list of ontologies to the sync_reasoner() function:

```
>>> sync_reasoner([onto])
```

Finally, the optional parameters infer_property_values and infer_data_property_values (supported only by the Pellet reasoner) make it possible to infer the values of the properties of individuals (object properties and data properties, respectively, for the two options):

```
>>> sync_reasoner(infer_property_values = True)
>>> sync_reasoner_pellet(infer_data_property_values = True)
```

These two options can also be used simultaneously:

```
>>> sync_reasoner_pellet(infer_property_values = True,
...                      infer_data_property_values = True)
```

7.3 Reasoning in a closed world or in a local closed world

OWL reasoners operate according to the *Open-World hypothesis*: anything that is not prohibited is considered possible (see section 3.5). However, it is often desirable to limit the reasoning to known facts, for the whole of the ontology or for certain entities only. This is called reasoning "in a closed world" or sometimes "negation as failure": that is to say that everything that is not explicitly known is considered false.

In Owlready, the close_world() function allows to "close the world" and to limit the reasoning to the facts present in the ontology, for the individual, the class, or the ontology passed in an argument. This function automatically adds the necessary constraints, in the form of constructors. We speak of "reasoning in a closed world" when all the ontology is closed and "reasoning in a local closed world" when only some entities are closed.

We had already encountered a problem of "open or closed world" with the Streptococcus class in Chapter 3 (see point 2 at the end of section 3.5): a round-shaped bacterium, grouped in chain and having a Gram positive coloring, is classified as a Coccus but not as a Streptococcus, because the reasoner cannot prove that there is no other grouping (unknown and therefore absent in the ontology) which would be of Isolated type.

In the following example, we create the unknown_bacterium2 which corresponds to the preceding criteria:

```
>>> with onto:
...     unknown_bacterium2 = onto.Bacterium(
...                 gram_positive = True,
...                 has_shape     = onto.Round(),
...                 has_grouping  = [onto.InSmallChain()] )
```

For the reason explained earlier, when the reasoner is executed, the bacterium is reclassified in the Coccus class but not in the Streptococcus class:

```
>>> sync_reasoner()
>>> unknown_bacterium2.__class__
bacteria.Coccus
```

Indeed, although only a small chain grouping is asserted for this bacterium, the reasoner works in an open world. He hypothesizes that another type of grouping may exist, but which is not known (the has_grouping property is not functional; thus, it can have several values for the same individual). However, we had defined the Streptococcus class as having no isolated grouping. Here, no isolated grouping is known for the unknown_bacterium2, but nothing prevents us from assuming that such a grouping exists.

To prohibit this hypothesis and solve our problem, we must "close the world", that is to say, when we say that this bacterium has a grouping in a small chain, it necessarily has this grouping, and it has no other grouping than this one. The close_world() function does this, as the following example shows:

```
>>> close_world(unknown_bacterium2)
>>> unknown_bacterium2.is_a
[bacteria.Coccus,
 bacteria.has_grouping.only(OneOf([bacteria.insmallchain1]))]
```

We note that a universal restriction (i.e., *only*) has been added to the individual by close_world(): this restriction indicates that the bacterium only has the grouping inSmallChain1. Note that close_world() has not added any restriction for the properties "gram_positive" and "has_shape", because these are functional: there can be only one value for each of them, and therefore the closing is not necessary.

Now, if we run the reasoner again, we find that the bacterium is well classified as a Streptococcus:

```
>>> sync_reasoner()
>>> unknown_bacterium2.__class__
bacteria.Streptococcus
```

Similarly, the close_world() function can be used to close an entire class or ontology. The complete syntax for this function is as follows:

```
close_world(entity, Properties = None, close_instance_list =↲
True, recursive = True)
```

entity is the entity to be considered in a closed world. Properties is the list of properties to consider (if the value is None, which is the default, all properties will be closed). If close_instance_list is True (default value), the instances of the closed class (or classes) are restricted to the instances asserted in the ontology. If recursive is `True` (default value) when the entity to close is a class, `close_world()` is applied recursively to all descendant classes.

7.4 Inconsistent classes and inconsistent ontologies

During reasoning, the reasoner may detect inconsistent classes. These classes are illogical, and, therefore, there should be no individuals belonging to these classes. For example, in our bacteria ontology, the following class, inheriting from the Streptococcus class and associated with a Rod form (*via* a restriction), would be inconsistent:

```
>>> with onto:
...     class RodStreptococcus(onto.Streptococcus):
...         is_a = [onto.has_shape.some(onto.Rod)]
```

As long as there is no individual belonging to this class, this is not a problem. The inconsistent classes are reclassified as equivalent to `Nothing` by the reasoner. It is therefore possible to test whether a class is inconsistent in Python by testing whether `Nothing` is an equivalent class, for example, to check if the RodStreptococcus class is consistent, we can do:

```
>>> sync_reasoner()

>>> if Nothing in RodStreptococcus.equivalent_to:
...     print("The class is inconsistent!")
... else:
...     print("The class is consistent.")
The class is inconsistent!
```

In addition, the default_world.inconsistent_classes() method provides a generator to iterate over all inconsistent classes.

On the contrary, when there exists at least one individual belonging to an inconsistent class, the entire ontology becomes inconsistent. An inconsistent ontology contains a logical problem that makes it absurd. Any reasoning on the ontology then becomes impossible. Be careful not to confuse an inconsistent class and an inconsistent ontology! In the first case, this does not prevent the reasoner from doing his job, while in the second, reasoning becomes impossible.

In case of an inconsistent ontology, the sync_reasoner() function raises the exception OwlReadyInconsistentOntologyError. Let's continue the previous example and create an individual of the RodStreptococcus class:

```
>>> rod_strepto = onto.RodStreptococcus()
>>> sync_reasoner()
Traceback (most recent call last):
  File "<stdin>", line 1, in <module>
  File "/home/jiba/src/owlready2/reasoning.py", line 120,↲
                                              in sync_reasoner_hermit
    raise OwlReadyInconsistentOntologyError()
owlready2.base.OwlReadyInconsistentOntologyError
```

This exception can be caught in Python, as follows:

```
>>> try:
...     sync_reasoner()
...     print("Ok, the ontology is consistent.")
... except OwlReadyInconsistentOntologyError:
...     print("The ontology is inconsistent!")
The ontology is inconsistent!
```

The ontology of bacteria became inconsistent following the addition of the "rod_strepto" individual. As it stands, we can no longer perform reasoning on the quadstore until this inconsistency is resolved! This is why we are going to delete the ontology of bacteria (modified with the addition of "rod_strepto"), in order to be able to continue using the reasoner in the rest of the chapter.

```
>>> onto.destroy()
```

We can then reload the bacteria ontology in the next chapters from the OWL file (so without the "rod_strepto" individual).

7.5 Restriction and reasoning on numbers and strings

The `ConstrainedDatatype` class is used to create a constrained datatype according to one or more facets, for example, a positive integer or a character string of at least three characters. The syntax is as follows:

```
ConstrainedDatatype(base_datatype, facet1 = value1, facet2 =
value2,...)
```

`base_datatype` is the initial datatype, for example, `int`, `float`, `bool`, `str`, `norm_str`, and so on (see Table 4-1).

The following facets are proposed by XMLSchema and supported by Owlready:

- For numeric types:
  - `max_inclusive`: Maximum value, included (the value must be inferior of equal to the given value)
  - `max_exclusive`: Maximum value, not included (the value must be strictly inferior to the given value)

- `min_inclusive`: Minimum value, included (the value must be superior of equal to the given value)
- `min_exclusive`: Minimum value, not included (the value must be strictly superior to the given value)
- `total_digits`: Number of digits present
- `fraction_digits`: Number of digits present after the decimal point

- For character strings:
  - `length`: Exact number of characters
  - `min_length`: Minimum number of characters
  - `max_length`: Maximum number of characters
  - `pattern`: A regular expression to constrain the possible values for the character string
  - `white_space`: Indicates how white spaces are treated, with three possible values:
    - `preserve`: Spaces are preserved as is.
    - `replace`: All white spaces (space, tabulation, line feed, etc.) are replaced by spaces.
    - `collapse`: As replace, but the spaces at the beginning/end of the chain are removed, and the consecutive multiple white spaces are replaced by a single space.

Please note Owlready allows the definition of facets, but does not take them into account: for example, spaces will not be replaced even if `white_space` is used. On the other hand, other tools can take this into account (including reasoners).

For example, for an integer in the range [0, 20] (inclusive), we will do:

```
>>> ConstrainedDatatype(int, min_inclusive = 0, max_inclusive = 20)
```

These constrained datatypes can be used in OWL restrictions (*some* and *only*), in particular to indicate ranges or restrictions of the form "property value greater than/less than X". In this case, Owlready also offers a shortened notation "property > value" (or >=, <, <=) which allows to automatically create an existential restriction ("some") with the appropriate constrained datatype.

The following example creates an ontology with a `Person` class and two `age` and `size` numeric properties. Then we create the `Elderly` and `TallPerson` classes, which are defined using restrictions on the `age` and `size` properties with constrained datatypes (for the second restriction, we used a shortened notation instead of `size.some (ConstrainedDatatype (int, max_inclusive = 1.8))`).

```
>>> onto_person = get_ontology("http://test.org/person.owl#")

>>> with onto_person:
...     class Person(Thing): pass
...     class age (Person >> int  , FunctionalProperty): pass
...     class size(Person >> float, FunctionalProperty): pass
...     class Elderly(Person):
...       equivalent_to = [
...         Person & age.some(ConstrainedDatatype(int,
...                                        min_inclusive = 65))
...         ]
...     class TallPerson(Person):
...       equivalent_to = [
...         Person & (size >= 1.8) # Shortened notation
...         ]
...
```

```
...       p1 = Person(age = 25, size = 2.0)
...       p2 = Person(age = 39, size = 1.7)
...       p3 = Person(age = 65, size = 1.6)
...       p4 = Person(age = 71, size = 1.9)
```

Attention, when combining the operator "&" for an intersection with the preceding shortened notation, it is necessary to use parentheses because, in the Python language, the order of priority between these operators is not the right one (in Python, & takes precedence over <, >, <=, and >=). This is why in the previous example, we wrote "`Person & (size >= 1.8)`" with the parentheses around "`size >= 1.8`".

We can then run the reasoner to reclassify the four persons we have created:

```
>>> sync_reasoner(onto_person)
```

Finally, we display their new classes (note that the individual `p4` now belongs to two classes, i.e., multiple instantiation, which is permitted in OWL):

```
>>> print("p1", p1.is_a)
p1 [person.TallPerson]

>>> print("p2", p2.is_a)
p2 [person.Person]

>>> print("p3", p3.is_a)
p3 [person.Elderly]

>>> print("p4", p4.is_a)
p4 [person.Elderly, person.TallPerson]
```

Attention, in Protégé, if you want to define classes with constrained datatypes using floating-point values, remember that Owlready associates by default the "decimal" XML Schema datatype with floating numbers of Python. Therefore, the `TallPerson` class should be defined with decimals in Protégé:

```
Person and (size some decimal[>= "1.8"^^decimal])
```

But not with floats.

Here is the result in Protégé:

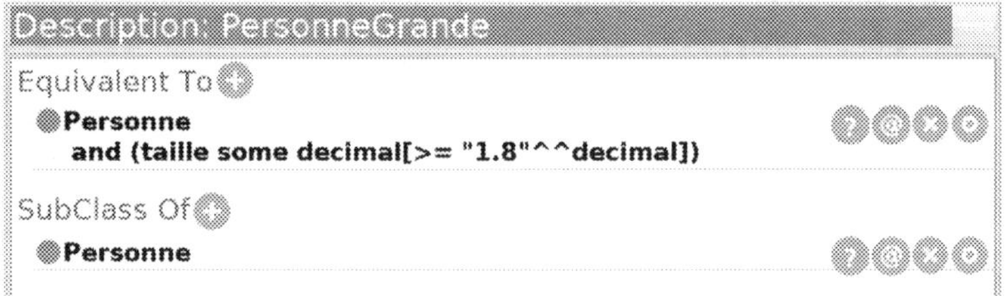

Alternatively, you can also modify the datatype used by Owlready for floats, as follows:

```
>>> set_datatype_iri(float, "http://www.w3.org/2001/↲
XMLSchema#float")
```

7.6 SWRL rules

SWRL (Semantic Web Rule Language) is a language that allows you to integrate inference rules into ontologies. Rules can be written in the Protégé editor or in Python, using Owlready, and then executed *via* the integrated HermiT or Pellet reasoners.

In the ontology of bacteria, the following example rule makes it possible to classify as Staphylococcus all Gram positive bacteria of round shape and grouped in clusters:

```
Bacterium(?b),
gram_positive(?b, true),
has_shape(?b, ?f), Ronde(?f)
has_grouping(?b, ?r), InCluster(?r)
-> Staphylococcus(?b)
```

7.6.1 SWRL syntax

A SWRL rule includes one or more conditions and one or more consequences, separated by an arrow "->" (composed of the two characters: minus and greater than). If the rule has several conditions or consequences, they are separated from each other by a comma "," which has implicitly the meaning of a logical "and". The elements that make up conditions and consequences are called *atoms*, and the same atoms can be used in conditions and in consequences.

In addition, SWRL rules use variables, whose names start with "?", for example, "?b" in the preceding example. These variables can represent individuals or values (whole numbers, real numbers, character strings, booleans, etc.), but never classes or properties.

The atoms available are:

- Membership of a class: "Class (?x)", which means:
  - "if the individual ?x belongs to the class Class" (when the atom is used as a condition)
  - "the individual ?x now belongs to the class Class, in addition to his/her current class(es)" (when used as a consequence)

- Object property value: “object_property(?x, ?y)”, which means:
  - “if the individual ?x has property_object ?y” (condition)
  - “add relation ?x object_property ?y” (consequence)

  Variables can also be replaced by specific individual names, for example, “object_property(?x, individual1)” or “object_property (individual2, ?y)”.
- Data property value: “data_property(?x, ?y)”, which means:
  - “if individual ?x has data_property ?y” (condition)
  - “add relation ?x data_property ?y” (consequence)

  Variables can also be replaced by a specific individual name (for ?x) or by a specific value (for ?y), for example, “data_property(?x, 9.2)” or “data_property(?x, charactersstring)”.
- Identical individuals: “SameAs(?x, ?y)”, which means:
  - “if individual ?x is the same as individual ?y” (condition)
  - “individual ?x is now the same as individual ?y” (consequence)
- Distinct individuals: “DifferentFrom(?x, ?y)”, which means:
  - “if individual ?x is distinct from individual ?y” (condition)
  - “individual ?x is now distinct from individual ?y” (consequence)
- Membership in a datatype: “datatype(?x)”, which means:
  - “if value ?x is of the given datatype” (condition)

The most common datatypes are "int", "decimal" (for floating-point numbers), "bool", "string", and "normalizedString".

- Predefined functions (*built-ins*): "function(?x, ?y,...)". A large number of predefined functions exist; here are the most frequently used:
  - add(?result, ?x, ?y): Computes ?result = ?x + ?y.
  - subtract(?result, ?x, ?y): Computes ?result = ?x - ?y.
  - multiply(?result, ?x, ?y): Computes ?result = ?x × ?y.
  - divide(?result, ?x, ?y): Computes ?result = ?x / ?y.
  - equal(?x, ?y): Tests whether ?x = ?y.
  - notEqual(?x, ?y): Tests whether ?x ≠ ?y.
  - lessThan(?x, ?y): Tests whether ?x < ?y.
  - greaterThan(?x, ?y): Tests whether ?x > ?y.
  - lessThanOrEqual(?x, ?y): Tests whether ?x ≤ ?y.
  - greaterThanOrEqual(?x, ?y): Tests whether ?x ≥ ?y.
  - stringConcat(?result, ?x, ?y): Concatenates ?x and ?y and puts the result in ?result.
  - substring(?result, ?str, ?start, ?length): Tests if the part of the character string ?str starting at ?start and with length ?length is equal to ?result. ?length is optional.
  - stringLength(?length, ?str): Computes the length of the character string ?str and puts the result in ?length.
  - contains(?str, ?part): Tests if the character string ?part is included in ?str.

- containsIgnoreCase(?string, ?part): Same as contains(), but ignoring case.
- startsWith(?str, ?start): Tests if the character string ?str starts with the character string ?start.
- endsWith(?str, ?end): Tests if the character string ?str ends with the character string ?end.

7.6.2 SWRL rules with Protégé

SWRL rules can be entered in Protégé, in the "Active ontology" tab and the "Rules" subtab, as in the following image. Please note that Protégé does not always preserve the order of elements in the rules; however, this does not change their meaning. Attention, **Owlready can only read SWRL rules in ontologies saved in the RDF/XML or N-Triples file formats**. The OWL/XML format is not supported for SWRL rules!

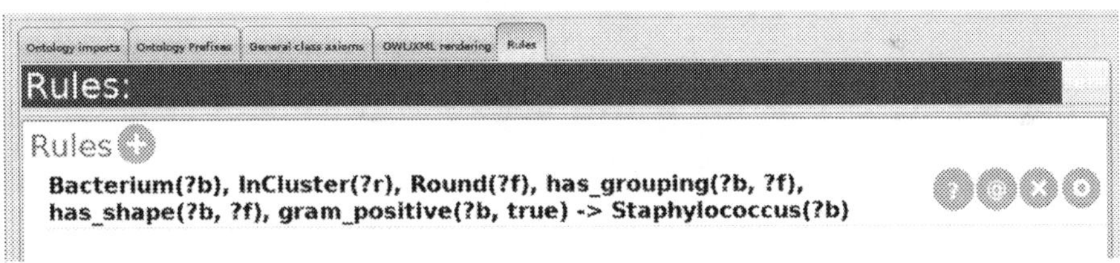

The rules defined in Protégé can then be executed with reasoners (e.g., using the `sync_reasoner()` function with Owlready). When the consequences of rules create new relationships for object properties, it is necessary to run the reasoner with the option `infer_property_value = True`. When they create new relationships for data properties, it is necessary to run the reasoner with the `infer_data_property_value = True` option and to use the Pellet reasoner. HermiT does not allow inferring the values of data properties (see 7.2).

When the rules are defined in Protégé and they use real numbers, Protégé defaults to floats where Owlready expects decimals (see 7.5). It is then necessary to force the decimal type, as in the following example: 2.2^^decimal.

7.6.3 SWRL rules with Owlready

In Owlready, the `Imp` class allows you to create SWRL rules, "Imp" being the abbreviation of "implies". Owlready allows you to create SWRL rules either from a written rule with a syntax equivalent to that of Protégé or by manually creating each of the atoms (which is more complex).

In the following example, we are going to create an ontology of people with a rule to calculate the Body Mass Index (BMI) from the size and weight of the person. The formula for calculating BMI is as follows:

$$BMI = \frac{weight}{size^2} = \frac{weight}{size \times size}$$

BMI is important because it determines obesity: a person is considered obese if his BMI is greater than or equal to 30.

We first create the ontology, with a Person class and three data properties: weight, size, and bmi.

```
>>> onto_person = get_ontology("http://test.org/person2.owl#")

>>> with onto_person:
...     class Person(Thing): pass
...     class weight(Person >> float, FunctionalProperty): pass
...     class size  (Person >> float, FunctionalProperty): pass
...     class bmi   (Person >> float, FunctionalProperty): pass
```

Then, we create a defined class for obese people: anyone with a BMI greater than or equal to 30 will be reclassified in the Obese class.

```
>>> with onto_person:
...     class Obese(Person):
...         equivalent_to = [Person & (bmi >= 30.0)]
```

Finally, we create a SWRL rule. This rule will use the following variables:

- ?x: An individual of the class Person
- ?w: His weight
- ?s: His size
- ?s2: His size squared
- ?b: His BMI

The Imp class allows you to create a new rule in the ontology. Then, the method set_as_rule() makes it possible to define the rule using a Protégé-like syntax:

```
>>> with onto_person:
...     imp = Imp()
...     imp.set_as_rule("Person(?x), weight(?x, ?w),↲
                         size(?x, ?s),↲
                         multiply(?s2, ?s, ?s),↲
                         divide(?b, ?w, ?s2)↲
                         -> bmi(?x, ?b)")
```

We can then create two individuals of the Person class:

```
>>> p1 = Person(size = 1.7, weight = 65.0)
>>> p2 = Person(size = 1.7, weight = 90.0)
```

And run the Pellet reasoner:

```
>>> sync_reasoner_pellet(infer_property_values = True,
...                      infer_data_property_values = True)
```

And finally, question the BMIs and the classes to which the two persons were reclassified:

```
>>> p1.bmi
22.491348
>>> p1.is_a
[person2.Person]

>>> p2.bmi
31.141868
>>> p2.is_a
[person2.Obese]
```

The `str()` Python function displays the rule in the Protégé-like syntax:

```
>>> str(imp)
'Person(?x), weight(?x, ?w), size(?x, ?s),↲
multiply(?s2, ?s, ?s), divide(?b, ?w, ?s2) -> bmi(?x, ?b)'
```

Owlready also provides access to the conditions and consequences of the rule via the body (for conditions) and head (for consequences) attributes:

```
>>> imp.body
[Person(?x), weight(?x, ?w), size(?x, ?s),↲
multiply(?s2, ?s, ?s), divide(?b, ?w, ?s2)]
>>> imp.head
[bmi(?x, ?b)]
```

It is then possible to access each of the atoms. For example, we can retrieve the first atom from the condition part and request its class and attributes:

```
>>> atom = imp.body[0]
>>> atom
Person(?x)
>>> atom.is_a
[swrl.ClassAtom]
>>> atom.class_predicate
person2.Person
>>> atom.arguments
[?x]
```

The reference manual (see C.7) gives the list of classes of atoms and the attributes of each. Attention, Owlready systematically uses the attribute "arguments" to access the arguments of the atom (i.e., the elements placed in parentheses), where SWRL sometimes uses "arguments" and sometimes "argument1" and "argument2". As usual with Owlready, these attributes can be changed directly.

Finally, the `rules()` and `variables()` methods make it possible to obtain a generator to iterate over all the SWRL rules and the SWRL variables in an ontology.

```
>>> list(onto_person.variables())
[?x, ?w, ?s, ?s2, ?b]

>>> list(onto_person.rules())
[Person(?x), weight(?x, ?w), size(?x, ?s),↵
multiply(?s2, ?s, ?s), divide(?b, ?w, ?s2) -> bmi(?x, ?b)]
```

7.6.4 Advantages and limits of SWRL rules

SWRL rules allow reasoning involving several variables (called "free variable"). On the contrary, the class definitions (via equivalence relations, see 3.4.8) have no variables and in fact correspond to "pseudo-rules" with a single free variable. Therefore, some complex reasoning cannot be achieved by class definitions. For example, if we consider people with friendship and enmity relationships, we can create the "AmbiguousPerson" class corresponding to any person with a friend who is also his enemy. This class cannot be defined by an equivalence relation: indeed, we can define a class of People having a friend and having an enemy, but OWL does not allow indicating that this friend and this enemy are the same person. For this, we would need two free variables: one for the AmbiguousPerson and another for his friend/enemy.

On the other hand, this type of reasoning can be easily carried out with a SWRL rule, as follows:

```
Person(?a),
Person(?b),
friend(?a, ?b),
enemy(?a, ?b),
-> AmbiguousPerson(?a)
```

However, the SWRL rules have a major drawback: they are dependent on a given application, which is contrary to the objective of independence of the ontologies (see 3.3). For example, imagine that we use the SWRL rule earlier to recognize Staphylococcus instead of the formal definition (created in 3.4.8). In this case, we cannot deduce the properties of a Staphylococcus: the rule states that all Gram positive bacteria, round and in clusters, are Staphylococcus, but it does not affirm that all Staphylococci are Gram positive, round, and in clusters. Therefore, the SWRL rule allows recognizing Staphylococci, but it does not allow other applications for which we could reuse our bacteria ontology.

It is therefore preferable to use formal definitions when both options are possible and SWRL rules when the reasoning is too complex for the definitions.

7.7 Example: an ontology-based decision support system

A decision support system helps an expert to make a decision, for example, by making proposals. Here, we are interested in the identification of bacteria: from the characteristics observed on the bacteria (Gram status, shape, grouping, etc.) and the knowledge expressed in the ontology of bacteria, the system tries to determine the type of bacteria. The system can also abstain: when the data are insufficient, no determination is made.

This decision support system is implemented in the form of a dynamic website with Flask (which we have already used in section 4.12). It includes two pages: a "data entry" page which contains a form to describe the bacteria observed and a "result" page which performs the reasoning and displays the result.

The following program creates the decision support website:

```
# File decision_support.py
from owlready2 import *
onto = get_ontology("bacteria.owl").load()

from flask import Flask, request
app = Flask(__name__)

@app.route('/')
def entry_page():
    html  = """<html><body>
<h3>Enter the bacteria characteristics:</h3>
<form action="/result">
```

```
    Gram:<br/>
    <input type="radio" name="gram" value="True"/> Positive<br/>
    <input type="radio" name="gram" value="False"/> Negative<br/>
    <br/>
    Shape:<br/>
    <input type="radio" name="shape" value="Round"/> Round<br/>
    <input type="radio" name="shape" value="Rod"/> Rod<br/>
    <br/>
    Groupings:<br/>
    <select name="groupings" multiple="multiple">
        <option value="Isolated">Isolated</option>
        <option value="InPair">InPair</option>
        <option value="InCluster">InCluster</option>
        <option value="InSmallChain">InSmallChain</option>
        <option value="InLongChain">InLongChain</option>
    </select><br/>
    <br/>
    <input type="submit"/>
</form>
</body></html>"""
    return html

ONTO_ID = 0

@app.route('/result')
def page_result():
    global ONTO_ID
    ONTO_ID = ONTO_ID + 1

    onto_tmp = get_ontology("http://tmp.org/onto_%s.owl#" %↵
    ONTO_ID)
```

```
    gram      = request.args.get("gram", "")
    shape     = request.args.get("shape", "")
    groupings = request.args.getlist("groupings")

    with onto_tmp:
        bacterium = onto.Bacterium()

        if   gram == "True": bacterium.gram_positive = True
        elif gram == "False": bacterium.gram_positive = False

        if shape:
            shape_class = onto[shape]
            bacterium.has_shape = shape_class()

        for grouping in groupings:
            grouping_class = onto[grouping]
            bacterium.has_grouping.append(grouping_class())

        close_world(bacterium)

        sync_reasoner([onto, onto_tmp])

    class_names = []
    for bacterium_class in bacterium.is_a:
        if isinstance(bacterium_class, ThingClass):
            class_names.append(bacterium_class.name)
    class_names = "," .join(class_names)

    html  = """<html><body>
<h3>Result: %s</h3>
</body></html>""" % class_names

    onto_tmp.destroy()

    return html

import werkzeug.serving
werkzeug.serving.run_simple("localhost", 5000, app)
```

The first page of the site, for data entry, is a simple HTML page with a form of three fields (we could have used a static HTML page). For Gram status and for shape, "radio button" fields are used. For grouping, it is a "select" field, in order to allow the selection of several values.

The second page, for displaying the results, performs the following steps:

1. Create a new temporary ontology (in order not to "pollute" the ontology of bacteria), with an IRI of the form "`http://tmp.org/onto_XXX.owl#`" where XXX is a number.

2. Retrieve the values of the form parameters. This is done with the functions `request.args.get()` (when the parameter can only take one value) and `request.args.getlist()` (when the parameter can have several values; here, this is the case for groupings).

3. Create an individual bacterium corresponding to the values entered.

4. Close the world for this new bacterium. This will prevent the reasoner from making assumptions about values other than those entered (see section 7.3).

5. Execute the reasoner on two ontologies: the bacteria ontology and the temporary ontology (on the other hand, the other temporary ontologies, created by other threads or processes, will not be taken into account). Inferences are placed in the temporary ontology (for the same reason as before: in order to avoid polluting the main ontology of bacteria).

6. Retrieve the names of the classes to which the bacteria belong after reasoning. The condition "`isinstance(bacterium_class, ThingClass)`" allows you to limit yourself to "true" classes, excluding constructors (and in particular restrictions created by `close_world()`).

7. Destroy the temporary ontology (this destroys the bacterium that we created but also its possible shape and groupings, as well as inferences).

During the execution of the program, the website can be consulted at the address "`http://127.0.0.1:5000`". The following screenshots show the site obtained, with the "entry" page and the "result" page. We entered a Gram positive bacterium, round, grouped in a small chain. After validation, the system tells us that it is a Streptococcus.

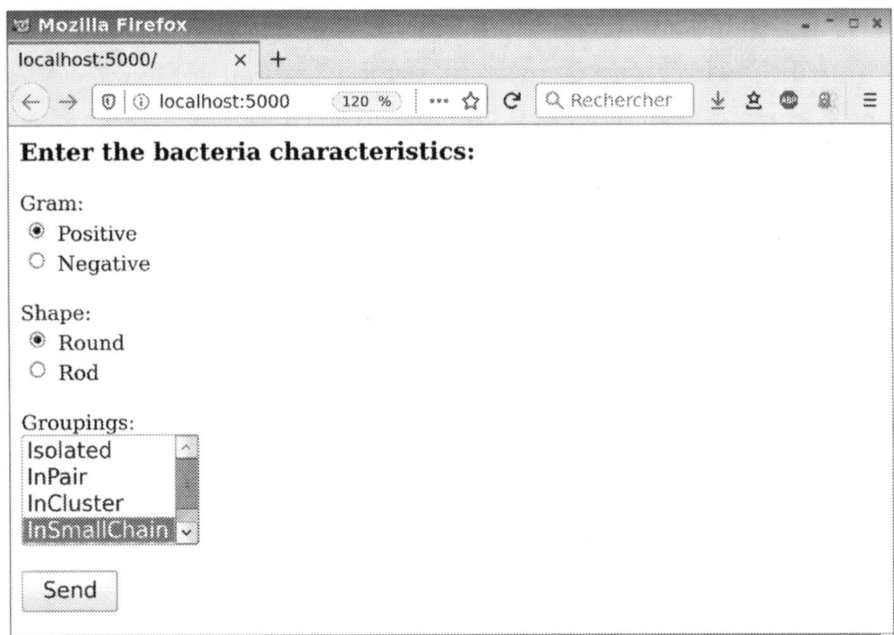

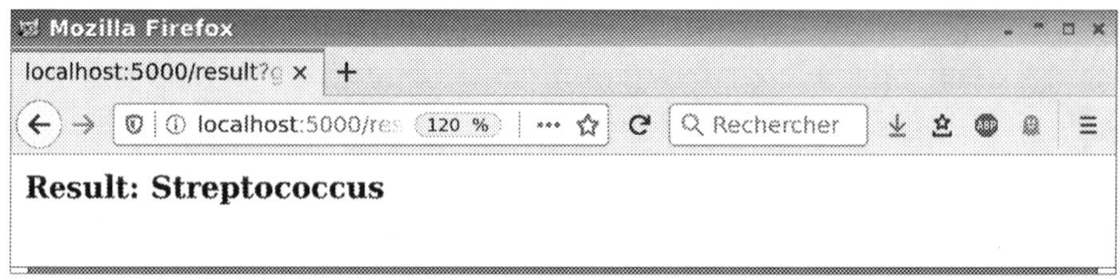

Only the defined classes (by equivalence relations: "equivalent_to") allow reclassifying individuals. As the only classes defined in the ontology of bacteria in Chapter 3 are Staphylococcus, Streptococcus, Coccus, and Bacillus, our system can currently identify only Staphylococci, Streptococci, Cocci, and Bacilli. However, if the ontology were enriched with other classes and other definitions, it would be possible to identify a greater number of bacteria. This would possibly require taking into account more parameters (anaerobic, other colors, etc.) to describe the bacteria in a more detailed way.

Note that the web server is multithreaded and that we write in the quadstore. In this case, we saw in section 5.13 that it is necessary to take synchronization into account. Owlready automatically synchronizes the `get_ontology()` and `ontology.destroy()` instructions, as well as the "with ontology: ..." blocks. So we don't have much left to do to synchronize!

The only point where we have to take synchronization into account is the following: each temporary ontology must necessarily have a different name. We named them with numbers (onto_1.owl, onto_2.owl, etc.). This is necessary because the `page_result()` function can be called simultaneously by several threads. Everyone must therefore have their own ontology: indeed, if they shared the same, when the first thread destroys the ontology (`onto_tmp.destroy()`), the second could no longer continue to work on it.

7.8 Summary

In this chapter, you have learned how to perform automatic reasoning with the Pellet and HermiT OWL reasoners. You have also learned how to perform reasoning in a closed world, or a local closed world, and to use SWRL rules in complement to class definitions.

CHAPTER 8

Annotations, multilingual texts, and full-text search

In this chapter, we will see how to handle annotations in Python with Owlready. We will also see how to handle multilingual texts, often used in annotations, and how to optimize full-text searches.

8.1 Annotating entities

Annotations allow you to add metadata about the entities and the relationships of an ontology. They can describe the authors, the modification dates, as well as the description of the entities, with the possibility of having texts in different languages. Annotations differ from properties in that they do not interfere with the reasoning. In particular, when defined on classes, annotations are not inherited by subclasses.

The following annotation properties are defined by default in OWL:

- label (the entity label)
- comment (any comment you may add about an entity or relation)
- seeAlso

L. Jean-Baptiste, *Ontologies with Python*, https://doi.org/10.1007/978-1-4842-6552-9_8

- versionInfo (versioning information)
- priorVersion
- deprecated (used to indicate an entity which should no longer exist and which is kept only for compatibility purposes)
- incompatibleWith
- backwardCompatibleWith (compatible with an entity of an earlier version)
- isDefinedBy

Annotations can be accessed with the dotted notation, like any relationship. Note that annotations are never functional, so their value is always a list. It is possible to add to the list with the `append()` method or to redefine the entire list:

```
>>> from owlready2 import *
>>> onto = get_ontology("bacteria.owl").load()

>>> onto.unknown_bacterium.label.append("An unknown bacterium")
>>> onto.unknown_bacterium.comment = [
...         "Found in the lab at the bottom of a drawer.",
...         "Remember to analyze it soon." ]
```

In this example, we reused the unknown_bacterium individual that we created previously in Protégé, in Chapter 3.

Any type of entity can be annotated: individuals but also classes and properties.

Annotations can be obtained with dotted notation, like any relationship. To remove an annotation, just remove it from the list (with the Python `del` statement or the `remove()` method; see 2.4.4).

8.2 Multilingual texts

The character strings in the annotations can be associated with a language (e.g., English, French, etc.). The `locstr` object (localized string) makes it possible to associate a character string with its language (identified by its two-letter code: "en" for English, "fr" for French, etc.):

```
>>> s = locstr("An unknown bacterium", "en")
>>> s.lang
'en'
```

`locstr` objects can be used as Python strings. They are often used in annotations:

```
>>> onto.unknown_bacterium.label = [
...         locstr("An unknown bacterium", "en"),
...         locstr("Une bactérie inconnue", "fr") ]
```

In addition, it is possible to filter an annotation list by language, as follows:

```
>>> onto.unknown_bacterium.label
['An unknown bacterium', 'Une bactérie inconnue']
>>> onto.unknown_bacterium.label.en
['An unknown bacterium']
>>> onto.unknown_bacterium.label.fr
['Une bactérie inconnue']
```

As with other Owlready lists, the `first()` method returns the first element (or None if the list is empty):

```
>>> onto.unknown_bacterium.label.en.first()
'An unknown bacterium'
```

Lists filtered by language allow you to add new annotations, without the need to create a locstr object. In the following example, the comment string will be automatically associated with the English language (as if a locstr object was used):

```
>>> onto.unknown_bacterium.comment.en.append("Comment in↲
English.")
```

8.3 Annotating constructs

Constructors can also be annotated, using the alternative syntax "annotation[constructor]". The following example creates a new subclass of Bacterium with a restriction and annotates this restriction:

```
>>> with onto:
...     class GramPositiveBacterium(onto.Bacterium):
...         is_a = [onto.gram_positive.value(True)]
>>> comment[GramPositiveBacterium.is_a[-1]].append(
...         "comment on the value restriction on gram_↲
            positive.")
```

8.4 Annotating properties and relations

Properties and relationships can also be annotated. Properties can be annotated like any other entity:

```
>>> onto.has_shape.comment = ["A comment on the has_shape↲
property."]
```

OWL also makes it possible to annotate relations, that is, you may annotate an RDF triple linking a subject to an object *via* a property (or predicate). This is useful if you want to provide additional details on a relationship, in the form of metadata, for example, to indicate the author or the date of the relation. We can do this with Owlready using the special syntax "annotation[subject, property, object]", for example:

```
>>> shape = onto.unknown_bacterium.has_shape
>>> comment[onto.unknown_bacterium, onto.has_shape, shape] =↲
    ["A comment on the fact that the bacterium has this shape."]
```

For relationships involving OWL built-in properties, the special values rdf_type, rdfs_subclassof, owl_equivalentclass, and so on can be used:

```
>>> comment[onto.unknown_bacterium, rdf_type, onto.Bacterium] =↲
    ["a comment on belonging to the Bacterium class."]
```

8.5 Creating new annotation classes

New annotation properties can be created in the same way as other properties, inheriting from the `AnnotationProperty` class, for example:

```
>>> with onto:
...     class observer(AnnotationProperty): pass
>>> onto.unknown_bacterium.observer = ["Observed by JB Lamy."]
>>> observer[onto.unknown_bacterium, rdf_type,↲
onto.Bacterium] = [
...      "Also observed by JB Lamy."
... ]
```

8.6 Ontology metadata

The metadata of the ontology consists of annotations placed directly on the ontology (which can be added in Protégé in the "Annotations" list of the "Active ontology" tab). They may describe the version number, the history of the ontology, the names of the authors, and so on. In Owlready, these annotations are available via the metadata attribute of the ontology. For example, the annotation "comment" of Gene Ontology (GO) is obtained as follows:

```
>>> go = get_ontology("http://purl.obolibrary.org/obo/go.owl").↲
load()
```

```
>>> go.metadata.comment
['cvs version: $Revision: 38972 $',
'Includes Ontology(OntologyID(OntologyIRI(<http://purl.↲
obolibrary.org/obo/go/never_in_taxon.owl>))) [Axioms: 18↲
Logical Axioms: 0]']
```

Metadata can also be modified with Owlready:

```
>>> go.metadata.comment.append("Here is a new comment!")
>>> go.metadata.comment
['cvs version: $Revision: 38972 $',
'Includes Ontology(OntologyID(OntologyIRI(<http://purl.↲
obolibrary.org/obo/go/never_in_taxon.owl>))) [Axioms: 18↲
Logical Axioms: 0]',
'Here is a new comment!']
```

8.7 Full-text search

Full-text search allows you to optimize text searches in an ontology. The speed gain can reach a factor of 1000 on large ontologies.

By default, full-text search is not activated because it increases the size of the quadstore. It is necessary to activate it for each property on which it will be used. The default_world.full_text_search_properties list contains the list of properties for which full-text search is enabled. It is empty by default. To activate full-text search on a property, simply add it to the list.

For example, to activate the full-text search on the OWL comment property:

```
>>> default_world.full_text_search_properties.append(comment)
```

We can now perform full-text searches with the `search()` method, using `FTS` objects (abbreviation for "full-text search") containing the texts to be searched. Unlike the normal search, the full-text search is done from a list of keywords (and not the exact value sought) and ignores the case (that is to say, it does not distinguish between upper- and lowercase). For example, to search for all entities with a comment including the word "English", we will do:

```
>>> default_world.search(comment = FTS("English"))
[bacteria.unknown_bacterium]
```

It is possible to give several keywords (the order of the keywords does not matter) and to use the character "*" as a wildcard, but only at the end of a keyword. For example, to search for all entities with a comment with the word "English" and a word starting with "comm", we will do:

```
>>> default_world.search(comment = FTS("English comm*"))
[bacteria.unknown_bacterium]
```

The `FTS` objects also allow you to specify the language of the search (by default, the search is performed in all languages). The following example searches only in English comments:

```
>>> default_world.search(comment = FTS("English comm*", "en"))
```

Please note if you are not using `FTS` objects, Owlready performs a normal, nonoptimized, search, as in the following example:

```
>>> default_world.search(comment = "English comm*") # Without
FTS !
[]
```

To deactivate full-text search, simply remove the property from the `default_world.full_text_search_properties` list using `remove()`.

8.8 Example: Using DBpedia in Python

DBpedia is an automatic extraction of structured data, derived from the free and open Wikipedia encyclopedia. DBpedia notably contains the relationships between Wikipedia pages but also more specific data, such as the date of birth of people appearing on Wikipedia. An OWL ontology structures all of the data. It is therefore a general dataset-oriented "general culture". The most recent version dates from 2016 and can be downloaded at the following address: `https://wiki.dbpedia.org/downloads-2016-10`. The 2020 version of DBpedia is still under development, and some important features are still missing.

DBpedia is in the form of several files (see the following screenshot of the website): the ontology part proper to download in OWL format (file "dbpedia_2016-10.owl") and the data to download in TTL format (equivalent to N-Triples) in their canonized version (noted "ttl *" on the DBpedia site). Several languages are available; we will work with the English version.

The ontology version used while extracting all datasets can be downloaded here:

File	Serialization
DBpedia Ontology	owl nt

[...]

Dataset	en	de	es	fr	ja	nl
Anchor Texts	tql ? ttl ?					
Article Categories	tql ? tql* ? ttl ? ttl* ?	tql ? tql* ? ttl ? ttl* ?	tql ? tql* ? ttl ? ttl* ?	tql ? tql* ? ttl ? ttl* ?	tql ? tql* ? ttl ? ttl* ?	tql ? tql* ? ttl ? ttl* ?
Article Templates	tql ? ttl ? Canonicalized version of http://dbpedia.org/dataset/article_categories; Triples: 23.1 M; File size: 106.5 M					
Category Labels.	tql ? tql* ? ttl ? ttl* ?	tql ? tql* ? ttl ? ttl* ?	tql ? tql* ? ttl ? ttl* ?	tql ? tql* ? ttl ? ttl* ?	tql ? tql* ? ttl ? ttl* ?	tql ? tql* ? ttl ? ttl* ?

8.8.1 Loading DBpedia

Because DBpedia is very large, not all files are commonly used. The following table lists the main ones, which you can download (please note the data is large: about 20 GB will be required).

Name in DBpedia	Filename and description
Ontology OWL	dbpedia_2016-10.owl The ontology (containing classes, but no individuals)
Instance Types	instance_types_wkd_uris_en.ttl.bz2 The "is_instance_of" relations between individuals and classes (corresponding to the RDF "type" relation)
Article Categories	article_categories_wkd_uris_en.ttl.bz2 The relation between Wikipedia articles and categories ("subject" property)
Mappingbased Literals	mappingbased_literals_wkd_uris_en.ttl.bz2 DataProperty present in the Wikipedia information box
Mappingbased Objects	mappingbased_objects_wkd_uris_en.ttl.bz2 ObjectProperty present in the Wikipedia information box
Category Labels	category_labels_wkd_uris_en.ttl.bz2 The labels for categories
Labels	labels_wkd_uris_en.ttl.bz2 Entity labels (needed for full-text search)
Person data	persondata_wkd_uris_en.ttl.bz2 Data relative to persons (date of birth, etc.)
Page Links	page_links_wkd_uris_en.ttl.bz2 Relations corresponding to the link between Wikipedia pages ("wikiPageWikiLink" property)

DBpedia is an OWL ontology and can therefore be loaded with Owlready. However, DBpedia is much less “clean” than the usual ontologies. In particular, the IRIs of the entities are not constant from one file to another, the following prefixes being used interchangeably:

- `http://dbpedia.org/ontology`
- `http://wikidata.dbpedia.org/ontology`
- `http://www.wikidata.org/entity`

A pretreatment step will therefore be necessary in order to clean up these inconsistencies, before loading the ontology.

In addition, DBpedia is a very voluminous ontology. This requires taking several precautions:

1. Save the quadstore on the disk (see 4.7) to avoid having to reload the ontology each time you use it.
2. Place temporary files on disk in a directory that can accommodate several gigabytes of data. In particular, under Linux, temporary files are by default placed in /tmp, but /tmp is often stored in RAM, which limits the available space. This can lead to an error of type “database or disk is full”.

For very large ontologies, it is therefore preferable to place temporary files elsewhere than in /tmp. This can be done with the `sqlite_tmp_dir` when defining the quadstore:

```
default_world.set_backend(
    filename = "/path/to/quadstore.sqlite3",
    sqlite_tmp_dir = "/path/to/temporary/files",
)
```

The following program is used to load DBpedia into an Owlready quadstore:

```
# File import_dbpedia.py
from owlready2 import *
import io, bz2

# DBPEDIA_DIR is the directory where you downloaded DBpedia
DBPEDIA_DIR = "/home/jiba/telechargements/dbpedia/"
TMP_DIR     = "/home/jiba/tmp"
QUADSTORE   = "dbpedia.sqlite3"

default_world.set_backend(filename = QUADSTORE,↲
sqlite_tmp_dir = TMP_DIR)

dbpedia = get_ontology("http://wikidata.dbpedia.org/ontology/")
contenu = open(os.path.join(DBPEDIA_DIR, "dbpedia_2016-10.↲
owl")).read()
contenu = contenu.replace("http://dbpedia.org/ontology,↲
          "http://wikidata.dbpedia.org/ontology")
contenu = contenu.replace("http://www.wikidata.org/entity,↲
          "http://wikidata.dbpedia.org/resource")
dbpedia.load(fileobj = io.BytesIO(contenu.encode("utf8")))

for fichier in os.listdir(DBPEDIA_DIR):
    if fichier.endswith(".ttl.bz2"):
        print("Import de %s..." % fichier)
        onto = get_ontology("http://dbpedia.org/ontology/%s/" %↲
                            fichier.replace(".ttl.bz2", ""))
        f = bz2.open(os.path.join(DBPEDIA_DIR, fichier))
        onto.load(fileobj = f)
```

```
print("Indexing...")
default_world.full_text_search_properties.append(label)

default_world.save()
```

In this program, three global variables must be modified according to your configuration: `DBPEDIA_DIR` indicates the directory where you downloaded the files from DBpedia (OWL and TTL.BZ2 files), `TMP_DIR` indicates a temporary directory which can accommodate several GB of data (see earlier), and `QUADSTORE` is the name of the file where the Owlready quadstore will be stored (be careful, allow 13 GB for the quadstore with the preceding files and an hour or more for the loading time).

The DBpedia ontology (OWL file) is read as a text file and corrected using the `replace()` method, then loaded with Owlready. In order to avoid having to save the corrected version of the file, we load the ontology directly from the RAM: the corrected version of the ontology is in the variable contained as a character string. We transform this string into a file object in two stages: first, we encode the string in UTF8, and then we transform it into a file object with `io.BytesIO()`. Finally, we load the ontology from this file object, with `load(filobj = ...)` (see 4.2).

Then, a loop traverses all the files in the `DBPEDIA_DIR` directory and processes the TTL.BZ2 files. These are decompressed with the Python module `bz2`, then loaded from compressed file objects. We have chosen here to create a separate ontology for each file (which will allow you to reload each file separately or delete the ontologies if we no longer need them).

Note the penultimate line, which activates the full-text search on the `label` property.

Then we can load the resulting quadstore in the following way, for example, in Python console mode. (Be careful not to reuse a Python console where you have already loaded Owlready2 and created entities in the quadstore; otherwise, you will get an error. This is because it is not possible to load the quadstore from a file if the one in memory is not empty.)

```
>>> from owlready2 import *
>>> QUADSTORE   = "dbpedia.sqlite3"
>>> default_world.set_backend(filename = QUADSTORE)
* Owlready2 * WARNING: http://wikidata.dbpedia.org/ontology/
senator
belongs to more than one entity types (e.g. Class, Property,
Individual):
[owl.ObjectProperty, ontology.MemberOfParliament, DUL.
sameSettingAs];
I'm trying to fix it...
[...]
```

Note that loading is much faster than when importing from OWL and TTL.BZ2 files. The "Warning" indicates that certain properties are not properly declared in DBpedia; we can safely ignore them.

Also note that the initial loading of DBpedia and the first commands handling this ontology can take a long time to execute, because the underlying database is very large (around 12 GB). However, once the first orders are placed, the indexes and caches will be in RAM, and access to DBpedia will be much faster.

We can then load the DBpedia ontology:

```
>>> dbpedia = get_ontology("http://wikidata.dbpedia.org/↲
ontology/")
```

We modify the rendering of entities (see 4.9) to display their label:

```
>>> def render(e):
...     return "%s:%s" % (e.name, e.label.en.first())
>>> set_render_func(render)
```

We can now perform optimized full-text searches in DBpedia, for example, finding all articles with "French" and "revolution" in their label:

```
>>> default_world.search(label = FTS("french Revolution"))
[Q1154330:10 August (French Revolution),
 Q207318:French Revolutionary Wars,
 Q7216178:French Revolution,
 [...] ]
```

Note that the very first searches can be long and take a few seconds. However, when your computer has loaded the indexes into the cache memory, the following searches will go much faster!

To access the articles, we need to create a namespace (see 4.8) because these are defined in "`http://wikidata.dbpedia.org/resource/`" and not in "`http://wikidata.dbpedia.org/ontology/`":

```
>>> dbpedia_resource = default_world.get_namespace(↲
                        "http://wikidata.dbpedia.org/resource/")
```

We can now access the article Q207318 ("French Revolutionary Wars", which is one of the most complete) and request the list of its properties:

```
>>> revolution = dbpedia_resource.Q207318
>>> list(revolution.get_properties())
[combatant:combatant, date:date, result:result, commander:commander,
place:place of military conflict, territory:territory, label:None,
wikiPageWikiLink:Link from a Wikipage to another Wikipage]
```

Then we can display the list of people mentioned in the article on French Revolution Wars:

```
>>> persons = [i for i in revolution.wikiPageWikiLink
...            if isinstance(i, dbpedia.Person)]
```

```
>>> print(persons)
[Q10088:Tipu Sultan, Q1096347:Claude Lecourbe,
 Q112009:Michael von Melas, Q128019:Pope Pius VI,
 ...]
```

When using the DBpedia ontology, there is one point to pay attention to: DBpedia uses the classic RDFS "comment" annotation to comment on classes; however, it also redefines its own "comment" property. The confusion between the two makes it difficult to get comments using the "entity.comment" syntax! In the event of a collision of names, it is the last property loaded which takes precedence, therefore that of DBpedia. This is why, in the following example, we get no comments:

```
>>> dbpedia.SongWriter.comment  # DBpedia comments
[]
```

To force the use of the RDFS "comment" annotation, two options are possible. First, we can use the alternative syntax "property[entity]" as in the following example:

```
>>> comment[dbpedia.SongWriter]  # RDFS comments
['a person who writes songs.', 'een persoon die de muziek en/of
 de tekst voor populaire muzieknummers schrijft.']
```

We can also redefine the property used by the syntax "entity.annotation", as follows:

```
>>> default_world._props["comment"] = comment
>>> dbpedia.SongWriter.comment  # RDFS comments now!
['a person who writes songs.', 'een persoon die de muziek en/of
 de tekst voor populaire muzieknummers schrijft.']
```

8.8.2 A search engine for DBpedia

Using the previously created quadstore and full-text search functions, we can easily make a search engine for DBpedia. We will rely on a dynamic website with Flask (which we have already used in section 4.12).

The following program loads the DBpedia quadstore, then creates the dynamic website:

```
# File search_dbpedia.py
from flask import Flask, request
app = Flask(__name__)

from owlready2 import *

QUADSTORE = "dbpedia.sqlite3"
default_world.set_backend(filename = QUADSTORE)

dbpedia  = get_ontology("http://wikidata.dbpedia.org/↲
ontology/")
resource = default_world.get_namespace(↲
                    "http://wikidata.dbpedia.org/resource/")

@app.route('/')
def page_query():
    html = """
<html><body>
    <form action="/result">
        <input type="text" name="keywords"/>
        <input type="submit"/>
    </form>
</body></html>"""
    return html

@app.route('/result')
def page_result():
```

```
    keywords = request.args.get("keywords", "")
    html = """<html><body>Search results for "%s":<br/>\n""" %↲
    keywords

    keywords =" ".join("%s*" % keyword for keyword in↲
    keywords.split())
    articles = default_world.search(label = FTS(keywords))

    html += """<ul>"""
    for article in articles:
        html += """<li><a href=/article/%s>%s:%s</a></li>"""↲
        % (article.name, article.name, article.label.first())
    html += """</ul></body></html>"""
    return html

@app.route('/article/<name>')
def page_article(name):
    article = resource[name]

    html = """<html><body><h2>%s:%s</h2>"""↲
          % (article.name, article.label.first())
    html += """belongs to classes: %s<br/><br/>\n """↲
           % "," .join(repr(clazz) for clazz in article.is_a)
    html += """has link to page:<br/>\n"""
    html += """<ul>"""
    for cite in article.wikiPageWikiLink:
        html += """<li><a href=/article/%s>%s:%s</a></li>"""↲
                % (cite.name, cite.name, cite.label.first())
    html += """</ul></body></html>"""
    return html

import werkzeug.serving
werkzeug.serving.run_simple("localhost", 5000, app)
```

The website includes three types of pages:

- The "query" page (path "/" which corresponds to the root of the website) displays a search field in an HTML form. This page is not dynamic in itself; we could have made it entirely in plain HTML.
- The "results" page (path "/results?keywords=<XXX>") which displays the search results. We get the keywords entered by the user, and then we transform them by adding a star "*" at the end of each keyword. Then we perform the search with `search()` and `FTS`. Finally, we generate an HTML page displaying the list of results showing, for each article found, its identifier, its label, and a link to the corresponding article page.
- The "article" page (path "/article/<identifier>/") which displays the identifier and the title of the article, the class or classes to which the article belongs, as well as the other articles it cites (obtained with the relation "wikiPageWikiLink").

Once the program has been executed, the website can be consulted at the address "http://127.0.0.1:5000". Here again, the initial loading of DBpedia and the first searches can be long. However, once the first searches are done, the next ones will be almost immediate.

The following images show screenshots of the "query" page and the "results" page of the dynamic website:

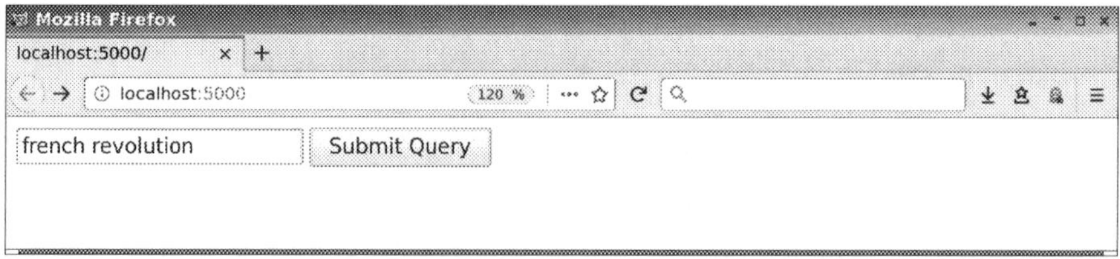

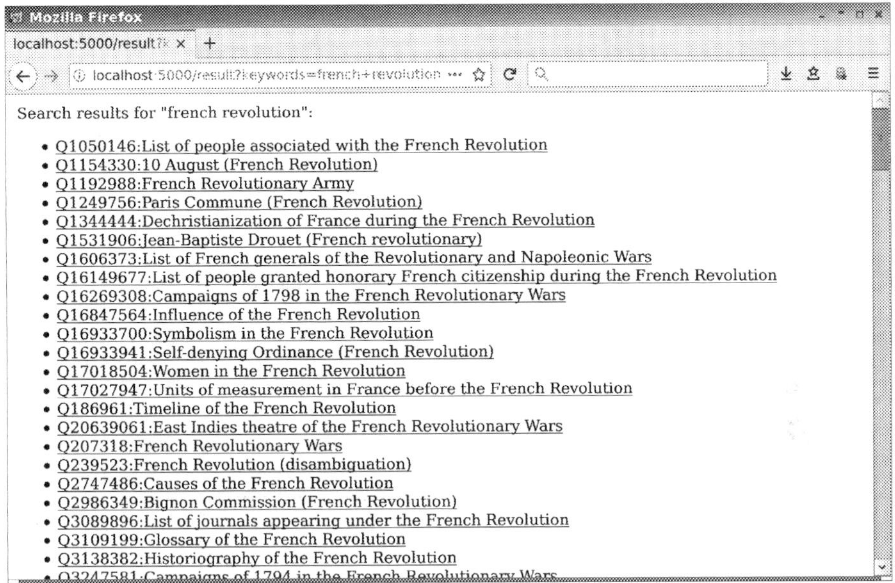

8.9 Summary

In this chapter, you have learned how to read and create OWL annotations and to use multilingual texts. We have also seen how to access DBpedia in Python with Owlready.

CHAPTER 9

Using medical terminologies with PyMedTermino and UMLS

In this chapter, we will see how to import into Python the main medical terminologies from UMLS, using PyMedTermino, a module allowing these terminologies to be integrated into Owlready. We will also see how to link these terminologies together using the UMLS unified concepts (CUI).

9.1 UMLS

UMLS (Unified Medical Language System) is a collection of more than 400 terminologies from the biomedical field. UMLS also integrates mappings between the different terminologies. UMLS is produced by the National Library of Medicine (NLM) in the United States and can be downloaded free of charge after registering online at the following address:

`www.nlm.nih.gov/research/umls/licensedcontent/umlsknowledgesources.html`

L. Jean-Baptiste, *Ontologies with Python*, https://doi.org/10.1007/978-1-4842-6552-9_9

Please note, however, that certain terminologies included in UMLS cannot be freely used in some countries. This is particularly the case of SNOMED CT, which is subject to a license paid either by the states or by institutions or companies.

As of this writing, the most recent version is 2019AB (Full Release (umls-2019AB-full.zip)). To use UMLS with Owlready and PyMedTermino, you need to download this file (about 4.8 GB). However, you don't need to decompress it (PyMedTermino will do it for you).

9.2 Importing terminologies from UMLS

PyMedTermino is a Python module allowing access to medical terminologies. Version 2 of PyMedTermino is directly included in Owlready, so you don't need to install it. Please note, however, that **importing UMLS data requires version 3.7 (or higher) of Python** (on the other hand, once UMLS data is imported, you can use it with Python 3.6 if you wish).

The `owlready2.pymedtermino2` module allows you to import all or part of UMLS data into an Owlready quadstore, via the global function `import_umls()`:

```
import_umls("./path/to/umls-2019AB-full.zip",↲
            terminologies = [...],↲
            langs = [...] )
```

The first parameter of the function is the path to the ZIP file containing UMLS data, which we downloaded previously. In the preceding example, this is a local path, but it can be a full path, for example, "/home/jblamy/download/umls-2020AA-full.zip" or "C:\\Downloads\\umls-2020AA-full.zip", depending on where you saved this file.

The second parameter is the list of terminologies to import. If this parameter is missing, all terminologies are imported. The following web page lists the terminologies available in UMLS and the associated codes:

www.nlm.nih.gov/research/umls/sourcereleasedocs/index.html

The third parameter indicates the languages to import, for example, "en" for English or "fr" for French. If this parameter is missing, all languages are imported.

We can, for example, import the terminologies CIM10 and SNOMED CT (in English versions, code ICD10 and SNOMEDCT_US in UMLS), as well as the CUI UMLS (considered as a pseudo-terminology), as follows:

```
>>> from owlready2 import *
>>> from owlready2.pymedtermino2 import *
>>> from owlready2.pymedtermino2.umls import *

>>> default_world.set_backend(filename = "pymedtermino.sqlite3")
>>> import_umls("umls-2020AA-full.zip",↲
                terminologies = ["ICD10", "SNOMEDCT_US", "CUI"])
>>> PYM = get_ontology("http://PYM/").load()
>>> default_world.save()
```

UMLS data import takes around 5–10 minutes. "PYM" is here the abbreviation for "PyMedTermino".

PyMedTermino activates by default the full-text search (see 8.7) for the annotation properties `label` (which corresponds to the terms of terminological concepts) and `synonyms` (which corresponds to synonyms). If you do not want to activate it, you must add the option `fts_index = False` when calling the `import_umls()` function.

Notice that UMLS includes several terminology translations, for example, ICD10 is available in German (code "DMDICD10") and Dutch (code "ICD10DUT"). However, the French translation is not included. PyMedTermino 2 has a specific module for importing French ICD10 (code "CIM10"), which can be used as follows:

```
>>> from owlready2.pymedtermino2.icd10_french import *
>>> import_icd10_french()
>>> default_world.save()
```

9.3 Loading terminologies after initial importation

Obviously, the next time we want to use the imported terminology, we will no longer need to call the import function. We will now only need the following three lines:

```
>>> from owlready2 import *
>>> default_world.set_backend(filename = "pymedtermino.sqlite3")
>>> PYM = get_ontology("http://PYM/").load()
```

These three lines reload the quadstore (with the `set_backend()` method) and the PYM (PyMedTermino) ontology. Do not forget the call to `load()`; it is necessary to load the Python methods associated with the ontology.

9.4 Using ICD10

PyMedTermino provides access to all terminologies using the same interface. We will see here the ICD10 and SNOMED CT terminologies, but, for the other terminologies, the functionalities remain similar.

The International Classification of Diseases, 10th edition (ICD10), is a classification of diseases that is widely used. For example, it is used in France for medico-economic coding in hospitals. ICD10 includes approximately 12,000 concepts. It is organized in a tree with 21 root concepts corresponding to the main chapters of diseases: cancer, infectious diseases, cardiovascular diseases, pulmonary diseases, and so on. (Notice that, in the United States, ICD9 (9th release) is still largely used. It can be obtained using the terminology code "ICD9CM".)

We can obtain the English ICD10 terminology as follows:

```
>>> ICD10 = PYM["ICD10"]

>>> ICD10
PYM["ICD10"] # ICD10

>>> ICD10.name
'ICD10'
```

PyMedTermino displays the concepts in the following way: "terminology[code] # concept label" (for concepts with several labels, only one is displayed, chosen from the preferred labels). Notice that the concept label is preceded by a # character and thus is treated as a comment if you copy-paste the concept in Python. This allows the copy-paste of PyMedTermino concepts or list of concepts.

Terminology objects and terminology concepts are Owlready classes. We can therefore use the class methods to manipulate the terminology, for example, the `subclasses()` method to obtain the child classes of ICD10, that is to say, the 21 aforementioned chapters of diseases:

```
>>> list(ICD10.subclasses())
[ ICD10["K00-K93.9"] # Diseases of the digestive system
, ICD10["C00-D48.9"] # Neoplasms
...]
```

However, PyMedTermino offers additional attributes and methods to facilitate the manipulation of terminologies. For example, the `children` attribute directly returns the list of child concepts, without having to go through a generator as before. In addition, the child concepts are sorted by code (which is not always the case in UMLS), as in the following example:

```
>>> ICD10.children
[ ICD10["A00-B99.9"] # Certain infectious and parasitic diseases
, ICD10["C00-D48.9"] # Neoplasms
, ICD10["D50-D89.9"] # Diseases of blood and blood-forming organs and
                     # certain disorders involving the immune mechanisms
, ICD10["E00-E90.9"] # Endocrine, nutritional and metabolic diseases
, ICD10["F00-F99.9"] # Mental, behavioural disorders
, ICD10["G00-G99.9"] # Diseases of the nervous system
, ICD10["H00-H59.9"] # Diseases of the eye and adnexa
, ICD10["H60-H95.9"] # Diseases of the ear and mastoid process
, ICD10["I00-I99.9"] # Diseases of the circulatory system
, ICD10["J00-J99.9"] # Diseases of the respiratory system
, ICD10["K00-K93.9"] # Diseases of the digestive system
, ICD10["L00-L99.9"] # Diseases of the skin and subcutaneous tissue
, ICD10["M00-M99.9"] # Diseases of the musculoskeletal system and
                     # connective tissue
, ICD10["N00-N99.9"] # Diseases of the genitourinary system
, ICD10["O00-O99.9"] # Pregnancy, childbirth and the puerperium
, ICD10["P00-P96.9"] # Certain conditions originating in the
                     # perinatal period
, ICD10["Q00-Q99.9"] # Congenital malformations, deformations
                     # and chromosomal abnormalities
, ICD10["R00-R99.9"] # Symptoms, signs and abnormal clinical and
                     # laboratory findings, not elsewhere classified
, ICD10["S00-T98.9"] # Injury, poisoning and certain other
                     # consequences of external causes
```

```
, ICD10["V01-Y98.9"] # External causes of morbidity and mortality
, ICD10["Z00-Z99.9"] # Factors influencing health status and
                     # contact with health services
]
```

We can go down in the hierarchy and display, for example, the children of the first chapter (infectious diseases):

```
>>> ICD10.children[0].children
[ ICD10["A00-A09.9"] # Intestinal infectious diseases
, ICD10["A15-A19.9"] # Tuberculosis
, ICD10["A20-A28.9"] # Certain zoonotic bacterial diseases
, ICD10["A30-A49.9"] # Other bacterial diseases
, ICD10["A50-A64.9"] # Infections with a predominantly sexual mode
                     # of transmission
...]
```

To directly access a concept from its code, we can index the terminology. For example, in ICD10, the concept coded "I10" corresponds to essential hypertension:

```
>>> ICD10["I10"]
ICD10["I10"] # Essential (primary) hypertension
```

PyMedTermino associates IRI with each concept, in the form "http://PYM/<terminology>/<code>", for example:

```
>>> ICD10["I10"].iri
'http://PYM/ICD10/I10'
```

The name (or identifier) of the concept therefore corresponds to its code:

```
>>> ICD10["I10"].name
'I10'
```

The terminology attribute is used to obtain the terminology to which a concept belongs:

```
>>> ICD10["I10"].terminology
PYM["ICD10"] # ICD10
```

The concept labels are accessible via the label annotation for the preferred labels and the synonyms annotation for the others; these OWL annotations can be accessed as Python attributes:

```
>>> ICD10["I10"].label
['Essential (primary) hypertension']
>>> ICD10["I10"].synonyms
[]
```

Depending on terminologies, the concepts can have one or more labels and zero or more synonyms (in ICD10, concepts have a single label and no synonym).

The parents attribute gives access to the parent concepts (i.e., more general):

```
>>> ICD10["I10"].parents
[ICD10["I10-I15.9"] # Hypertensive diseases
]
```

ICD10 is a monoaxial classification, that is to say that each concept has only one parent (except the major chapters which do not have one). However, PyMedTermino is made to be able to handle all terminologies with the same interface; this is why the parents attribute returns a list of only one parent in CIM10.

The ancestor_concepts() and descendant_concepts() methods return the list of ancestor and descendant concepts, respectively. They are similar to ancestors() and descendants(); however, they return lists (and not sets), and they only return UMLS concepts (in particular, the list returned by ancestor_concepts() does not include Thing).

```
>>> ICD10["I10"].ancestor_concepts()
[ ICD10["I10"]       # Essential (primary) hypertension
, ICD10["I10-I15.9"] # Hypertensive diseases
, ICD10["I00-I99.9"] # Diseases of the circulatory system
]
>>> ICD10["I00-I99.9"].descendant_concepts()
[ ICD10["I00-I99.9"] # Diseases of the circulatory system
, ICD10["I00-I02.9"] # Acute rheumatic fever
, ICD10["I00"] # Rheumatic fever without mention of heart↲
  involvement
, ICD10["I01"] # Rheumatic fever with heart involvement
, ICD10["I01.0"] # Acute rheumatic pericarditis
, ICD10["I01.1"] # Acute rheumatic endocarditis
, ICD10["I01.2"] # Acute rheumatic myocarditis
, ICD10["I01.8"] # Other acute rheumatic heart disease
, ICD10["I01.9"] # Acute rheumatic heart disease, unspecified
, ICD10["I02"] # Rheumatic chorea
, ICD10["I02.0"] # Rheumatic chorea with heart involvement
...]
```

By default, these two methods include the initial concept in the lists they return. If you want to avoid this, you must use the optional parameter `include_self = False`, for example:

```
>>> ICD10["I10"].ancestor_concepts(include_self = False)
[ ICD10["I10-I15.9"] # Hypertensive diseases
, ICD10["I00-I99.9"] # Diseases of the circulatory system
]
```

The `descendant_concepts()` method also makes it possible to browse all the concepts of the terminology, when it is applied to the terminology object (note that this requires loading all CIM10 concepts, i.e., more than 10,000 concepts in memory, which can take some time!):

```
>>> ICD10.descendant_concepts(include_self = False)
[ ICD10["A00-B99.9"] # Certain infectious and parasitic↲
diseases
, ICD10["A00-A09.9"] # Intestinal infectious diseases
, ICD10["A00"] # Cholera
, ICD10["A00.0"] # Cholera due to Vibrio cholerae 01, biovar↲
cholerae
...]
```

It is possible to test if one concept is a descendant of another with the Python function issubclass():

```
>>> issubclass(ICD10["I10"], ICD10["I00-I99.9"])
True
```

The search() method allows you to search for concepts by label and synonym. The character "*" can be used as a wildcard at the end of a word, and it is possible to include several keywords separated by spaces (as for the full-text search, on which this method is based, see 8.7). For example, we can search for all concepts with a word starting with "hypertension":

```
>>> ICD10.search("hypertension*")
[ ICD10["K76.6"] # Portal hypertension
, ICD10["I15.0"] # Renovascular hypertension
, ICD10["G93.2"] # Benign intracranial hypertension
, ICD10["I10"] # Essential (primary) hypertension
, ICD10["I27.0"] # Primary pulmonary hypertension
, ICD10["I15"] # Secondary hypertension
, ICD10["I15.9"] # Secondary hypertension, unspecified
...]
```

Similarly, we can search for all concepts with one word starting with "hypertension" and another with "pulmo":

```
>>> ICD10.search("hypertension* pulmo*")
[ICD10["I27.0"] # Primary pulmonary hypertension
]
```

9.5 Using SNOMED CT

The SNOMED CT (Systematized Nomenclature of Medicine—Clinical Terms) is a richer and more complete medical terminology than ICD10. Attention, as mentioned previously, the SNOMED CT cannot be used freely in some countries.

In the same way as for ICD10, we can access the SNOMED CT terminology and its concepts, as well as the labels, the parents, children, ancestors, and descendants concepts.

```
>>> SNOMEDCT_US = PYM["SNOMEDCT_US"]

>>> SNOMEDCT_US["45913009"]
SNOMEDCT_US["45913009"]  # Laryngitis

>>> SNOMEDCT_US["45913009"].parents
[ SNOMEDCT_US["129134004"] # Inflammatory disorder of
                           # upper respiratory tract
, SNOMEDCT_US["363169009"] # Inflammation of specific body organs
, SNOMEDCT_US["60600009"] # Disorder of the larynx
]

>>> SNOMEDCT_US["45913009"].children
[ SNOMEDCT_US["1282001"] # Perichondritis of larynx
, SNOMEDCT_US["14969004"] # Catarrhal laryngitis
, SNOMEDCT_US["17904003"] # Hypertrophic laryngitis
...]
```

SNOMED CT defines labels (label) but also synonyms (synonyms):

```
>>> SNOMEDCT_US["45913009"].label
['Laryngitis']
```

```
>_>_> SNOMEDCT_US["45913009"].synonyms
['Laryngitis (disorder)']
```

Unlike ICD10, SNOMED CT authorizes a concept to have several parents: it is therefore a multiaxial terminology. In the previous example, the concept "Laryngitis" has three parents: "inflammatory upper respiratory disease", "specified organ inflammation", and "larynx disease".

In addition, SNOMED CT is not limited to diseases: it also describes the anatomical structures (organs, parts of organs, etc., called "body structure" or "finding site"), morphologies (that is to say, the types of diseases, "associated morphology"), living species, chemical substances, and so on. SNOMED CT also includes transversal links connecting these different elements.

This information is found in the concept's parent classes, in the form of restrictions (of the type *some* or *only*):

```
>>> SNOMEDCT_US["45913009"].is_a
[ SNOMEDCT_US["363169009"] # Inflammation of specific body organs
, SNOMEDCT_US["60600009"]  # Disorder of the larynx
, SNOMEDCT_US["129134004"] # Inflammatory disorder
                           # of upper respiratory tract
, PYM.unifieds.some(CUI["C0023067"]  # Laryngitis
), PYM.mapped_to.some(ICD10["J04.0"] # Acute laryngitis
), PYM.groups.some(<Group 22731_0>   # mapped_to=Acute↲
   laryngitis
), PYM.has_associated_morphology.some(SNOMEDCT_US["23583003"]
   #Inflammation
), PYM.groups.some(<Group 22731_1>
#has_associated_morphology=Inflammation;↲
                              has_finding_site=Laryngeal structure
```

```
), PYM.has_finding_site.some(SNOMEDCT_US["4596009"] # Laryngeal↲
structure
), PYM.unifieds.only(CUI["C0023067"] # Laryngitis
)]
```

However, restrictions are not easy to deal with. Fortunately, Owlready allows accessing them as class properties (see 6.3). For example, from a disease like laryngitis, we can obtain the corresponding anatomical structures and morphologies:

```
>>> SNOMEDCT_US["45913009"].has_finding_site
[SNOMEDCT_US["4596009"] # Laryngeal structure
]
```

```
>>> SNOMEDCT_US["45913009"].has_associated_morphology
[SNOMEDCT_US["409774005"] # Inflammatory morphology
]
```

The `get_class_properties()` method allows you to obtain all the properties available for a given concept:

```
>>> SNOMEDCT_US["45913009"].get_class_properties()
{PYM.mapped_to,
 PYM.unifieds,
 PYM.has_associated_morphology,
 PYM.groups,
 PYM.has_finding_site,
 PYM.terminology, rdf-schema.label,
 PYM.synonyms,
 PYM.subset_member,
 PYM.ctv3id,
 PYM.type_id,
 PYM.case_significance_id,
 PYM.definition_status_id,
 PYM.active,
 PYM.effective_time}
```

We find in the set of properties the annotations label and synonyms, as well as has_associated_morphology and has_finding_site.

When several anatomical structures and/or morphologies are involved, it is interesting to know which morphology applies to which anatomical structure. Groups allow this. In the following example, the concept "hepatosplenomegaly" is associated with two anatomical structures and one morphology:

```
>>> SNOMEDCT_US["36760000"]
SNOMEDCT_US["36760000"] # Hepatosplenomegaly

>>> SNOMEDCT_US["36760000"].has_finding_site
[ SNOMEDCT_US["181268008"] # Entire liver
, SNOMEDCT_US["181279003"] # Entire spleen
]

>>> SNOMEDCT_US["36760000"].has_associated_morphology
[SNOMEDCT_US["442021009"] # Enlargement
]
```

We may wonder whether the morphology is associated with the first anatomical structure (i.e., liver), the second (i.e., spleen), or both. Groups allow answering this question; they are available through the group property:

```
>>> SNOMEDCT_US["36760000"].groups
[ <Group 18807_4> # has_finding_site=Entire liver ;
                  # has_associated_morphology=Enlargement
, <Group 18807_3> # has_finding_site=Entire spleen ;
                  #has_associated_morphology=Enlargement
, <Group 18807_0> # mapped_to=Hepatomegaly with splenomegaly,
                  # not elsewhere classified
]
```

In the preceding example, we have three groups:

- The first describes an enlargement of the liver.
- The second describes an enlargement of the spleen.
- The third describes a correspondence with another terminology, but does not contain an anatomical structure or morphology.

Therefore, here, the morphology concerns both anatomical structures. Please note that the exact order of the groups may vary: you will have the same groups but not necessarily in the same order.

Each group can be queried individually, for example, for the second group earlier:

```
>>> SNOMEDCT_US["36760000"].groups[0].get_class_properties()
{PYM.has_associated_morphology,
 PYM.has_finding_site}
```

```
>>> SNOMEDCT_US["36760000"].groups[0].has_associated_morphology
[SNOMEDCT_US["442021009"] # Enlargement
]
```

```
>>> SNOMEDCT_US["36760000"].groups[0].has_finding_site
[SNOMEDCT_US["181268008"] # Entire liver
]
```

PyMedTermino also allows you to navigate in the other direction, that is to say, starting from anatomical structures or morphologies to go toward diseases. For example, we can get all the diseases involving the vitreous as follows:

```
>>> SNOMEDCT_US["181268008"].finding_site_of
[ SNOMEDCT_US["80660001"] # Mauriac's syndrome
, SNOMEDCT_US["93369005"] # Congenital microhepatia
, SNOMEDCT_US["192008"] # Congenital syphilitic hepatomegaly
, SNOMEDCT_US["80378000"] # Neonatal hepatosplenomegaly
...]
```

A full-text search is, of course, possible in SNOMED CT and works in the same way as for CIM10.

9.6 Using UMLS unified concepts (CUI)

UMLS defines unified concepts (CUI, Concept Unique Identifier) allowing the navigation between terminologies. These CUIs can be imported with PyMedTermino, using the special terminology code "CUI". Please note, when only certain terminologies are imported, PyMedTermino only imports the CUIs used by the selected terminologies. If you want to have access to all of the CUIs, you will need to import all UMLS.

```
>>> CUI = PYM["CUI"]
```

The `unifieds` property makes it possible to obtain the unified concept(s) associated with a concept of any terminology (here we have taken ICD10):

```
>>> ICD10["I10"]
ICD10["I10"] # Essential (primary) hypertension
```

```
>>> ICD10["I10"].unifieds
[CUI["C0085580"] # Essential hypertension
]
```

The unified concepts all have a label and synonyms (from imported terminologies and therefore dependent on the choice of these):

```
>>> CUI["C0085580"].synonyms
['Essential (primary) hypertension',
 'Idiopathic hypertension',
 'Primary hypertension',
 'Systemic primary arterial hypertension',
 'Essential hypertension (disorder)']
```

The `originals` property is the inverse property of `unifieds`: it allows to obtain the concepts of the original terminologies with which a unified concept is associated:

```
>>> CUI["C0085580"].originals
[ SNOMEDCT_US["59621000"] # Essential hypertension
, ICD10["I10"] # Essential (primary) hypertension
]
```

These unified concepts allow to navigate between terminologies, as we will see in the next section.

Finally, the "SRC" pseudo-terminology (abbreviation of sources) lists all the terminologies available in UMLS and/or PyMedTermino. It is sort of a "terminology of terminologies". So, the root concept of PyMedTermino is `http://PYM/SRC/SRC`:

```
>>> PYM["SRC"]["SRC"]
PYM["SRC"] # Metathesaurus Source Terminology Names

>>> PYM["SRC"]["SRC"].iri
'http://PYM/SRC/SRC'
```

9.7 Mapping between terminologies

The >> operator allows you to convert from one terminology to another, using the links existing in UMLS. Note that this operator should not be confounded with the Python prompt >>> (three > characters vs. two). This operation is often called "mapping", "transcoding", or "correspondence". For mapping concepts, PyMedTermino uses UMLS "mapped_to" relationships when they exist. When they are not present, PyMedTermino uses the unified concepts (CUI) to navigate between terminologies. The following example maps the ICD10 concept "E11" to SNOMED CT:

```
>>> ICD10["E11"]
ICD10["E11"] # Non-insulin-dependent diabetes mellitus

>>> ICD10["E11"] >> SNOMEDCT_US
Concepts([
  SNOMEDCT_US["44054006"] # Type 2 diabetes mellitus
])
```

Here, the ICD10 concept "E11" corresponds to the SNOMEDCT concept "44054006", both representing type 2 diabetes. The concept CIM10 "E11" has no "mapped_to" relation; we can verify it as follows:

```
>>> ICD10["E11"].mapped_to
[]
```

It is therefore the CUIs that were used to perform the mapping.

We can also map in the reverse direction, from SNOMED CT to ICD10:

```
>>> SNOMEDCT_US["44054006"] >> ICD10
Concepts([
  ICD10["E11.9"] # Non-insulin-dependent diabetes mellitus↲
  without complications
])
```

We note that the concept obtained is not the one we had previously in ICD10 ("E11", Non-insulin-dependent diabetes mellitus). Indeed, SNOMED CT considers that the general concept "Type 2 diabetes mellitus" without any specification of complications corresponds to diabetes without complications. UMLS has a "mapped_to" relationship for this SNOMED CT concept, which we can verify as follows:

```
>>> SNOMEDCT_US["44054006"].mapped_to
[ICD10["E11.9"] # Non-insulin-dependent diabetes mellitus↲
                  without complications
]
```

PyMedTermino used this relation when mapping from SNOMED CT to ICD10.

Mapping always returns a set of concepts (described in the next section). This set can contain several concepts when the starting concept corresponds to several concepts in the terminology of arrival, as in this example:

```
>>> ICD10["N80.0"]
ICD10["N80.0"] # Endometriosis of uterus

>>> ICD10["N80.0"] >> SNOMEDCT_US
Concepts([
  SNOMEDCT_US["784314006"] # Uterine adenomyosis
, SNOMEDCT_US["76376003"] # Endometriosis of uterus
, SNOMEDCT_US["237115002"] # Endometriosis of myometrium
, SNOMEDCT_US["198247003"] # Endometriosis interna
])
```

9.8 Manipulating sets of concepts

The PYM.Concepts class is used to create a set of concepts. This class inherits from Python's set class (see 2.4.7) and therefore has the same methods to compute the intersection, union, subtraction, and so on of two sets. It adds specific methods to terminologies. For example, the lowest_common_ancestors() method allows computing the closest common ancestor(s) to several concepts:

```
>>> PYM.Concepts([ICD10["E11.1"], ICD10["E12.0"]]).lowest_↲
common_ancestors()
Concepts([
  ICD10["E10-E14.9"] # Diabetes mellitus
])
```

This method is practical for "generalizing" several concepts and grouping them into a single, higher-level, concept.

The find() method makes it possible to seek the first concept of a set which is a descendant of a given concept (including the concept itself). For example, we can create a set of four concepts:

```
>>> cs = PYM.Concepts([
...     SNOMEDCT_US["49260003"], SNOMEDCT_US["371438008"],
...     SNOMEDCT_US["373137001"], SNOMEDCT_US["300562000"],
... ])
>>> cs
Concepts([
  SNOMEDCT_US["300562000"] # Genitourinary tract problem
, SNOMEDCT_US["373137001"] # Immobile heart valve
, SNOMEDCT_US["49260003"]  # Idioventricular rhythm
, SNOMEDCT_US["371438008"] # Urolith
])
```

Then, we can search for the presence of a cardiac concept (here, 301095005 is the SNOMED CT code for "Cardiac finding"):

```
>>> cs.find(SNOMEDCT_US["301095005"])
SNOMEDCT_US["373137001"] # Immobile heart valve
```

The extract() method is similar, but returns the subset of all the concepts descending from the concept passed as a parameter, for example, here, all cardiac concepts:

```
>>> cs.extract(SNOMEDCT_US["301095005"])
Concepts([
  SNOMEDCT_US["373137001"] # Immobile heart valve
, SNOMEDCT_US["49260003"]  # Idioventricular rhythm
])
```

The `subtract()` method returns a new set containing the same concepts, except those which descend from the concept passed in a parameter. The `subtract_update()` method performs the same operation, but modifies the set passed in a parameter in place, instead of returning a new one.

The `keep_most_generic()` and `keep_most_specific()` methods allow only the most generic or specific concepts to be kept, respectively. In the following example, the concept SNOMED CT 300562000 ("Genitourinary tract problem") has been removed because it is less specific than 371438008 ("Urolith"):

```
>>> cs.keep_most_specific()
>>> cs
Concepts([
  SNOMEDCT_US["373137001"] # Immobile heart valve
, SNOMEDCT_US["371438008"] # Urolith
, SNOMEDCT_US["49260003"]  # Idioventricular rhythm
])
```

The `all_subsets()` method returns all the possible subsets of the set, for example:

```
>>> cs = PYM.Concepts([
...       SNOMEDCT_US["49260003"],
...       SNOMEDCT_US["371438008"],
...       SNOMEDCT_US["373137001"],
... ])
>>> cs.all_subsets()
[Concepts([
]), Concepts([
  SNOMEDCT_US["373137001"] # Immobile heart valve
]), Concepts([
  SNOMEDCT_US["371438008"] # Urolith
]), Concepts([
```

```
  SNOMEDCT_US["373137001"] # Immobile heart valve
, SNOMEDCT_US["371438008"] # Urolith
]), Concepts([
  SNOMEDCT_US["49260003"] # Idioventricular rhythm
]), Concepts([
  SNOMEDCT_US["373137001"] # Immobile heart valve
, SNOMEDCT_US["49260003"] # Idioventricular rhythm
]), Concepts([
  SNOMEDCT_US["49260003"] # Idioventricular rhythm
, SNOMEDCT_US["371438008"] # Urolith
]), Concepts([
  SNOMEDCT_US["373137001"] # Immobile heart valve
, SNOMEDCT_US["49260003"] # Idioventricular rhythm
, SNOMEDCT_US["371438008"] # Urolith
])]
```

The methods `is_semantic_subset()`, `is_semantic_superset()`, `is_semantic_disjoint()`, and `semantic_intersection()` are similar to homonymous methods of Python sets, but they took into account hierarchical *is-a* relations between concepts. In the following example, the intersection of the two sets is empty but not the semantic intersection, because the urolith is a urinary problem:

```
>>> cs1 = PYM.Concepts([SNOMEDCT_US["371438008"]])
>>> cs2 = PYM.Concepts([SNOMEDCT_US["106098005"]])
>>> cs1
Concepts([
  SNOMEDCT_US["371438008"] # Urolith
])
>>> cs2
Concepts([
  SNOMEDCT_US["106098005"] # Urinary system finding
])
```

```
>>> cs1.intersection(cs2)
Concepts([
])
>>> cs1.semantic_intersection(cs2)
Concepts([
  SNOMEDCT_US["371438008"] # Urolith
])
```

Be careful, however, these semantic operations do not take into account the possible common descendants of the concepts. In the following example, the intersection of the concepts "infectious diseases" and "urinary problems" is empty, while urinary tract infections do exist:

```
>>> cs1 = PYM.Concepts([SNOMEDCT_US["40733004"]])
>>> cs2 = PYM.Concepts([SNOMEDCT_US["106098005"]])
>>> cs1
Concepts([
  SNOMEDCT_US["40733004"] # Disorder due to infection
])
>>> cs2
Concepts([
  SNOMEDCT_US["106098005"] # Urinary system finding
])
>>> cs1.semantic_intersection(cs2)
Concepts([
  ])
```

We will see later (at 10.7) how to achieve a real semantic intersection that takes into account the common descendants.

PyMedTermino also allows mapping a set of concepts, always with the operator ">>". As the mapping operations themselves return a set of concepts, it is possible to chain these operations. For example, we can map from SNOMED CT to CIM10 by forcing the passage through the CUI, as follows:

```
>>> SNOMEDCT_US["44054006"] >> CUI >> ICD10
Concepts([
  ICD10["E11"] # Non-insulin-dependent diabetes mellitus
])
```

On the contrary, the direct mapping (as seen earlier) may return a different result, when the "mapped_to" relationships are present in UMLS:

```
>>> SNOMEDCT_US["44054006"] >> ICD10
Concepts([
  ICD10["E11.9"] # Non-insulin-dependent diabetes
                 # mellitus without complications
])
```

The passage through the CUI then guarantees a reversible mapping.

9.9 Importing all terminologies in UMLS

When the `terminologies` parameter is missing, the `import_umls()` function imports all the terminologies present in UMLS. We can therefore import all UMLS as follows (be careful, this requires at least 20 GB of disk space, 16 GB of RAM, and more than an hour):

```
>>> from owlready2 import *
>>> from owlready2.pymedtermino2 import *
>>> from owlready2.pymedtermino2.umls import *

>>> default_world.set_backend(filename = "pymedtermino.sqlite3",
...                           sqlite_tmp_dir = "/home/jiba/tmp")
>>> import_umls("umls-2020AA-full.zip")
>>> PYM = get_ontology("http://PYM/").load()
```

Note that, when calling the `set_backend()` method, we added the optional `sqlite_tmp_dir` parameter, which indicates a path to a directory where to store large temporary files (see 8.8.1).

Then, to search for concepts in all terminologies at once, the `PYM.search()` method can be used:

```
>>> PYM.search("hypertension*")
[ SNOMEDCT_US["123800009"] # Goldblatt hypertension
, SNOMEDCT_US["70272006"] # Malignant hypertension
, ICD10["K76.6"]# Portal hypertension
, SNOMEDCT_US["34742003"] # Portal hypertension
, SNOMEDCT_US["70995007"] # Pulmonary hypertension
, SNOMEDCT_US["28119000"] # Renal hypertension
, ICD10["I15.0"] # Renovascular hypertension
...]
```

9.10 Example: Linking the ontology of bacteria with UMLS

We can now take up the ontology of bacteria and link it to UMLS. For this, we will create relationships between the concepts of this ontology and the unified concepts (CUI) of UMLS. Since these are classes, we will use Owlready's class properties (see 6.3).

The following lines of code make it possible to link the three classes of bacteria (Pseudomonas, Streptococcus, and Staphylococcus) to the corresponding CUI (which we searched for using `search()`). These relationships are placed in a new ontology, named "bacteria_umls.owl".

```
>>> onto = get_ontology("bacteria.owl").load()
>>> onto_bacteria_umls = get_ontology("http://↲
lesfleursdunormal.fr/static/_downloads/bacteria_umls.owl")

>>> CUI = PYM["CUI"]
```

```
>>> with onto_bacteria_umls:
...     onto.Pseudomonas    .mapped_to = [ CUI["C0033808"] ]
...     onto.Streptococcus .mapped_to = [ CUI["C0038402"] ]
...     onto.Staphylococcus.mapped_to = [ CUI["C0038170"] ]

>>> onto_bacteria_umls.save("bacteria_umls.owl")
```

We have reused the UMLS mapped_to object property for our relationships.

We can verify that it is indeed a class property, that is to say, an OWL restriction:

```
>>> onto.Pseudomonas.mapped_to
[CUI["C0033808"] # Pseudomonas
]
>>> onto.Pseudomonas.is_a
[bacteria.Bacterium,
 bacteria.has_shape.some(bacteria.Rod),
 bacteria.has_shape.only(bacteria.Rod),
 bacteria.has_grouping.some(bacteria.Isolated | bacteria.InPair),
 bacteria.gram_positive.value(False),
 PYM.mapped_to.some(CUI["C0033808"] # Pseudomonas
)]
```

It is possible to map these CUIs, for example, to SNOMED CT:

```
>>> SNOMEDCT_US = PYM["SNOMEDCT_US"]

>>> onto.Pseudomonas.mapped_to[0] >> SNOMEDCT_US
Concepts([
  SNOMEDCT_US["5274006"] # Chryseomonas
, SNOMEDCT_US["57032008"] # Pseudomonas
])
```

Here, the concept "Pseudomonas" of UMLS corresponds to Pseudomonas in SNOMED CT, but also to Chryseomonas, a genus of bacteria which was later attached to the genus Pseudomonas (under the name of Pseudomonas luteola).

It is also possible to translate the unified concept CUI toward SNOMED CT and then to recover the associated diseases, via the "causative_agent_of" relation (which is the inverse of "has_causative_agent"):

```
>>> diseases = [
...     disease
...     for snomedct in onto.Pseudomonas.mapped_to[0] >>↲
        SNOMEDCT_US
...     for disease in snomedct.causative_agent_of
... ]
>>> diseases
[ SNOMEDCT_US["127201000119101"] # Septic shock co-occurrent
     # with acute organ dysfunction due to Pseudomonas
, SNOMEDCT_US["16664009"]  # Malignant otitis media
, SNOMEDCT_US["448813005"] # Sepsis due to Pseudomonas
...]
```

This gives us a list of the diseases that the bacteria can cause.

9.11 Example: A multi-terminology browser

The consultation of medical terminologies is quite possible in a Python terminal with PyMedTermino; however, it quickly becomes laborious. We will therefore build a multi-terminological "mini-browser" allowing both to search for concepts by keywords and to navigate among the various terminologies. This browser will use the Python `Flask` module to make a dynamic website (see 4.12) and will integrate all the terminologies available in PyMedTermino.

The following program describes the multi-terminology "mini-browser":

```
# File termino_browser.py
from owlready2 import *
default_world.set_backend(filename = "pymedtermino.sqlite3")
PYM = get_ontology("http://PYM/").load()

from flask import Flask, url_for, request
app = Flask(__name__)

def repr_concept(concept):
    return """[<a href="%s">%s:%s</a>] %s""" % (
        url_for("concept_page", iri = concept.iri),
        concept.terminology.name,
        concept.name,
        concept.label.first() )

def repr_relations(entity, border = False):
    if border: html = """<table style="border: 1px solid
#aaa;">"""
    else:      html = """<table>"""
    for Prop in entity.get_class_properties():
        for value in Prop[entity]:
            if issubclass(value, PYM.Concept):
                value = repr_concept(value)
            elif issubclass(value, PYM.Group):
                value = repr_relations(value, True)
            html += """<tr><td>%s:""" % Prop.name
            html += """</td><td> %s</td></tr>""" % value
    html += """</table>"""
    return html
```

```
@app.route('/')
def homepage():
    html ="""
<html><body>
  Search in all terminologies:
  <form action="/search">
    <input type="text" name="keywords"/>
    <input type="submit"/>
  </form>
  Or <a href="%s">browse the entire hierarchy</a>
</body></html>""" % url_for("concept_page", iri = "http://PYM/↲
SRC/SRC")
    return html

@app.route('/search')
def search_page():
    keywords = request.args.get("keywords", "")
    html = """<html><body>Recherche "%s":<br/>\n""" % keywords
    keywords = " " .join("%s"* % word for word in keywords.↲
    split())
    results = PYM.search(keywords)
    for concept in results:
        html += """%s<br/>""" % repr_concept(concept)
    html += """</body></html>"""
    return html

@app.route('/concept/<path:iri>')
def concept_page(iri):
    concept = IRIS[iri]
    html  = """<html><body>"""
    html += """<h2>%s</h2>""" % repr_concept(concept)
    html += """<h3>Ancestor concept (except parents)</h3>"""
```

```
    html += """%s<br/>""" % repr_concept(concept.terminology)
    ancestors = set(concept.ancestor_concepts(include_self =↲
    False))
    ancestors = ancestors - set(concept.parents)
    ancestors = list(ancestors)
    ancestors.sort(key = lambda t: len(t.ancestor_concepts()))
    for ancestor in ancestors:
        html += """%s<br/>""" % repr_concept(ancestor)

    html += """<h3>Parent concepts</h3>"""
    for parent in concept.parents:
        html += """%s<br/>""" % repr_concept(parent)

    html += """<h3>Relations</h3>"""
    html += repr_relations(concept)

    if not concept.name == "CUI":
        html += """<h3>Child concepts</h3>"""
        for child in concept.children:
            html += """%s<br/>""" % repr_concept(child)

    html += """</body></html>"""
    return html

import werkzeug.serving
werkzeug.serving.run_simple("localhost", 5000, app)
```

The program starts by importing Owlready and loading the quadstore with PyMedTermino, and then it imports Flask. Then it creates two utility functions:

- `repr_concept()`, which will be used to represent a concept in HTML, using its label, terminology, and code, with a link to the concept page.

- `repr_relations()`, which will be used to represent in HTML the (nonhierarchical) relationships of a concept or a group. The function returns an HTML table with one row per property and property value. This function is recursive: if it is called for a concept, it will call itself for each of the groups of the concept, if necessary.

Then, the program creates three web pages:

- The root page (path "/"), which proposes a search field and a link to the root concept of PyMedTermino.
- The search page (path "/search?keywords=entered_keywords"), which lists the results of the text search. This page works similarly to the one we created for DBpedia (see 8.8.2).
- The concept page (path "/concept/concept_IRI"), which displays the properties of a given concept: ancestor concepts (excluding parents), parent concepts, relationships, and child concepts.

  In order to facilitate the reading, we have removed the ancestors' parents, and we have sorted the list of ancestors according to the number of ancestor concepts that the ancestor himself has. This allows having at the beginning of the list the concepts having fewer ancestors, therefore the most general, and at the bottom of the list the most specific.

  In addition, the display of child concepts has been deactivated for the "CUI" classification, because it is not hierarchical. Consequently, all CUIs (more than 20,000) are direct children of the classification, which would lead to a page that is far too long!

The following screenshots show the resulting terminology browser:

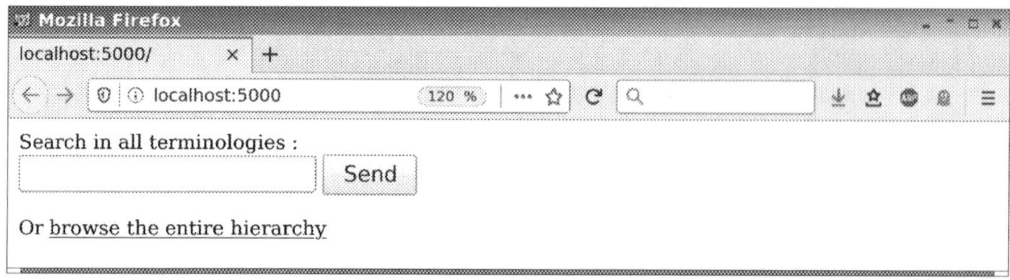

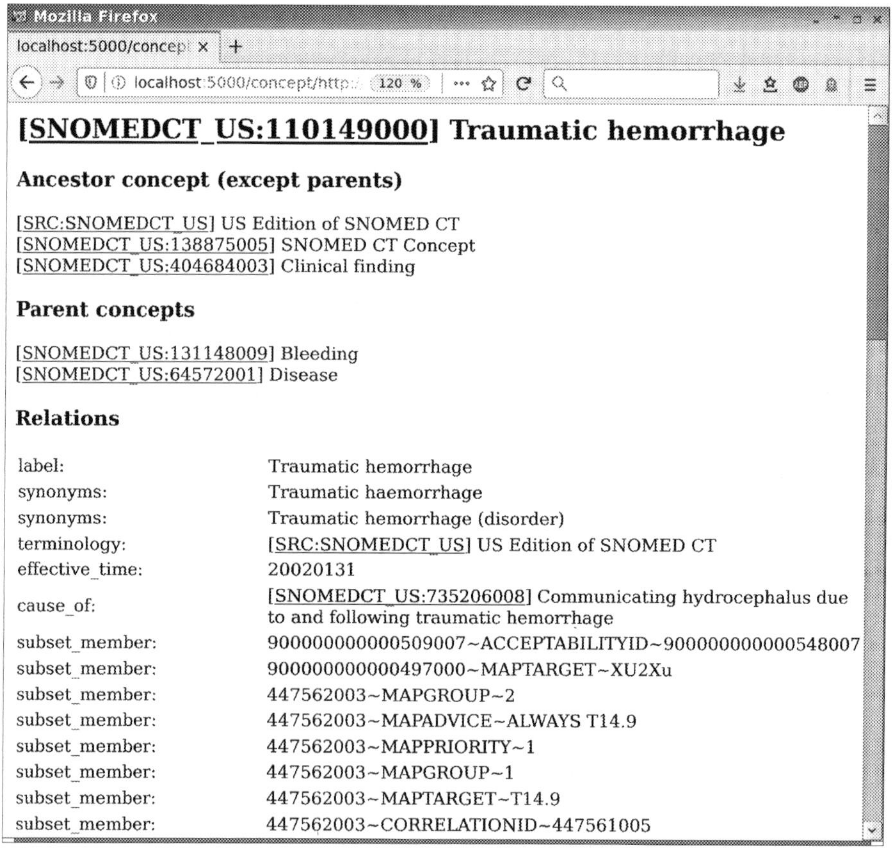

Mozilla Firefox
localhost:5000/
localhost:5000
120 %
Search in all terminologies :
Send
Or browse the entire hierarchy

Mozilla Firefox
localhost:5000/concep
localhost:5000/concept/http
120 %
[SNOMEDCT_US:110149000] Traumatic hemorrhage
Ancestor concept (except parents)
[SRC:SNOMEDCT_US] US Edition of SNOMED CT
[SNOMEDCT_US:138875005] SNOMED CT Concept
[SNOMEDCT_US:404684003] Clinical finding
Parent concepts
[SNOMEDCT_US:131148009] Bleeding
[SNOMEDCT_US:64572001] Disease
Relations
label: Traumatic hemorrhage
synonyms: Traumatic haemorrhage
synonyms: Traumatic hemorrhage (disorder)
terminology: [SRC:SNOMEDCT_US] US Edition of SNOMED CT
effective_time: 20020131
cause_of: [SNOMEDCT_US:735206008] Communicating hydrocephalus due to and following traumatic hemorrhage
subset_member: 900000000000509007~ACCEPTABILITYID~900000000000548007
subset_member: 900000000000497000~MAPTARGET~XU2Xu
subset_member: 447562003~MAPGROUP~2
subset_member: 447562003~MAPADVICE~ALWAYS T14.9
subset_member: 447562003~MAPPRIORITY~1
subset_member: 447562003~MAPGROUP~1
subset_member: 447562003~MAPTARGET~T14.9
subset_member: 447562003~CORRELATIONID~447561005

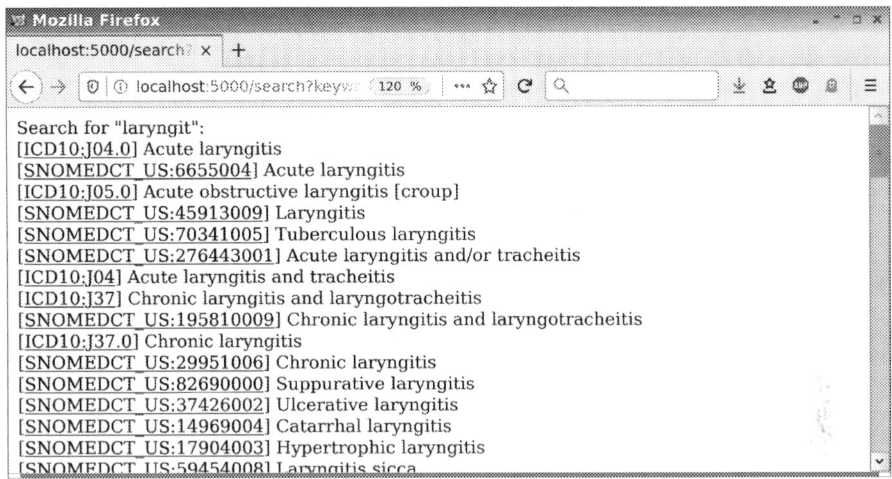

9.12 Summary

In this chapter, you have learned how to import medical terminologies from UMLS and how to access them as an ontology. We have seen how to map concepts from one terminology to another and to design a simple terminology browser.

CHAPTER 10

Mixing Python and OWL

In this chapter, we will see how to mix Python methods and OWL logical constructors within the same class.

10.1 Adding Python methods to OWL classes

With Owlready, OWL classes are Python classes (almost) like the others. It is therefore possible to include Python methods in these classes. Here is a simple example to calculate the price per tablet of a drug from its unit price (per box) and the number of tablets in the box:

```
>>> from owlready2 import *
>>> onto = get_ontology("http://test.org/drug.owl#")
>>> with onto:
...     class Drug(Thing): pass
...
...     class price(Drug >> float, FunctionalProperty):
...         pass
...     class nb_tablet(Drug >> int, FunctionalProperty):
...         pass
```


L. Jean-Baptiste, *Ontologies with Python*, https://doi.org/10.1007/978-1-4842-6552-9_10

```
...
...     class Drug(Thing):
...         def get_price_per_tablet(self):
...             return self.price / self.nb_tablet
```

Note that the Drug class is defined twice: the first definition is a forward declaration in order to be able to use the class in the definitions of the properties (see 5.8). Note also that, since we create a new ontology, we integrated the separator (here, #) at the end of the ontology IRI (see 5.1).

The method can then be called on the individuals of the class:

```
>>> my_drug = Drug(price = 10.0, nb_tablet = 5)
>>> my_drug.get_price_per_tablet()
2.0
```

In ontologies, it is common to use only classes and subclasses, instead of individuals (this is the case in, e.g., Gene Ontology), because the power of class representation is greater. In this case, Python allows you to define "class methods" which will be called on the class (or one of its subclasses) and which take this class (or subclass) as the first parameter.

Here is the same example as before, but using classes:

```
>>> with onto:
...     class Drug(Thing): pass
...
...     class price(Drug >> float, FunctionalProperty):
...         pass
...     class nb_tablet(Drug >> int, FunctionalProperty):
...         pass
...
...     class Drug(Thing):
...         @classmethod
...         def get_price_per_tablet(self):
...             return self.price / self.nb_tablet
```

The method can then be called on the class and its subclasses:

```
>>> class MyDrug(Drug): pass
>>> MyDrug.price = 10.0
>>> MyDrug.nb_tablet = 5
>>> MyDrug.get_price_per_tablet()
2.0
```

Be careful, however, to make the two types of method (individual and class) coexist together; it is necessary to use different method names.

10.2 Associating a Python module to an ontology

When the ontologies are not created entirely in Python (as we did in the preceding example) but loaded from an OWL file, the Python methods can be defined in a separate Python module (.py file). This file can be imported manually or linked to the ontology via an annotation; in this case, Owlready will automatically import the Python module when the ontology is loaded.

For example, the following file, named "bacteria.py", adds a method in the Bacterium and Staphylococcus classes of the bacteria ontology:

```
# File bacteria.py
from owlready2 import *

onto = get_ontology("http://lesfleursdunormal.fr/static/↲
_downloads/bacteria.owl#")

with onto:
    class Bacterium(Thing):
        def my_method(self):
            print("It is a bacterium!")
```

```
class Staphylococcus(Thing):
    def my_method(self):
        print("It is a staphylococcus!")
```

Note that we have not loaded the bacteria ontology (i.e., we have not called `.load()`) because it will be done by the main program. Note also that we have not indicated the superclass of Staphylococcus (which is Bacterium): indeed, it already appears in the OWL file, so there is no need to assert it a second time here! On the other hand, it is necessary to mention Thing as a superclass to state that the new class is an OWL class managed by Owlready and not a usual Python class. Generally, when creating a separate Python file with the methods, it is preferable to put only the methods inside and to keep the rest of the ontology (superclasses, properties, relations, *etc.*) in OWL to limit redundancy.

10.2.1 Manual import

We can then load the ontology and manually import the file "bacteria.py":

```
>>> from owlready2 import *
>>> onto = get_ontology("bacteria.owl").load()
>>> import bacteria
```

Then, we create a Staphylococcus, and we call our method:

```
>>> my_bacterium = onto.Staphylococcus()
>>> my_bacterium.my_method()
It is a staphylococcus!
```

10.2.2 Automatic import

For this, it is necessary to edit the ontology with Protégé and add an annotation indicating the name of the associated Python module. This annotation is called python_module, and it is defined in the ontology "owlready_ontology.owl", which it is necessary to import. Here are the steps:

1. Launch Protégé and load the bacteria ontology.
2. Go to the "Active Ontology" tab of Protégé.
3. Import the ontology "owlready_ontology" by clicking the "+" button to the right of "Direct imports". The ontology can be imported from the local copy which is in the installation directory of Owlready or from its IRI: `www.lesfleursdunormal.fr/static/_downloads/owlready_ontology.owl`.

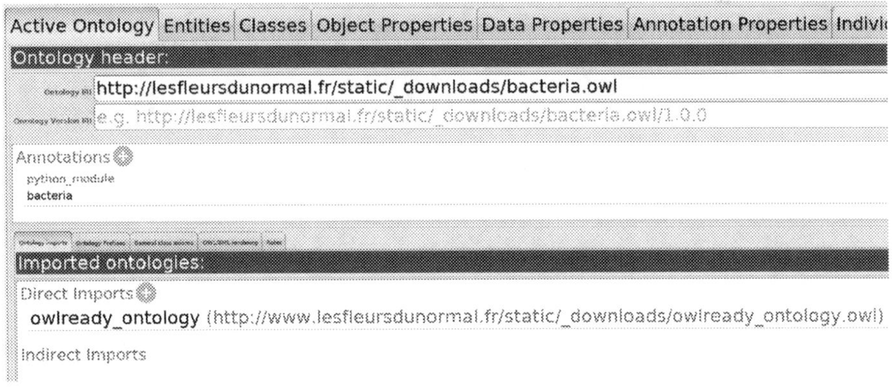

Figure 10-1. "python_module" annotation in Protégé

4. Add an annotation in the “Ontology header” section. The annotation type is “python_module”, and the value is the name of the module, here bacteria (see Figure 10-1). You may also use a Python package, for example, “my_module.my_package”.

Now, we no longer need to import the “bacteria” module: Owlready does this automatically each time the bacteria ontology is loaded. In the following example, we have saved the bacteria ontology (with the annotation “python_module”) in a new OWL file called “bacteria_owl_python.owl”:

```
>>> from owlready2 import *
>>> onto = get_ontology("bacteria_owl_python.owl").load()
>>> my_bacterium = onto.Staphylococcus()
>>> my_bacterium.my_method()
It is a staphylococcus!
```

10.3 Polymorphism with type inference

We have seen in section 7.2 that, during the reasoning, the classes of individuals and the superclasses of classes could be modified. In this case, the available methods may change. In addition, in the case of polymorphism, that is to say, when several classes implement the same method differently, the implementation of the method for a given individual or class may change. This is “polymorphism with type inference”.

Here is a simple example:

```
>>> my_bacterium = onto.Bacterium(gram_positive = True,
...         has_shape = onto.Round(),
...         has_grouping = [onto.InCluster()] )
>>> my_bacterium.my_method()
It is a bacterium!
```

We created a bacteria. When we execute the method, it is the implementation of the class Bacterium which is therefore called. We will now call the reasoner.

```
>>> sync_reasoner()
```

The reasoner deduced that the bacterium is in fact a Staphylococcus (due to its relationships). Now, if we call the method, it is the implementation of the Staphylococcus class which is called:

```
>>> my_bacterium.my_method()
It is a staphylococcus!
```

10.4 Introspection

Introspection is an advanced object programming technique which consists in "analyzing" an object without knowing it, for example, in order to obtain the list of its attributes and their values.

For the introspection of individuals, the `get_properties()` method allows obtaining the list of properties for which the individual has at least one relation.

```
>>> onto.unknown_bacterium.get_properties()
{bacteria.has_shape,
 bacteria.has_grouping,
 bacteria.gram_positive,
 bacteria.nb_colonies}
```

It is then possible to obtain and/or modify these relations. The getattr(object, attribute) and setattr(object, attribute, value) Python functions allow you to read or write an attribute of any Python object when the name of the attribute is known in a variable (see 2.9.4), for example:

```
>>> for prop in onto.unknown_bacterium.get_properties():
...     print(prop.name, "=",
...           getattr(onto.unknown_bacterium, prop.python_name))
has_grouping = [bacteria.in_cluster1]
has_shape = bacteria.round1
gram_positive = True
nb_colonies = 6
```

The returned values are the same as with the usual syntax "individual. property": it is a single value for the functional properties and a list of values for the other properties. However, when doing introspection, it is often easier to treat all properties generically, whether they are functional or not. In this case, the alternative syntax "property[individual]" is preferable because it always returns a list of values, even when called on functional properties, for example:

```
>>> for prop in onto.unknown_bacterium.get_properties():
...     print(prop.name, "=", prop[onto.unknown_bacterium])
has_grouping = [bacteria.in_cluster1]
has_shape = [bacteria.round1]
gram_positive = [True]
nb_colonies = [6]
```

For class introspection, the get_class_properties() method works similarly to that of individuals. It returns the properties for which the class has at least one existential restriction (or universal, depending on the type of class property; see 6.3):

```
>>> onto.Pseudomonas.get_class_properties()
{bacteria.gram_positive,
 bacteria.has_shape,
 bacteria.has_grouping}
```

Owlready considers the parent classes, but also the equivalent classes. The syntax "property[class]" can be used to obtain and/or modify the existential restrictions of classes.

Finally, the `INDIRECT_get_properties()` and `INDIRECT_get_class_properties()` methods work in the same way, but also return indirect properties (i.e., inherited from a parent class).

In addition, the `constructs()` method allows you to browse all the constructors that refer to a class or a property. For example, we can look for the constructors referring to the InSmallChain class:

```
>>> list(onto.InSmallChain.constructs())
[  bacteria.Bacterium
 & bacteria.has_shape.some(bacteria.Round)
 & bacteria.has_shape.only(bacteria.Round)
 & bacteria.has_grouping.some(bacteria.InSmallChain)
 & bacteria.has_grouping.only(Not(bacteria.Isolated))
 & bacteria.gram_positive.value(True)]
```

Here, we get only one construct, which is an intersection including an existential restriction with the class InSmallChain as value. We can then use this constructor's `subclasses()` method to get a list of all the classes that use it:

```
>>> constructor = list(onto.InSmallChain.constructs())[0]
>>> constructor.subclasses()
[bacteria.Streptococcus]
```

We thus find the Streptococcus class in which we had placed this restriction (see 3.4.8).

10.5 Reading restrictions backward

The restrictions make it possible to define relationships at the level of the classes of the ontology, for example, "Pseudomonas has_shape some Rod". Owlready provides easy access to these relationships with the syntax "Class.property" (see 4.5.4):

```
>>> onto.Pseudomonas.has_shape
bacteria.Rod
```

But how to read this existential restriction "backward", that is to say, from the Rod class, go back to the Pseudomonas class? Even if we had defined the reverse property, which we could call "is_shape_of", it would not answer our question, as the following example shows:

```
>>> with onto:
...     class is_shape_of(ObjectProperty):
...         inverse = onto.has_shape

>>> onto.Rod.is_shape_of
[]
```

Indeed, from a logical point of view, the following two propositions are different:

- "Pseudomonas has_shape some Rod"
- "Rod is_shape_of some Pseudomonas"

The first indicates that all Pseudomonas have a Rod shape, which is true. The second indicates that all Rod shapes are the shape of a Pseudomonas, which is not the same meaning (and is not true). For example, the Rod shape of a rugby ball is not the shape of a Pseudomonas.

Similarly, for the following two propositions:

- "Nucleus is_part_of some Cell"
- "Cell has_part some Nucleus"

The first indicates that every nucleus is part of a cell. The second indicates that every cell has a nucleus, which is different: in biology, the first proposition is true, while the second is false (e.g., bacteria are cells without nuclei).

However, it is sometimes useful to be able to read existential relationships backward. Owlready allows it: this can be done by combining the `constructs()` and `subclasses()` methods, as we did in the previous section. The `inverse_restrictions()` method automates this:

```
>>> set(onto.Rod.inverse_restrictions(onto.has_shape))
{bacteria.Pseudomonas, bacteria.Bacillus}
```

Note that we used `set()` to display the generator returned by `inverse_restrictions()`, after removing the duplicates.

10.6 Example: Using Gene Ontology and managing "part-of" relations

Gene Ontology (GO) is an ontology widely used in bioinformatics (see 4.7). GO consists of three parts: biological processes, molecular functions, and cell components. This third part describes the different elements of a cell: membranes, nucleus, organelles (such as mitochondria), and so on. It is particularly complex to manage because it includes both a hierarchy of "classic" inheritance using is-a relationships and a "part-of" relationship hierarchy. In this second hierarchy, called meronymy, the cell is decomposed into subparts, then into sub-subparts, and so on. The root of this hierarchy is therefore the entire cell, and the leaves the indivisible parts.

OWL and Owlready have relationships and methods to manage the inheritance hierarchy (`subclasses()`, `descendants()`, `ancestors()`, etc.; see 4.5.3). On the other hand, there is no standard OWL relation for meronymy nor specific methods in Owlready. We will see here how to add to the GO classes methods to access the subparts and super-parts, taking into account both the part-of and the is-a relations.

GO being quite large (almost 200 MB), loading takes several tens of seconds or even a few minutes, depending on the power of the computer and the download time of the OWL file. We will therefore load GO and store the Owlready quadstore in a file (see 4.7). In addition, we will use manual import here to associate our Python methods with OWL classes (see 10.2.1), so as not to have to modify GO by adding a "python_module" annotation.

GO uses arbitrary identifiers which are not directly understandable by humans. The following table summarizes the GO identifiers that we will need later:

GO identifier	Label
GO_0005575	*cellular_component*
BFO_0000050	*part of*
BFO_0000051	*has_part*

```
# File go_part_of.py
from owlready2 import *

default_world.set_backend(filename = "quadstore.sqlite3")
go = get_ontology("http://purl.obolibrary.org/obo/go.owl#").↲
load()
obo = go.get_namespace("http://purl.obolibrary.org/obo/")
default_world.save()
```

```
def my_render(entity):
    return "%s:%s" % (entity.name, entity.label.first())
set_render_func(my_render)

with obo:
    class GO_0005575(Thing):
        @classmethod
        def subparts(self):
            results = list(self.BFO_0000051)
            results.extend(self.inverse_restrictions↲
            (obo.BFO_0000050))
            return results

        @classmethod
        def transitive_subparts(self):
            results = set()
            for descendant in self.descendants():
                results.add(descendant)
                for subpart in descendant.subparts():
                    results.update(subpart.transitive_↲
                    subparts())
            return results

        @classmethod
        def superparts(self):
            results = list(self.BFO_0000050)
            results.extend(self.inverse_restrictions(obo.↲
            BFO_0000051))
            return results

        @classmethod
        def transitive_superparts(self):
            results = set()
            for ancestor in self.ancestors():
```

```
            if not issubclass(ancestor, GO_0005575):↲
            continue
            results.add(ancestor)
            for superpart in ancestor.superparts():
                if issubclass(superpart, GO_0005575):
                    results.update(superpart.transitive_↲
                    superparts())
        return results
```

This module defines four class methods in the class GO_0005575 (i.e., cellular_component). `subparts()` allows obtaining all the subparts of the component. This method takes into account the relationships BFO_0000051 (has-part) but also the relationships BFO_0000050 (part-of) read backward, contrary to what we would have obtained with .INDIRECT_BFO_0000051 (see 6.3). The `transitive_subparts()` method returns the subparts in a transitive manner, taking into account the child classes and the transitivity (if A is a subpart of B and B is a subpart of C, then A is also a subpart of C). The `superparts()` and `transitive_superparts()` methods work the same way for super-parts.

We can then import this module and access GO and "part-of" relationships. In the following example, we are looking at the part-of relationships of the nucleolus, which is a component located in the nucleus of the cell:

```
>>> from owlready2 import *
>>> from go_part_of import *

>>> nucleolus = go.search(label = "nucleolus")[0]

>>> print(nucleolus.subparts())
[GO_0005655:nucleolar ribonuclease P complex,
 GO_0030685:nucleolar preribosome,
 GO_0044452:nucleolar part,
```

```
 GO_0044452:nucleolar part,
 GO_0101019:nucleolar exosome (RNase complex)]

>>> print(nucleolus.superparts())
[GO_0031981:nuclear lumen]
```

Here, direct relationships (without taking transitivity into account) are not very informative. Transitive relationships are much richer:

```
>>> nucleolus.transitive_subparts()
{GO_0034388:Pwp2p-containing subcomplex of 90S preribosome,
 GO_0097424:nucleolus-associated heterochromatin,
 GO_0005736:DNA-directed RNA polymerase I complex,
 GO_0005731:nucleolus organizer region,
 GO_0101019:nucleolar exosome (RNase complex),
 [...] }

>>> nucleolus.transitive_superparts()
{GO_0031981:nuclear lumen,
 GO_0005634:nucleus,
 GO_0043226:organelle,
 GO_0044464:cell part,
 GO_0005623:cell,
 GO_0005575:cellular_component,
 [...] }
```

10.7 Example: A "dating site" for proteins

Now, we will use the functionality of the "go_part_of.py" module to create a "dating site" for proteins. This site allows you to enter two protein names, and the site determines in which compartments of the cell they can meet (if an encounter is possible!). From a biological point of view, this is important because two proteins that do not have a common "meeting site" cannot interact together.

For this, we will use

- The Flask Python module to make a dynamic website (see 4.12).
- The MyGene Python module to perform searches on the MyGene server and retrieve the GO concepts associated with each of the two proteins. This module allows you to do search on genes (and the proteins they code). MyGene is used as follows:

```
import mygene
mg = mygene.MyGeneInfo()
dico = mg.query('name:"<gene_name>"',
                fields = "<searched fields>",
                species = "<species>",
                size = <number of genes to
                search for>)
```

The call to MyGene returns a dictionary which itself contains lists and other dictionaries. For example, we can search for all of the GO terms associated with insulin as follows:

```
>>> import mygene
>>> mg = mygene.MyGeneInfo()
>>> dict = mg.query('name:"insulin"',
...     fields = "go.CC.id,go.MF.id,go.BP.id,"
...     species = "human",
...     size = 1)
>>> dict
{'max_score': 13.233688, 'took': 17, 'total': 57,
'hits': [{'_id': '3630', '_score': 13.233688,
```

```
'go': {'BP': [{'id': 'GO:0002674'},
              {'id': 'GO:0006006'}, [...]
              ]}}]}
```

"Go.CC.id", "go.MF.id", and "go.BP.id" represent the three main parts of GO (cellular components, molecular functions, and biological process, respectively). For our dating site, we will only use "CC". Although they originate from Gene Ontology, these actually describe the localization in the cell of the gene product, that is, the protein (in general), and not the gene itself (the genes normally remain in the nucleus, for eukaryotic cells).

More information is available on the MyGene website:

`http://docs.mygene.info/en/latest/`

- Owlready and Gene Ontology (GO) to make the *semantic intersection* of the GO terms describing the cellular compartments of the two proteins. A "simple" intersection (in the set sense of the term) is not sufficient: the intersection must take into account both the "is-a" relations of inheritance and the "part-of" relations. For example, a protein A present only in the membranes and a protein B present only in the mitochondria may meet in the membrane of the mitochondria. Indeed, the mitochondria membrane is a membrane, and it is a part of the mitochondria, as shown in the following diagram:

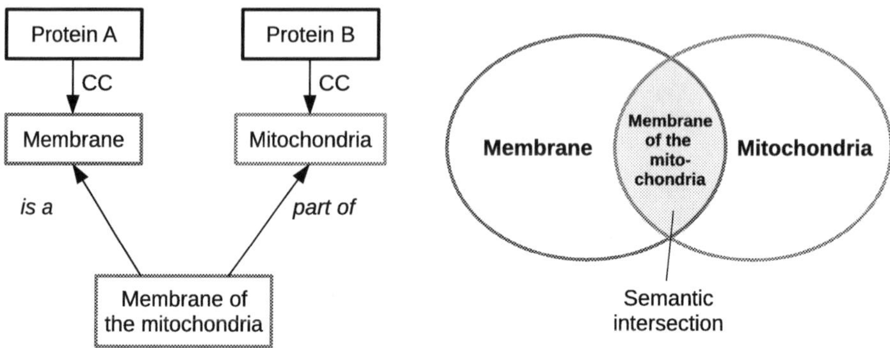

The following program describes the protein dating site. It begins by importing and initializing all of the modules:

- Owlready
- The "go_part_of" module that we created in the previous section
- Flask
- MyGene

Then, the `search_protein()` function is defined. It takes as input a protein name (in English), such as "insulin", and returns all of the GO terms of the cellular component type ("CC") associated with it in MyGene. For this, we check that at least one result (hit in English) is found, and then we get the "CC". If only one CC is found, MyGene returns it; otherwise, it is a list. To facilitate processing, we systematically create a list called `cc`. Then we go through this list and extract the GO identifier. The identifiers returned by MyGene are of the form "GO: 0002674" and not "GO_0002674" as in the OWL version of GO. So we replace all ":" with "_". Finally, we recover the concept of the corresponding ontology using the `obo` namespace (which was imported from the go_part_of module).

The `semantic_intersection()` function performs the semantic intersection of two sets containing GO concepts of cellular components in four steps:

1. We create two sets, subparts1 and subparts2, containing the components associated with each of the two proteins as well as their subparts in a transitive way. For this, we reuse the static method transitive_subparts() that we defined in the module go_part_of.py in the previous section. We then have the sets of all the components where each of the two proteins can be encountered, taking into account the is-a and part-of relations.

2. We compute the intersection of these two sets with the operator "&" (see 2.4.7 for sets in Python), and we call the result `common_components`.

3. We now have to simplify the `common_components` set. Indeed, it includes the concepts that we are looking for, but also all their descendants and their subparts (in the previous example with "membrane" and "mitochondria", we therefore have "membrane of the mitochondria" but also "inner membrane of the mitochondria" and "outer membrane of the mitochondria"). In order to speed up the processing of the next step, we first create a cache (using a dictionary). This cache matches each GO concept in `common_components` with all of its (transitive) subparts.

4. We create a new set, `largest_common_components`, which is empty at the beginning. We add to it all the concepts of `common_components` which is not a

subpart of another concept in common_components. Note the use of "else" in the "for" loop, which allows you to execute instructions when the loop has iterated over all items (that is to say, no "break" has been encountered; see 2.6). Finally, we return largest_common_components.

The rest of the program defines two web pages with Flask. The first (path "/") is a basic form with two text fields to enter the names of the proteins and a button to validate. The second (path "/result") computes and displays the result. It first calls the search_protein() function twice, once for each protein, then the semantic_intersection() function. Finally, it generates a web page displaying the components associated with the first protein, the second, and the components where they are likely to meet.

```
# File dating_site.py
from owlready2 import *
from go_part_of import *

from flask import Flask, request
app = Flask(__name__)

import mygene
mg = mygene.MyGeneInfo()

def search_protein(protein_name):
    r = mg.query('name:"%s"' % protein_name, fields =↲
    "go.CC.id", sspecies = "human", size = 1)
    if not "go" in r["hits"][0]: return set()

    cc = r["hits"][0]["go"]["CC"]
    if not isinstance(cc, list): cc = [cc]
```

```
    components = set()
    for dict in cc:
        go_id = dict["id"]
        go_term = obo[go_id.replace(":", "_")]
        if go_term: components.add(go_term)

    return components

def semantic_intersection(components1, components2):
    subparts1 = set()
    for component in components1:
        subparts1.update(component.transitive_subparts())

    subparts2 = set()
    for component in components2:
        subparts2.update(component.transitive_subparts())

    common_components = subparts1 & subparts2

    cache = { component: component.transitive_subparts()↲
              for component in common_components }

    largest_common_components = set()
    for component in common_components:
        for component2 in common_components:
            if (not component2 is component) and↲
               (component in cache[component2]): break
        else:
            largest_common_components.add(component)

    return largest_common_components

@app.route('/')
def entry_page():
    html  = """
```

```
<html><body>
  <form action="/result">
    Protein 1: <input type="text" name="prot1"/><br/><br/>
    Protein 2: <input type="text" name="prot2"/><br/><br/>
    <input type="submit"/>
  </form>
</body></html>"""
    return html

@app.route('/result')
def result_page():
    prot1 = request.args.get("prot1", " ")
    prot2 = request.args.get("prot2", " ")

    components1 = search_protein(prot1)
    components2 = search_protein(prot2)

    common_components = semantic_intersection(components1,↵
    components2)

    html  = """<html><body>"'"
    html += """<h3>Components for protein #1 (%s)</h3>""" % prot1
    if components1:
        html += "<br/>".join(sorted(str(component)↵
                                for component in components1))
    else:
        html += "(none)<br/>"

    html += """<h3>Components for protein #2 (%s)</h3>""" %↵
    prot2
    if components2:
        html += "<br/>".join(sorted(str(component)↵
                                for component in components2))
```

```
    else:
        html += "(none)<br/>"

    html += """<h3>Possible dating sites</h3>"""
    if common_components:
        html += "<br/>".join(sorted(str(component)↲
                                    for component in common_components))
    else:
        html += "(none)<br/>"

    html += """</body></html>"""
    return html

import werkzeug.serving
werkzeug.serving.run_simple("localhost", 5000, app)
```

In order to test our dating site, here are some examples of protein names: trypsin, cytochrome C, insulin, insulin-degrading enzyme, insulin receptor, glucagon, hemoglobin, elastase, granzyme B, decorin, beta-2-microglobulin, and so on.

The following screenshots show the dating site obtained and its use:

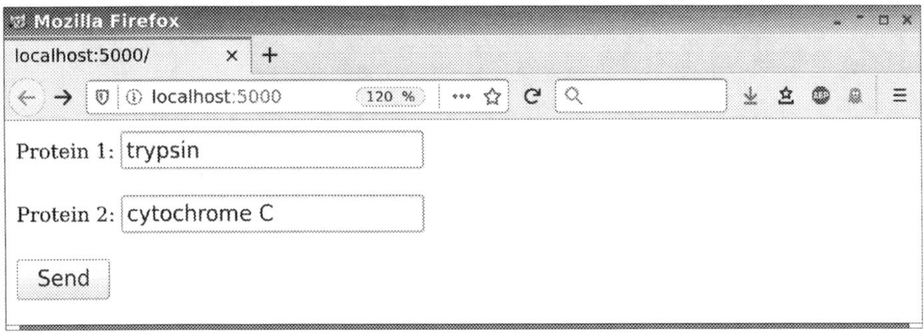

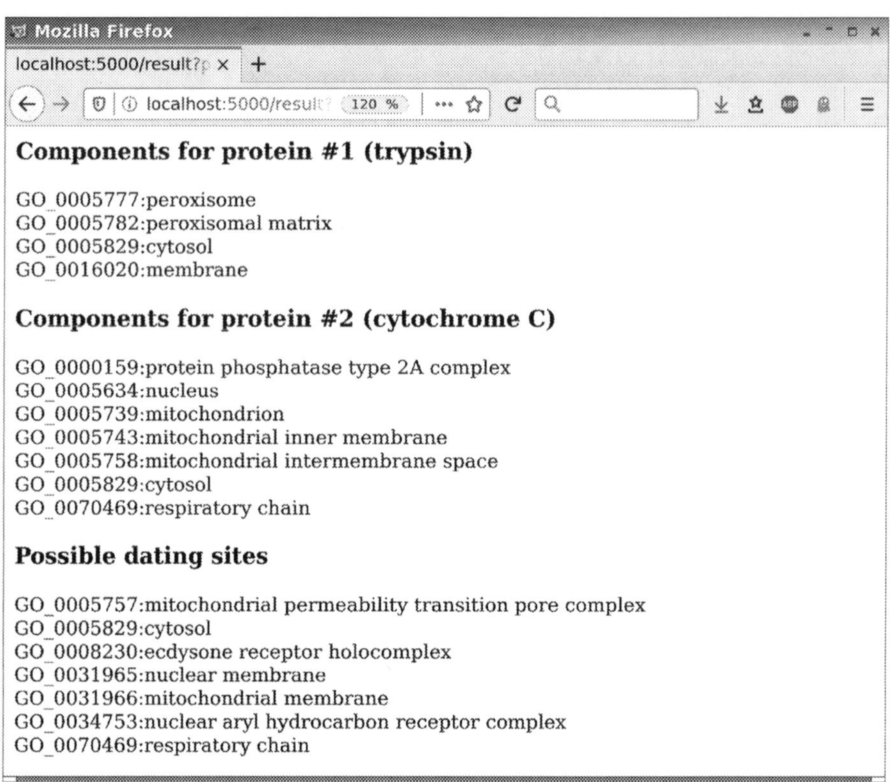

10.8 Summary

In this chapter, you have learned how to mix Python and OWL in order to associate Python methods with an OWL class having a rich semantics. We have also seen how to perform introspection on OWL classes and entities.

CHAPTER 11

Working with RDF triples and worlds

In this chapter, we will see how to directly access Owlready's RDF quadstore and how to create several isolated "worlds", each having their own quadstore.

11.1 RDF triples

RDF (Resource Description Framework) is a graph model for the formal description of resources and metadata. In particular, any OWL ontology can be expressed in the form of an RDF graph. An RDF graph consists of a set of RDF triples of the form (subject, predicate, object). The predicate corresponds to a property in the OWL sense. In the ontology of bacteria, two examples of triples describing the individual "unknown_bacterium" are

```
(http://lesfleursdunormal.fr/static/_downloads/bacteria.↲
owl#unknown_bacterium,
 http://www.w3.org/1999/02/22-rdf-syntax-ns#type,
 http://lesfleursdunormal.fr/static/_downloads/bacteria.↲
 owl#Bacterium)
```

```
(http://lesfleursdunormal.fr/static/_downloads/bacteria.↲
owl#unknown_bacterium,
```


L. Jean-Baptiste, *Ontologies with Python*, https://doi.org/10.1007/978-1-4842-6552-9_11

```
http://lesfleursdunormal.fr/static/_downloads/bacteria.↲
owl#gram_positive, true)
```

The first triple indicates the class to which the individual belongs, via the RDF predicate "type", and the second indicates the Gram status of the bacterium.

Other more complex OWL constructors, such as class restrictions, can be described using several RDF triples and blank nodes in the graph. For example, the restriction "gram_positive value false" of the Pseudomonas class is translated into four RDF triples, as follows:

```
(http://lesfleursdunormal.fr/static/_downloads/bacteria.↲
owl#Pseudomonas,
 http://www.w3.org/1999/02/22-rdf-syntax-ns#type,
 _:7)

(_:7,
 http://www.w3.org/1999/02/22-rdf-syntax-ns#type,
 http://www.w3.org/2002/07/owl#Restriction)

(_:7,
 http://www.w3.org/2002/07/owl#onProperty,
 http://lesfleursdunormal.fr/static/_downloads/bacteria.↲
 owl#gram_positive)

(_:7,
 http://www.w3.org/2002/07/owl#hasValue,
 false)
```

Here, "_:7" is a blank node (i.e., an anonymous entity). The name of this node is not meaningful (and may vary from execution to execution); only the relationships in which it participates are important.

Owlready allows displaying all RDF triples of an ontology with the `dump()` method:

```
>>> from owlready2 import *
>>> onto = get_ontology("bacteria.owl").load()

>>> onto.graph.dump()
<http://lesfleursdunormal.fr/static/_downloads/bacteria.owl>↲
    <http://www.w3.org/1999/02/22-rdf-syntax-ns#type>↲
    <http://www.w3.org/2002/07/owl#Ontology> .
<http://lesfleursdunormal.fr/static/_downloads/bacteria.↲
owl#Shape>↲
    <http://www.w3.org/1999/02/22-rdf-syntax-ns#type>↲
    <http://www.w3.org/2002/07/owl#Class> .
[...]
```

`dump()` can also be called on `default_world` in order to display all the RDF triples present in the quadstore (i.e., `default_world.graph.dump()`)

11.2 Manipulating RDF triples with RDFlib

11.2.1 Reading RDF triples

RDFlib is a Python module that allows you to manipulate RDF graphs and triples. For the OWL ontologies being stored in an RDF graph, we can use RDFlib to manipulate this graph. However, unlike Owlready, RDFlib does not take into account the semantics specific to OWL and therefore does not allow to take advantage of the expressiveness of OWL or to carry out automatic reasoning.

Owlready uses a different quadstore than that of RDFlib. However, the Owlready quadstore can be made compatible with RDFlib with the `as_rdflib_graph()` method, as follows:

```
>>> from rdflib import *
>>> graph = default_world.as_rdflib_graph()
```

The resulting graph object is an RDFlib-compatible quadstore.

RDFlib graphs are composed of three elements: entities (identified by a URI and created with the `URIRef()` function), blank nodes (created with the `BNode()` function), and data (integer or real numbers, character strings, etc. grouped under the name literals and created with the `Literal()` function). The `triples(subject, predicate, object)` method of the RDF graph allows you to browse a subset of the triples; each of the three parameters can take the value `None`, which is treated as a wildcard. So, to browse the set of triples having a given subject, we will pass the value `None` for the two parameters `predicate` and `object`.

For example, we can display all RDF triples about the Staphylococcus class, as follows (NB: line breaks have been added for easier reading, but will not appear on the screen if you run this example):

```
>>> list(graph.triples((URIRef("http://lesfleursdunormal.fr/↲
static/_downloads/bacteria.owl#Staphylococcus"), None, None)))
[(rdflib.term.URIRef('http://lesfleursdunormal.fr/static/↲
                      _downloads/bacteria.owl#Staphylococcus'),
  rdflib.term.URIRef('http://www.w3.org/1999/02/22-rdf-syntax-↲
  ns#type'),
  rdflib.term.URIRef('http://www.w3.org/2002/07/owl#Class')),

 (rdflib.term.URIRef('http://lesfleursdunormal.fr/static/↲
                      _downloads/bacteria.owl#Staphylococcus'),
  rdflib.term.URIRef('http://www.w3.org/2000/01/rdf-↲
  schema#subClassOf'),
```

```
  rdflib.term.URIRef('http://lesfleursdunormal.fr/static/↲
                      _downloads/bacteria.owl#Coccus')),
 (rdflib.term.URIRef('http://lesfleursdunormal.fr/static/↲
                      _downloads/bacteria.owl#Staphylococcus'),
  rdflib.term.URIRef('http://www.w3.org/2002/07/↲
  owl#equivalentClass'),
  rdflib.term.BNode('20'))
]
```

11.2.2 Creating new RDF triples with RDFlib

RDFlib allows you to access triples, but also to create new ones with the add((subject, predicate, object)) method. When adding triples, it is necessary to indicate in which ontology they will be added. This can be done in two different ways:

- Either in the manner of Owlready, with a "with ontology: ..." block:

```
>>> with onto:
...     graph.add((
...       URIRef("http://www.test.org/t.owl#MyClass"),
...       URIRef("http://www.w3.org/1999/02/22-rdf-↲
          syntax-ns#type"),
...       URIRef("http://www.w3.org/2002/07/↲
          owl#Class"),
... ))
```

- Or like RDFlib, using a contextual graph that we obtain with the get_context() method:

```
>>> graph2 = graph.get_context(onto)
>>> graph2.add((
```

```
...      URIRef("http://www.test.org/t.owl#MyClass2"),
...      URIRef("http://www.w3.org/1999/02/22-rdf-↲
         syntax-ns#type"),
...      URIRef("http://www.w3.org/2002/07/owl#Class"),
... ))
```

The get_context() method takes as a parameter either the Owlready ontology as in the preceding example or its IRI (in the form of a URIRef object from RDFlib), as in the following example:

```
>>> graph2 = graph.get_context(URIRef("http://↲
lesfleursdunormal.fr/static/_downloads/bacteria.owl"))
```

RDF blank nodes can be created using the graph.BNode() method, as follows:

```
>>> with onto:
...     new_blank_node = graph.BNode()
```

The blank node can then be used with RDFlib:

```
>>> with onto:
...     graph.add((
...       URIRef("http://www.test.org/t.owl#MyClass"),
...       URIRef("http://www.w3.org/1999/02/22-rdf-syntax-↲
          ns#type"),
...       new_blank_node,
... ))
```

Please note adding RDF triples via RDFlib may not update the corresponding objects in Owlready if they have already been loaded from the quadstore. On the other hand, if the objects have not been loaded, it is possible to do so after their creation using RDFlib.

11.2.3 Removing RDF triples with RDFlib

Finally, RDFlib allows you to delete triples with the `remove((subject, predicate, object))` method:

```
>>> graph.remove((
...     URIRef("http://www.test.org/t.owl#MyClass"),
...     URIRef("http://www.w3.org/1999/02/22-rdf-syntax-↲
        ns#type"),
...     URIRef("http://www.w3.org/2002/07/owl#Class"),
... ))
```

The `remove()` method accepts the use of `None` as a wildcard for the subject, the predicate, and/or the object. For example, we can delete all triples with the subject "`http://www.test.org/t.owl#MyClass2`" as follows:

```
>>> graph.remove((
...     URIRef("http://www.test.org/t.owl#MyClass2"),
...     None,
...     None,
... ))
```

Be careful, again, deleting RDF triples via RDFlib may not update the corresponding objects in Owlready.

11.3 Performing SPARQL requests

SPARQL (SPARQL Protocol and RDF Query Language) is a query language for searching in an RDF graph. This language is a bit like the SQL (Structured Query Language) of relational databases, but it is devoted to RDF graph databases.

RDFlib includes a SPARQL engine, which can be used with Owlready.

11.3.1 Searching with SPARQL

SPARQL allows you to do more complex searches than the `search()` method of Owlready; however, for simple searches, it is better to use `search()` because the performance is better.

The `query()` method of the RDFlib graph object allows you to perform a SPARQL query and returns the result in RDFlib format (that is to say, in the form of `URIRef`, `BNode`, and `Literal`). The WHERE clause of the query is made of one or more RDF triples, which can contain entities (identified by their IRI) but also variables, whose names are prefixed with "?". In the following example, we are looking for all the entities ?b being of the class Bacterium, where ?b is a variable:

```
>>> graph = default_world.as_rdflib_graph()
>>> list(graph.query("""
... SELECT ?b WHERE {
... ?b
... <http://www.w3.org/1999/02/22-rdf-syntax-ns#type>
... <http://lesfleursdunormal.fr/static/_downloads/bacteria.↲
    owl#Bacterium>.
... }""" ))
[(rdflib.term.URIRef('http://lesfleursdunormal.fr/static/↲
_downloads/bacteria.owl#unknown_bacterium'),)]
```

The `query_owlready()` method works the same way, but returns the result in Owlready format (i.e., as an Owlready object or as Python datatypes):

```
>>> list(graph.query_owlready("""
... SELECT ?b WHERE {
... ?b
... <http://www.w3.org/1999/02/22-rdf-syntax-ns#type>
```

```
... <http://lesfleursdunormal.fr/static/_downloads/bacteria.↲
    owl#Bacterium>.
... }""" ))
[[bacteria.unknown_bacterium]]
```

SPARQL allows you to perform searches involving several variables. For example, we can look for all bacteria with a grouping whose type is InCluster. This research requires two variables, noted here ?b (the bacterium) and ?r (its grouping), and three triples. It can be done as follows:

```
>>> list(graph.query_owlready("""
... SELECT ?b WHERE {
... ?b
... <http://www.w3.org/1999/02/22-rdf-syntax-ns#type>
... <http://lesfleursdunormal.fr/static/_downloads/bacteria.↲
    owl#Bacterium>.
...
... ?b
... <http://lesfleursdunormal.fr/static/_downloads/bacteria.↲
    owl#has_grouping>
... ?r .
...
... ?r
... <http://www.w3.org/1999/02/22-rdf-syntax-ns#type>
... <http://lesfleursdunormal.fr/static/_downloads/bacteria.↲
    owl#InCluster>.
... }""" ))
[[bacteria.unknown_bacterium]]
```

Finally, the default_world.sparql_query() method is a shortcut for directly performing a SPARQL search and retrieving the result in Owlready format (as with query_owlready()):

```
>>> list(default_world.sparql_query("""..."""))
```

It is possible to easily integrate Owlready objects into a SPARQL query using their IRI between angle brackets (<...>), for example:

```
>>> individual = onto.unknown_bacterium
>>> list(default_world.sparql_query("""
... SELECT ?class WHERE {
...     <%s> a ?class .
...     ?class a <http://www.w3.org/2002/07/owl#Class> .
... }""" % individual.iri))
[[bacteria.Bacterium]]
```

This SPARQL query searches for all the classes to which the individual "unknown_bacterium" belongs. In this example, the property "a" is a shortcut for "<http://www.w3.org/1999/02/22-rdf-syntax-ns#type>".

11.3.2 SPARQL prefixes

Owlready and RDFlib also allow the use of SPARQL prefix in order to simplify the writing of SPARQL queries and to shorten the IRIs. Prefixes are declared with the bind() method, as follows:

```
graph.bind("prefix", "base IRI")
```

Then, the IRIs starting with the basic IRI can be written in the form "prefix:end_of_the_IRI", without the angle brackets. In the following example, we define a prefix for OWL, and then we resume the previous example using this prefix:

```
>>> graph = default_world.as_rdflib_graph()
>>> graph.bind("owl", "http://www.w3.org/2002/07/owl#")
```

```
>>> individual = onto.unknown_bacterium
>>> list(default_world.sparql_query("""
... SELECT ?class WHERE {
...     <%s> a ?class .
...     ?class a owl:Class .
... }""" % individual.iri))
[[bacteria.Bacterium]]
```

11.3.3 Creating RDF triples with SPARQL

SPARQL queries of type "INSERT" allow the creation of RDF triples. They are executed with the update() method of the RDFlib graph object. As previously with RDFlib (see 11.2.2), it is necessary to indicate in which ontology the triples will be created. This can be done in two different ways:

- Either in the manner of Owlready, with a "with ontology: ..." block:

```
>>> with onto:
...     graph.update("""
... INSERT {
...     <http://www.test.org/t.owl#MyClass>
...     <http://www.w3.org/1999/02/22-rdf-syntax-↲
        ns#type>
...     <http://www.w3.org/2002/07/owl#Class> .
... } WHERE {}""")
```

- Or like RDFlib, using a contextual graph that we obtain with the get_context() method:

```
>>> graph  = default_world.as_rdflib_graph()
>>> graph2 = graph.get_context(onto)
>>> graph2.update("""
```

```
... INSERT {
...     <http://www.test.org/t.owl#MyClass2>
...     <http://www.w3.org/1999/02/22-rdf-syntax-ns↲
        #type>
...     <http://www.w3.org/2002/07/owl#Class> .
... } WHERE {}""")
```

More complex queries can include a “WHERE” part. The following example finds all the classes (“WHERE” part) and adds a comment to them (“INSERT” part):

```
>>> graph2.update("""
... INSERT {
...     ?class
...     <http://www.w3.org/2000/01/rdf-schema#comment>
...     "This entity is a class!."
... } WHERE {
...     ?class a <http://www.w3.org/2002/07/owl#Class> .
... }
... """)
```

Please note adding RDF triples *via* SPARQL may not update the corresponding objects in Owlready if they have already been loaded in Python.

11.3.4 Removing RDF triples with SPARQL

The `update()` method of the RDFlib graph object also allows executing “DELETE” queries to delete RDF triples. These requests can take a “WHERE” part. The following example deletes the comments added previously:

```
>>> graph2.update("""
... DELETE {
...     ?class
```

```
...     <http://www.w3.org/2000/01/rdf-schema#comment>
...     "This entity is a class!."
... } WHERE {
...     ?class a <http://www.w3.org/2002/07/owl#Class> .
... }
... """)
```

Please note removing RDF triples *via* SPARQL may not update the corresponding objects in Owlready if they have already been loaded in Python.

11.4 Accessing RDF triples with Owlready

Owlready also has methods to directly access the RDF quadstore. These methods are more complex and less standard than using RDFlib, but they are also faster.

In order to reduce the volume of the quadstore, Owlready replaces the IRIs of the entities with "abbreviated IRIs" called *storid* (store ID). These are arbitrary codes in the form of strictly positive integers. The `_abbreviate()` and `_unabbreviate()` methods allow translating an IRI to a storid or a storid to an IRI, respectively. If an IRI has not yet received an abbreviation, a new code is automatically created by `_abbreviate()` and saved in the quadstore.

In the following example, the IRI of the Staphylococcus class corresponds to the storid 324 (note: the exact value of the storid can vary from one quadstore to another, depending on the order of creation of the entities in the ontology):

```
>>> default_world._abbreviate(onto.Staphylococcus.iri)
323
>>> default_world._unabbreviate(323)
'http://lesfleursdunormal.fr/static/_downloads/bacteria.owl
#Staphylococcus'
```

The `storid` attribute of any entity allows you to retrieve its storid:

```
>>> onto.Staphylococcus.storid
323
```

The `_get_by_storid()` method allows the opposite operation, that is to say, to obtain an entity from its storid:

```
>>> default_world._get_by_storid(323)
bacteria.Staphylococcus
```

Blank nodes are also represented in the quadstore by storid, but these are strictly negative integers.

The Owlready quadstore stores relationships between two entities using RDF triples of the classic form (subject, predicate, object). On the other hand, the relations between an entity and a datatype value are stored in the form of quadruplets (or quad), of the form (subject, predicate, value, datatype). The value can be an integer (Python `int` type), a real number (Python `float` type), or a character string (Python `str` type). The type is either a character string which indicates the language for a localized character string, prefixed by "`@`" (e.g., "`@en`" or "`@fr`"), or the storid of the datatype (see supported IRIs by OWL in Table 4-1), or 0 if no datatype is specified (corresponding to PlainLiteral in OWL).

The `_get_triples_spod_spod(subject, predicate, object_or_value, datatype)` method behaves similarly to RDFlib's `triples()` method. We can obtain the triples present in the quadstore for the Staphylococcus class, as follows:

```
>>> default_world._get_triples_spod_spod(323, None, None, None)
[(323, 6, 11, None),
 (323, 9, 321, None),
 (323, 33, -20, None)]
```

Since these are triples corresponding to relations between two entities, the datatype (fourth value of each tuple) is not used and is equal to `None`.

The `_get_obj_triples_spo_spo(subject, predicate, object)` and `_get_data_triples_spod_spod(subject, predicate, value, type)` methods work like `_get_triples_spod_spod()`, but they are limited to relations between two entities (for the former) and between an entity and a datatype value (for the latter).

The `_unabbreviate()` method can then be used to decode the results obtained previously:

```
>>> default_world._unabbreviate(6)
'http://www.w3.org/1999/02/22-rdf-syntax-ns#type'
>>> default_world._unabbreviate(11)
'http://www.w3.org/2002/07/owl#Class'
[...]
```

The `default_world._to_rdf(entity_or_data)` method makes it possible to transform any entity or datatype value into RDF. It returns either a couple (storid, None), when called on an entity, or a couple (value, type), when called on a datatype value, as in the following examples:

```
>>> default_world._to_rdf(8)
(8, 43)
>>> default_world._to_rdf(onto.Staphylococcus)
(323, None)
```

Its counterpart, the `default_world._to_python(object_or_value, datatype)` method, performs the opposite operation.

```
>>> default_world._to_python(8, 43)
8
>>> default_world._to_python(323, None)
bacteria.Staphylococcus
```

The _has_obj_triple_spo(subject, predicate, object) and _has_data_triple_spod(subject, predicate, data, datatype) methods are used to verify the existence of an RDF triple in the quadstore. For example, we can verify the existence of the first triple of the Staphylococcus class as follows:

```
>>> default_world._has_obj_triple_spo(323, 6, 11)
True
```

The _del_obj_triple_spo(subject, predicate, object) and _del_data_triple_spod(subject, predicate, data, datatype) methods allow deleting one or more RDF triples (several triples are deleted in the case where a parameter is None, which acts as a joker). For example, we can delete the first triples of the Staphylococcus class as follows:

```
>>> default_world._del_obj_triple_spo(323, 6, 11)
```

Be careful, however, these methods do not update the corresponding Owlready objects: the Staphylococcus class is still a child of Coccus in Python:

```
>>> onto.Staphylococcus.is_a
[bacteria.Coccus]
```

The _add_obj_triple_spo(subject, predicate, object) and _add_data_triple_spod (subject, predicate, data, datatype) methods add an RDF triple. They must be applied to an ontology (and not to default_world) in order to specify the ontology in which the triple will be inserted. For example, to recreate the previously deleted triple, we will do:

```
>>> onto._add_obj_triple_spo(323, 6, 11)
```

Again, these two methods do not update Owlready Python objects.

Finally, Owlready has many optimized methods for performing a specific type of search in the quadstore. The names of these methods follow the following pattern:

```
_get_<element>_triple<plural>_<inputs>_<output>()
```

where

- <element> indicates in which part of the quadstore the search is made:
  - <element> = (empty): For searching in the entire quadstore
  - <element> = obj: For searching in the relations between two entities
  - <element> = data: For searching in the relations between an entity and a datatype value
- <plural> indicates how many results are returned:
  - <plural> = s: Returns all results found in the quadstore
  - <plural> = (empty): Returns the first result found in the quadstore
- <input> indicates the parameters of the method. It is a combination of the following characters:
  - c: The ontology identifier
  - s: The subjects of the triple (a storid for an entity or a blank node)
  - p: The predicate of the triple (a storid for a property)
  - o: The object of the triple (a storid for an entity or a blank node or a datatype value)

  - d: The datatype (an empty string, a storid for a datatype, or a two-letter language code prefixed by "@")

- <output> indicates the return values of the method. It is a combination of the same characters as for the entries.

The following optimized methods are available:

- `_get_triples_s_p()`, `_get_triples_s_pod()`, `_get_triples_sp_od()`, `_get_triples_spod_spod()`
- `_get_triple_sp_od()`
- `_get_obj_triples_sp_o()`, `_get_obj_triples_sp_co()`, `_get_obj_triples_spo_spo()`, `_get_obj_triples_cspo_cspo()`, `_get_obj_triples_s_po( )`, `_get_obj_triples_po_s()`
- `_get_obj_triple_po_s()`, `_get_obj_triple_sp_o()`
- `_get_data_triples_s_pod()`, `_get_data_triples_sp_od()`, `_get_data_triples_spod_spod()`
- `_get_data_triple_sp_od()`

For example, the `_get_obj_triples_sp_o()` method searches only among the relations between two entities ("objs"); it takes as parameters a subject and a predicate ("sp") and returns a list of objects ("o"). We can obtain the storids of the parent classes of the Staphylococcus class (storid 323) as follows (6 being the storid of the typical RDF property):

```
>>> list(default_world._get_obj_triples_sp_o(323, 6))
[11]
```

11.5 Interrogating the SQLite3 database directly

The Owlready quadstore is implemented as a SQLite3 database. It contains three main tables:

- resources, which maps IRIs to storids
- objs, which contains the quadruplets of the relations between two entities
- datas, which contains the quadruplets of the relations between an entity and a data

Finally, the "quads" view is a read-only pseudo-table that contains both the records from the objs table and the datas table (for objs, d = NULL).

The following tables show the schema of these tables:

resources table	
storid INTEGER	iri TEXT

objs table				
rowid INTEGER	c INTEGER	s INTEGER	p INTEGER	o INTEGER

datas table					
rowid INTEGER	c INTEGER	s INTEGER	p INTEGER	o BLOB	d INTEGER

quads view					
rowid INTEGER	c INTEGER	s INTEGER	p INTEGER	o BLOB	d INTEGER

The fields are

- storid: An identifier in the quadstore
- iri: The IRI associated with the storid
- rowid: A row identifier in the SQL table
- c: An ontology identifier—1 for the first ontology loaded, 2 for the second, and so on
- s: The subject of the triple, that is, a storid
- p: The predicate of the triple, that is, a storid for a property
- o: The object of the triple, that is, a storid (for the objs table), a datatype value (integer, float, or string for the datas table), or any of the two (for the quads view)
- d: The datatype for the value in o is either of the following:
  - `None` (`NULL` in SQL) for an entity (in the quads view)
  - A storid indicating the type of data (for the datas or quads table)
  - A two-letter language code of the form "@langue", for example, "`@en`" for English or "`@fr`" for French (for localized texts in the datas and quads tables)

The `execute()` method allows you to execute an SQL query directly on the database. As an example, the following SQL query makes it possible to search for all of the bacteria having a grouping whose type is InCluster (a query that we had already carried out in SPARQL in section 11.3.1):

```
>>> default_world.graph.execute("""
... SELECT q1.s
... FROM objs q1, objs q2, objs q3
```

```
... WHERE q1.p=%s AND q1.o=%s
...    AND q2.s=q1.s AND q2.p=%s
...    AND q3.s=q2.o AND q3.p=%s AND q3.o=%s
...   """% (rdf_type, onto.Bacterium.storid,
...          onto.has_grouping.storid,
...          rdf_type, onto.InCluster.storid)
... ).fetchall()
[(327,)]
>>> default_world.graph._unabbreviate(327)
'http://lesfleursdunormal.fr/static/_downloads/bacteria.owl#↲
unknown_bacterium'
```

This query uses the objs table three times (this corresponds to the three triples of the SPARQL query).

To help write SQL queries, it is possible to draw inspiration from queries produced by Owlready's `search()` method. The `sql_request()` method of the pseudo-list returned by `search()` displays the SQL query and the corresponding parameters (whose values will replace the "?" of the query). Here is an example:

```
>>> default_world.search(iri = "*Bacteri*").sql_request()
('SELECT DISTINCT q1_1.s FROM objs q1_1, resources↲
  WHERE resources.storid = q1_1.s AND resources.iri GLOB ?',↲
['*Bacteri*'])
```

11.6 Adding support for custom datatypes

The `declare_datatype()` global function allows declaring additional datatype in Owlready. The function takes four parameters: the datatype Python class, its IRI, a parser function, and a serializer function. The serializer function is in charge of the serialization of the datatype, that is to say, to translate it into a string. The parser function is in charge of the opposite operation: it reads the string and returns the Python datatype value.

The following example adds support for the "hexBinary" datatype (which is defined in XML-Schema). It first creates a Python class called "Hex" for managing a hexadecimal value. Then, it defines the parser function. This function reads a hexadecimal value (in the format of XML-Schema) and returns a Hex instance. The serializer function takes a Hex instance and returns a hexadecimal value formatted in a string (we remove the first two characters, with "[2:]", because Python adds "0x" at the beginning of a hexadecimal value, while XML-Schema does not). Finally, we declare the new datatype.

```
>>> class Hex(object):
...     def __init__(self, value):
...         self.value = value

>>> def parse_hex(s):
...     return Hex(int(s, 16))

>>> def serialize_hex(x):
...     h = hex(x.value)[2:]
...     if len(h) % 2 != 0: return "%s" % h
...     return h

>>> declare_datatype(Hex, "http://www.w3.org/2001/↲
XMLSchema#hexBinary", parse_hex, serialize_hex)
```

We can now create an ontology and use a Hex value in data properties:

```
>>> onto = get_ontology("http://www.test.org/test_hex.owl")

>>> with onto:
...     class has_hex(Thing >> Hex): pass
```

```
...     class MyClass(Thing): pass
...     c = MyClass()
...     c.has_hex.append(Hex(14))
```

We can verify the content of the quadstore:

```
>>> onto.graph.dump()
<http://www.test.org/t.owl>
      <http://www.w3.org/1999/02/22-rdf-syntax-ns#type>
      <http://www.w3.org/2002/07/owl#Ontology> .
[...]
<http://www.test.org/t.owl#myclass1>
      <http://www.test.org/t.owl#has_hex>
      0e^^<http://www.w3.org/2001/XMLSchema#hexBinary> .
```

Notice that the value is stored in the hexadecimal format in the quadstore (here, "0e" is the hexadecimal representation of 14).

We may also load ontologies using the XML-Schema hexBinary datatype. However, note that declare_datatype() must be called before loading such ontologies.

11.7 Creating several isolated worlds

Owlready makes it possible to create several isolated "worlds", sometimes called "universe of speech". This makes it possible in particular to load the same ontology several times, independently, that is to say, without the modifications made on one copy affecting the other copy. It can also be useful for simultaneously loading several incompatible versions of the same ontology.

By default, Owlready creates only one world, called default_world. The World class allows you to create a new world, independent from default_world.

```
>>> from owlready2 import *
>>> my_world = World()
```

Each world is stored in a separate quadstore. Each can be stored in RAM and/or on the disk in a different file *via* the set_backend() method (see section 4.7). Generally speaking, all of the methods we applied to default_world can be applied to worlds, such as search() or as_rdflib_graph(). In addition, several global functions are actually shortcuts to methods of default_world. When using several worlds, you must therefore call the methods and not the global shortcuts. Here is the list of these shortened functions and the corresponding methods:

Shortcut global function	Corresponding method
get_ontology()	World.get_ontology()
get_namespace()	World.get_namespace()
IRIS[iri]	World[iri]
sync_reasoner()	sync_reasoner(world)

The following example illustrates the isolation of the worlds, creating a new world separate from default_world, then loading the ontology of bacteria in each world. In default_world, we delete the Staphylococcus class, but it remains present in the other world.

```
>>> onto = get_ontology("http://lesfleursdunormal.fr/↲
static/_downloads/bacteria.owl#").load()
>>> onto2 = my_world.get_ontology("http://lesfleursdunormal.↲
fr/static/_downloads/bacteria.owl#").load()
```

```
>>> destroy_entity(onto.Staphylococcus)
>>> onto.Staphylococcus
None
>>> onto2.Staphylococcus
bacteria.Staphylococcus
```

Finally, the `subclasses()` and `descendants()` methods of the OWL `Thing` and `Nothing` classes assume that they are called for `default_world` (indeed, these classes are shared by all worlds). If it is not the case, it is necessary to pass as a parameter the desired world, for example:

```
>>> list(Thing.descendants(world = my_world))
```

11.8 Summary

In this chapter, you have learned how to access directly to RDF triples in the Owlready quadstore and to perform SPARQL queries. We have also seen how to create several isolated worlds, for instance, for loading several copies of the same ontology.

APPENDIX A

Description logics

Description logics (DL) are a family of logics used by ontologies to formalize knowledge of a domain by describing the different concepts of this domain and the associated semantics. Semantics is expressed using predicates of the first-order logic. In order to keep a decidable system, only a subset of the first-order logic is used. The subset is chosen according to the needs of the field. This is why we speak of "description logics" in the plural, because there are a large number of different logics, depending on the subsets selected: with or without negation, with or without unions, and so on.

The different description logics are named using letters representing the elements of the first-order logic that they authorize. For example, the $\mathcal{AL}$ logic allows the universal concept $\top$, the empty concept $\bot$, the negation of an atomic concept $\neg A$, the intersection $A \sqcap B$, the universal restriction $\forall R.\ C$, and the existential restriction $\exists R.\ \top$, limited to the universal concept $\top$. The $\mathcal{ALU}$ logic is an extension of the $\mathcal{AL}$ logic which also allows the union $A \sqcup B$ and so on.

Description logics correspond to fragments of the first-order predicate logic with a single free variable. They are equipped with formal semantics, based on logic. An ontology $\mathcal{O}$ can be defined as a set of logical axioms Φ. These axioms are constructed from a set of individuals $\mathbb{I} = \{i, j, \ldots\}$, from a set of concepts $C = \{C, D, \ldots\}$, a set of roles $\mathbb{R} = \{R, S, \ldots\}$, and a set of constructors $\mathbb{S}$. These constructors make it possible to combine concepts and/or roles (depending on the constructor) and to define new concepts or roles. The types of axioms and the constructors depend on

L. Jean-Baptiste, *Ontologies with Python*, https://doi.org/10.1007/978-1-4842-6552-9

the logic of description considered. The main types of axioms are $C \sqsubseteq D$ (subsumption), $C \equiv D$ (equivalence), $C(i)$ (instantiation), and $R(i,j)$ (relation) and, for the description logic $\mathcal{ALCI}$, $\mathbb{S} = \{\neg, \sqcap, \sqcup, \forall, \exists, R^{-}\}$. Table A-1 lists the main types of axioms and the constructors.

Description logics have a formal semantics, which is defined in terms of interpretations. For an ontology $\mathcal{O}$, an interpretation $\mathcal{I} = (\Delta, f)$ is a pair comprising an interpretation domain Δ (which is a nonempty set) and an interpretation function $f()$ which, for each individual, concept, role, compound expression (defined using constructors), and axiom, returns its interpretation in the Δ domain, as follows:

$$f(i \in \mathbb{I}) \in \Delta$$

$$f(A \in \mathbb{C}) \subseteq \Delta$$

$$f(R \in \mathbb{R}) \subseteq \Delta \times \Delta$$

Table A-1. *Syntax and semantics of an ontology in a description logic. A and B are concepts, R is a role, i and j of individuals. The disjointedness has been added to facilitate its understanding, but it can be obtained by combining the intersection and the subsumption*

	Syntax	Description	Semantics
Constants	$\top$	Thing/Top	Δ
	$\bot$	Nothing/Bottom	$\varnothing$ (empty set)
Axioms	$A \sqsubseteq B$	A is subsumed by B	$f(A) \subseteq f(B)$
	$A \equiv B$	A is equivalent to B	$f(A) = f(B)$

(*continued*)

Table A-1. *(continued)*

	Syntax	Description	Semantics
	$A(i)$	i is an instance of A	$f(i) \in f(A)$
	$R(i,j)$	i and j related by R	$(f(i), f(j)) \in f(R)$
Constructors	$\neg A$	Complement of A	$\Delta \setminus f(A)$
	$A \sqcap B$	Intersection of A and B	$f(A) \cap f(B)$
	$A \sqcup B$	Union of A and B	$f(A) \cup f(B)$
	$\exists R.\ B$	Existential restriction	$\{a \in \Delta \mid \exists\ b, (a, b) \in f(R) \wedge b \in f(B)\}$
	$\forall R.\ B$	Universal restriction	$\{a \in \Delta \mid \forall\ b, (a, b) \in f(R) \rightarrow b \in f(B)\}$
	R^-	Inverse role	$\{(a, b) \in \Delta \times \Delta \mid (b, a) \in f(R)\}$
Disjointedness	$A \sqcap B \sqsubseteq \bot$	A and B are disjoint	$f(A) \cap f(B) = \varnothing$

The last column of Table A-1 shows the interpretation associated with each axiom and constructor. Using the interpretation function, the logical axioms of an ontology can be transformed into set formulas, which express the semantics of the ontology. For example, the axiom $A \sqsubseteq B \sqcap C$ is translated to $f(A \sqsubseteq B \sqcap C) = f(A) \subseteq f(B) \cap f(C)$.

An interpretation $\mathcal{I}$ satisfies an ontology $\mathcal{O}$ if it satisfies all the axioms of $\mathcal{O}$ (i.e., $\forall \Phi \in \mathcal{O}, f(\Phi)$ is true). An ontology $\mathcal{O}$ is consistent if there exists at least one interpretation $\mathcal{I}$ which satisfies $\mathcal{O}$ ($\mathcal{O}$ is inconsistent otherwise). A concept C is satisfiable in $\mathcal{O}$ if (and only if) there exists at least one interpretation $\mathcal{I}$ which satisfies $\mathcal{O}$ such that $f(C) \neq \varnothing$ (i.e., there exists an individual i which belongs to C).

For an ontology $\mathcal{O}$, $\Phi \in \mathcal{O}$ means that the axiom Φ belongs to the set $\mathcal{O}$ (i.e., the axiom has been asserted in the ontology), and $\mathcal{O} \models \Phi$ means that the axiom Φ can be inferred from the axioms in $\mathcal{O}$. The simple transitivity between the subsumption relations is generally not considered as an inference from this point of view: for example, if $\mathcal{O} = \{A \sqsubseteq B, B \sqsubseteq C\}$, we consider that $A \sqsubseteq C \in \mathcal{O}$. In fact, indirect subsumption relationships can be easily calculated, and a reasoner is not required for this task.

If you wish to explore the question from a theoretical point of view, you can find more information on the description logics in the following book:

> F. Baader, D. Calvanese, D.L. McGuinness, D. Nardi, P.L. Patel-Schneider. ***The description logic handbook: theory, implementation and applications***. Cambridge University Press, 2007
>
> `https://www.researchgate.net/publication/230745455_The_Description_Logic_Handbook_Theory_Implementation_and_Applications`

APPENDIX B

Notations for formal ontologies

The tables on the following pages give the correspondence between different notations for the ontologies : Protégé, Owlready, the description logics, as well as the corresponding semantics in set logic and first-order logic. The following table, available for download from the Internet, can be printed as a one-page memory aid:

www.lesfleursdunormal.fr/static/_downloads/great_ontology_table.pdf

		Protégé
Const.	Top	Thing
	Bottom	Nothing
Axioms	Class subsumption	A subclass of B
	Property subsumption	R subproperty of S
	Equivalence	A equivalent to B
	Instantiation	i type A
	Relations	i object property assertion j i data property assertion j

(*continued*)

L. Jean-Baptiste, *Ontologies with Python*, https://doi.org/10.1007/978-1-4842-6552-9

		Protégé
Semantic constructors	Complement (negation)	not A
	Intersection (and)	A and B
	Union (or)	A or B
	Extension	{i, j,...}
	Inverse	inverse of R
	Transitive closure	-
	Composition	R o S
	Existential restriction	R some B
	Universal restriction	R only B
	Cardinality restrictions	R exactly 2 B R max 2 B R min 2 B
	Value restriction	R value j
Decomp.	Disjoint	A disjoint with B
	Domain	R domain A
	Range	R range B

		Python + Owlready2
Const.	Top	Thing
	Bottom	Nothing

(continued)

		Python + Owlready2
Axioms	Subsumption	class A(B): ... (assertion) A.is_a.append(B) (assertion) issubclass(A, B) (test)
	Equivalence	A.equivalent_to.append(B) (assertion) B in A.equivalent_to (test)
	Instantiation	i = A() (assertion) i.is_instance_of.append(A) isinstance(i, A) (test)
	Relations	i.R = j (R is functional) i.R.append(j) (otherwise)
Semantic constructors	Complement (negation)	Not(A)
	Intersection (and)	A & B (or) And([A, B,...])
	Union (or)	A | B (or) Or([A, B,...])
	Extension	OneOf([i, j,...])
	Inverse	Inverse(R) (constructor) S.inverse = R (assertion)
	Transitive closure	-
	Composition	PropertyChain([R, S])
	Existential restriction	R.some(B)
	Universal restriction	R.only(B)
	Cardinality restrictions	R.exactly(2, B) R.max(2, B) R.min(2, B)
	Value restriction	R.value(j)

(continued)

		Python + Owlready2	
Decomposable	Disjoint	AllDisjoint([A, B])	
	Domain	R.domain = [A]	
	Range	R.range = [B]	
	Class property: Existential restriction	A.R = B A.R.append(B)	(R is functional) (otherwise)
	Universal restriction	A.R = B A.R.append(B) A.R.append(C)	(R is functional) (otherwise)
	Value restriction	A.R = j A.R.append(j)	(R is functional) (otherwise)

		Description Logics (DL)
Const.	Top	$\top$
	Bottom	$\bot$
Axioms	Class subsumption	$A \sqsubseteq B$
	Property subsumption	$R \sqsubseteq S$
	Equivalence	$A \equiv B$
	Instantiation	$A(i)$
	Relations	$R(i, j)$

(*continued*)

		Description Logics (DL)
Semantic constructors	Complement (negation)	$\neg A$
	Intersection (and)	$A \sqcap B$
	Union (or)	$A \sqcup B$
	Extension	$i, j, \ldots$
	Inverse	R^{-}
	Transitive closure	R^{+}
	Composition	$R \circ S$
	Existential restriction	$\exists R.\ B$
	Universal restriction	$\forall R.\ B$
	Cardinality	$=2R.\ B$
	restrictions	$\leq 2R.\ B$ $\geq 2R.\ B$
	Value restriction	$\exists R.\ \{j\}$
Decomposable	Disjoint	$A \sqcap B \sqsubseteq \bot$
	Domain	$\exists R.\ \top \sqsubseteq A$
	Range	$\top \sqsubseteq \forall R.\ B$
	Class property: Existential restriction	$A \sqsubseteq \exists R.\ B$
	Universal restriction	$A \sqsubseteq \forall R.\ (B \sqcup C \sqcup \ldots)$
	Value restriction	$A \sqsubseteq \exists R.\ \{j\} \wedge (\exists R^{-}.\ A)(j)$

		First-order logic
Const.	Top	$\top$, such as $\forall x$, $\top(x) = true$
	Bottom	$\bot$, such as $\forall x$, $\bot(x) = false$
Axioms	Class subsumption	$\forall x, A(x) \rightarrow B(x)$
	Property subsumption	$\forall x \forall y, R(x,y) \rightarrow S(x,y)$
	Equivalence	$\forall x, A(x) \leftrightarrow B(x)$
	Instantiation	$A(i)$
	Relations	$R(i,j)$
Semantic constructors	Complement (negation)	$\neg A(x)$
	Intersection (and)	$A(x) \wedge B(x)$
	Union (or)	$A(x) \vee B(x)$
	Extension	$x \in \{i, j, \ldots\}$
	Inverse	$\forall i \forall j, S(i,j) = R(j,i)$
	Transitive closure	
	Composition	
	Existential restriction	$\exists y, R(x,y) \wedge B(y)$
	Universal restriction	$\forall y, R(x,y) \rightarrow B(y)$
	Cardinality restrictions	$\lvert\{y \mid R(x,y) \wedge B(y)\}\rvert = 2$ $\lvert\{y \mid R(x,y) \wedge B(y)\}\rvert \leq 2$ $\lvert\{y \mid R(x,y) \wedge B(y)\}\rvert \geq 2$
	Value restriction	$R(x,j)$
Decomp.	Disjoint	$\forall x, \neg (A(x) \wedge B(x))$
	Domain	$\forall x, (\exists y, R(x,y)) \rightarrow A(x)$
	Range	$\forall x \forall y, R(x,y) \rightarrow B(y)$

		Set notation
Const.	Top	Δ
	Bottom	$\varnothing$
Axioms	Class subsumption	$f(A) \subseteq f(B)$
	Property subsumption	$f(R) \subseteq f(S)$
	Equivalence	$f(A) = f(B)$
	Instantiation	$f(i) \in f(A)$
	Relations	$(f(i), f(j)) \in f(R)$
Semantic constructors	Complement (negation)	$\Delta \setminus f(A)$
	Intersection (and)	$f(A) \cap f(B)$
	Union (or)	$f(A) \cup f(B)$
	Extension	$\{f(i), f(j), \ldots\}$
	Inverse	$\{(a, b) \mid (b, a) \in f(R)\}$
	Transitive closure	$\cup i_{\geq 1}(f(R))i$
	Composition	$\{(a, c) \in \Delta \times \Delta \mid \exists b, (a, b) \in f(R) \wedge (b, c) \in f(S)\}$
	Existential restriction	$\{a \in \Delta \mid \exists b, (a, b) \in f(R) \wedge b \in f(B)\}$
	Universal restriction	$\{a \in \Delta \mid \forall b, (a, b) \in f(R) \rightarrow b \in f(B)\}$
	Cardinality restrictions	$\{a \in \Delta \mid \lvert\{b \mid (a, b) \in f(R) \wedge b \in f(B)\}\rvert = 2\}$ $\{a \in \Delta \mid \lvert\{b \mid (a, b) \in f(R) \wedge b \in f(B)\}\rvert \leq 2\}$ $\{a \in \Delta \mid \lvert\{b \mid (a, b) \in f(R) \wedge b \in f(B)\}\rvert \geq 2\}$
	Value restriction	$\{a \in \Delta \mid (a, f(j)) \in f(R)\}$
Decomp.	Disjoint	$f(A) \cap f(B) = \varnothing$
	Domain	$f(R) \subseteq \{(a, b) \mid a \in f(A)\}$
	Range	$f(R) \subseteq \{(a, b) \mid b \in f(B)\}$

APPENDIX C

Reference manual

C.1 World class

Attributes

- filename: The name of the file where the quadstore is saved or :memory: if it is stored in RAM. Read-only (use the set_backend() method to set the filename).
- full_text_search_properties: The list of properties for which full-text search is enabled. The list can be modified to add or remove properties.
- graph: The associated RDF graph object (not an RDFlib graph). Read-only.
- ontologies: A dictionary matching IRIs to ontologies currently loaded. Read-only.

Operators and special syntax

- world["<IRI>"]: Returns an entity from its IRI (or None if there is no entity with the requested IRI).

L. Jean-Baptiste, *Ontologies with Python*, https://doi.org/10.1007/978-1-4842-6552-9

Methods

- `search(_use_str_as_loc_str = True, _case_sensitive = True, iri, ...)`: Searches for entities and returns a (lazy) list with the entities found.

  `_use_str_as_loc_str`: If this parameter is `True`, Python strings to search for can be matched to localized strings (`locstr`).

  `_case_sensitive`: If this parameter is `True`, the case is taken into account when matching character strings (that is to say that the lowercase and uppercase letters are considered as different).

  iri (optional): The IRI of the concept sought, in the form of a character string which may contain wildcards ("*" character).

  type = **Class** (optional): Searches for individuals of the class Class. A list of classes can also be passed as a parameter.

  subclass_of = **Class** (optional): Searches for subclasses of the class Class. A list of classes can also be passed as a parameter.

  is_a = **Class** (optional): Matches both the `type` and `subclass_of` parameters (either one) and allows you to find both subclasses and individuals.

  <property> = **value** (optional): Searches for entities with the given value for the given property. The special value can be used as a wildcard to indicate the presence of a relation, whatever the value. The value None can be used to indicate that there is no relationship. A list of values can also be passed as a parameter.

- search_one(_use_str_as_loc_str = True, _case_sensitive = True, iri, ...): Searches for an entity. If several entities match the search criteria, only one is returned (according to an arbitrary choice). The parameters are the same as for the search() method earlier.
- get_ontology(base_iri): Creates a new ontology from its IRI (or returns the already existing ontology, if there is one).

  base_iri: The IRI of the ontology.
- get_namespace(base_iri): Creates a namespace (see 4.8).

  base_iri: The IRI of the namespace created.
- set_backend(filename = "/name/of/the/quadstore/file.sqlite3"): Saves the quadstore to the specified file.

  filename: The filename of the quadstore.
- save(file = None, format = "rdfxml"): Saves the quadstore. Without parameters, the quadstore is saved in its file (corresponds to the filename attribute) in SQLite3 format. The file and format parameters are used to export the quadstore in an OWL file.

  file: The filename for saving the quadstore or a Python file object.

  format: The file format.

- `close()`: Closes the quadstore.
- `get(iri, default = None)`: Returns an entity from its IRI (or `default` if there is no such entity).

  `iri`: The desired IRI.

  `default`: The value returned if the entity does not exist.
- `get_if_loaded(iri, default = None)`: Returns an entity from its IRI, only if the entity is already loaded in memory and available in cache. Otherwise, returns `default`.

  `iri`: The desired IRI.

  `default`: The value returned if the entity does not exist.
- `new_blank_node()`: Creates a new blank node.
- `as_rdflib_graph()`: Returns a graph object, compatible with RDFlib.
- `sparql_query()`: Performs a SPARQL query (see 11.3).
- `classes()`: Returns a generator for iterating all classes.
- `inconsistent_classes()`: Returns a generator for iterating all inconsistent classes (that is to say, equivalent to `Nothing`).
- `individuals()`: Returns a generator for iterating over all individuals.
- `properties()`: Returns a generator for iterating over all properties.
- `data_properties()`: Returns a generator for iterating over all data properties.

- `object_properties()`: Returns a generator for iterating over all object properties.
- `annotation_properties()`: Returns a generator for iterating over all annotation properties.
- `disjoints()`: Returns a generator for iterating over all disjoints (of classes and properties) and all distinctions (of individuals).
- `disjoints_classes()`: Returns a generator for iterating over all disjoints of classes (`AllDisjoint`).
- `disjoints_properties()`: Returns a generator for iterating over all disjoints of properties (`AllDisjoint`).
- `different_individuals()`: Returns a generator for iterating over all distinctions of individuals (`AllDifferent`).
- `rules()`: Returns a generator for iterating over all SWRL rules.
- `variables()`: Returns a generator for iterating over all SWRL variables.
- `general_axioms()`: Returns a generator for iterating over all general axioms.

C.2 Ontology class

Attributes

- `base_iri`: The IRI of the ontology (including the trailing character, "#" or "/"). Read-only.
- `name`: The name of the ontology (i.e., the last part of the base IRI).

- imported_ontologies: The list of imported ontologies. Can be modified, for adding or removing imports.
- loaded: True if the ontology has been loaded (with load()) and False otherwise. Read-only.
- graph: The associated RDF graph object (not an RDFlib graph). Read-only.
- metadata: The ontology metadata. Allows accessing or modifying the ontology's annotations (see 8.6).
- python_module: The name of the Python module that is loaded with the ontology (optional).
- storid: The ontology identifier in the Owlready quadstore.
- world: The world in which the ontology is defined (by default, it is default_world). Read-only.

Operators and special syntax

- ontology.<entity name>: Returns an entity of the ontology, whose IRI is the concatenation of the base IRI of the ontology and the entity name. Returns None if the entity does not exist.
- ontology["<entity name>: (idem)"].

Methods

- load(only_local = False, fileobj = None, reload = False, reload_if_newer = False): Loads the ontology from the file object passed as an argument, from a local cache directory (in onto_path), or from its IRI (in decreasing order of priority).

`only_local`: If this parameter is `True`, the ontology will not be downloaded from the Internet.

`fileobj`: A Python file object from which the ontology is loaded (optional, can be used to force the load from a given file).

`reload`: If this parameter is `True`, the ontology will be reloaded, even if it has already been loaded before.

`reload_if_newer`: If this parameter is `True`, the ontology will be reloaded, even if it has already been loaded before, but only if the local copy is newer than the one present in the quadstore.

- `save(file = None, format = "rdfxml")`: Saves the ontology in a file. Parameters are:

  `file`: The file where to save the ontology; it can be a filename or a Python file object.

  `format`: The file format (supported file format for writing: “rdfxml” and “N-Triples”).

- `destroy()`: Destroys the ontology from the quadstore.
- `get_namespace(base_iri)`: Creates a namespace in this ontology (see 4.8).

  `base_iri`: The IRI of the namespace.

- `search(_use_str_as_loc_str = True, iri, ...)`: Searches for some entities defined in this ontology and returns a (lazy) list with the entities. The parameters are the same as for the `search()` method of the `World` class.

- `search_one(_use_str_as_loc_str = True, iri, ...)`: Searches for some entities defined in this ontology and returns a (lazy) list with the entities. If several entities match the search criteria, only one is returned (according to an arbitrary choice). The parameters are the same as for the `search_one()` method of the `World` class.
- `classes()`: Returns a generator to iterate over all the classes defined in the ontology.
- `inconsistent_classes()`: Returns a generator to iterate over inconsistent classes defined in the ontology (i.e., classes equivalent to `Nothing`).
- `individuals()`: Returns a generator to iterate over all the individuals defined in the ontology.
- `properties()`: Returns a generator to iterate over all the properties defined in the ontology.
- `data_properties()`: Returns a generator to iterate over all the data properties defined in the ontology.
- `object_properties()`: Returns a generator to iterate over all the object properties defined in the ontology.
- `annotation_properties()`: Returns a generator to iterate over all the annotation properties defined in the ontology.
- `disjoints()`: Returns a generator for iterating over all disjoints (of classes and properties) and all distinctions (of individuals) defined in the ontology.

- `disjoints_classes()`: Returns a generator for iterating over all disjoints of classes (`AllDisjoint`) defined in the ontology.
- `disjoints_properties()`: Returns a generator for iterating over all disjoints of properties (`AllDisjoint`) defined in the ontology.
- `different_individuals()`: Returns a generator for iterating over all distinctions of individuals (`AllDifferent`) defined in the ontology.
- `rules()`: Returns a generator for iterating over all SWRL rules defined in the ontology.
- `variables()`: Returns a generator for iterating over all SWRL variables defined in the ontology.
- `general_axioms()`: Returns a generator for iterating over all general axioms defined in the ontology.

C.3 Classes (`ThingClass` class)

Attributes

- `name`: The name or identifier of the class (i.e., the last part of the IRI, after the trailing character "#" or "/").
- `iri`: The IRI of the class.
- `namespace`: The namespace in which the class is located; it can be an ontology (if the IRI of the class is the concatenation of the IRI of the ontology with the class name) or an object of the class `Namespace` otherwise. Read-only.

- `is_a`: The list of parent classes, including constructors. This list can be modified.
- `equivalent_to`: The list of equivalent classes, including constructors. This list can be modified.
- `storid`: The identifier of the class in the Owlready quadstore.
- `defined_class`: Boolean annotation indicating if the class is defined. The default value is `False`; if the value is set to `True`, Owlready generates a class definition when class properties are used (see 6.4).

Operators and special syntax

- `class.`<annotation_property_name>: Returns the list of annotation values for the class (e.g., `Class.label`, `Class.comment`, etc.).
- `class.INDIRECT_`<annotation_property_name>: Returns the list of annotation values for the class, including indirect values (due to annotation property inheritance).
- `class.`<data_or_object_property_name>: Returns the value or values of the existential and value restrictions on the class for this property. Returns a single value if the property is functional or returns a list otherwise.
- `class.INDIRECT_`<data_or_object_property_name>: Returns all the values of the existential and value restrictions on the class for this property, including indirect relations due to class inheritance, property inheritance, or transitive, symmetric, or reflexive properties.

Methods

- `ancestors(include_self = True, include_constructs = False)`: Returns the set of ancestor classes of the class (mother classes, grandmothers, etc.). The parameters are:

  `include_self`: If this parameter is `True`, the class itself is included in the returned set.

  `include_constructs`: If this parameter is `True`, constructors are included in the returned set.

- `subclasses(only_loaded = False, world = None)`: Returns a generator for iterating over the direct child classes of the given class. Parameters are:

  `only_loaded`: If this parameter is `True`, only classes already loaded in Python are considered.

  `world`: This parameter is used to indicate the world in which to look for the child classes; it is only used for the `Thing` and `Nothing` classes, when using a world other than `default_world`.

- `descendants(include_self = True, only_loaded = False, world = None)`: Returns the set of classes descending from the class (child classes, children of a child class, etc.). Parameters are:

  `include_self`: If this parameter is `True`, the class itself is included in the returned set.

  `only_loaded`: If this parameter is `True`, only classes already loaded in Python are considered.

`world`: This parameter is used to indicate the world in which to look for the descendant classes; it is only used for the `Thing` and `Nothing` classes, when using a world other than `default_world`.

- `instances(world = None)`: Returns the list of instances (or individuals) belonging to the class (or one of its descendant classes). The parameter is:

  `world`: This parameter is used to indicate the world in which to look for instances; it is only used for the `Thing` and `Nothing` classes, when using a world other than `default_world`.

- `direct_instances(world = None)`: Returns the list of instances (or individuals) directly belonging to the class, excluding those belonging to a descendant class. The parameter is:

  `world`: This parameter is used to indicate the world in which to look for instances; it is only used for the `Thing` and `Nothing` classes, when using a world other than `default_world`.

- `get_class_properties()`: Returns the set of properties for which the class has at least one relation (*via* a restriction). The value of these restrictions can then be obtained either with the dotted notation "Class.property_name" or with the alternative syntax "property[Class]".

- `INDIRECT_get_class_properties()`: Returns the set of properties for which the class has at least one direct or indirect relationship (*via* a restriction and taking into account class inheritance, property inheritance, and transitive, symmetric, and reflexive properties). The value of these restrictions can then be obtained with the dotted notation "Class.INDIRECT_property_name".

- `constructs()`: Returns a generator to iterate over the constructors that refer to the class.
- `inverse_restrictions(Prop = None)`: Returns a generator to iterate over the restrictions that reference the class. The parameter is:

  `Prop`: If this parameter is not `None`, the results are tailored to the restrictions on the property `Prop`.
- `disjoints()`: Returns a generator to iterate over disjoints that include the class.

C.4 Individuals (Thing class)

Attributes

- `name`: The name or identifier of the individual (i.e., the last part of the IRI, after the trailing character "#" or "/").
- `iri`: The IRI of the individual.
- `namespace`: The namespace in which the individual is located; it can be an ontology (if the IRI of the individual is the concatenation of the IRI of the ontology with the individual name) or an object of the class `Namespace` otherwise. Read-only.
- `is_a`: The list of the classes the individual belongs to, including constructors. This list can be modified.

- equivalent_to: The list of identical (i.e., equivalent) individuals (corresponds to the *same as* OWL relation). This list can be modified.
- storid: The identifier of the individual in the Owlready quadstore.

Operators and special syntax

- individual.<property_name>: Returns the individual's value(s) for this property. Returns a single value if the property is functional or a list otherwise. The returned values take into account the inverse properties.
- individual.INDIRECT_<property_name>: Returns all the values of the individual for this property, including the indirectly deducible relations (due to the class inheritance, property inheritance, and transitive, symmetric, and reflexive properties).

Methods

- differents(): Returns a generator to iterate over the distinction (i.e., disjoints) that includes the individual (corresponds to *different from* OWL relations).
- get_properties(): Returns the set of properties for which the individual has at least one relation. The value of these relations can then be obtained either with the dotted notation "individual.property_name" or with the alternative syntax "property[individual]".
- INDIRECT_get_properties(): Returns the set of properties for which the individual has at least one direct or indirect relation (due to the class inheritance, property inheritance, and transitive, symmetric, and

reflexive properties). The value of these relations can then be obtained with the dotted notation "individual. INDIRECT_property_name".

- `get_inverse_properties()`: Returns a generator to iterate over the properties for which the individual has at least one inverse relation (i.e., of which it is the object). The generator yields couples of the form (other_individual, Property), such that the relation "other_individual Property individual" exists.
- `generate_default_name()`: Returns a name for the individual. This method is called at the creation of an individual. The default implementation returns the class name in lowercase, followed by a number (1, then 2, 3, etc.). This method can be reimplemented.

C.5 Properties (`PropertyClass` class and its descendants)

Attributes

- `name`: The name or identifier of the property (i.e., the last part of the IRI, after the trailing character "#" or "/").
- `iri`: The IRI of the property.
- `namespace`: The namespace in which the property is located; it can be an ontology (if the IRI of the property is the concatenation of the IRI of the ontology with the property name) or an object of the class `Namespace` otherwise. Read-only.

- `is_a`: The list of parent properties, including constructors. This list can be modified.
- `equivalent_to`: The list of equivalent properties, including constructors. This list can be modified.
- `storid`: The identifier of the property in the Owlready quadstore.
- `python_name`: The name used in Python to access the property via the dotted notation "individual.property_name". It defaults to the name attribute, but can be modified.
- `inverse`: The inverse property of this property (or `None` if none has been declared).
- `domain`: The list of domains of the property. This list can be modified.
- `range`: The list of ranges of the property. This list can be modified.
- `range_iri`: The list of ranges of the property in the form of IRIs. Useful in particular for data properties to be able to distinguish between the different types of integer, float, and so on, datatypes recognized by OWL but not distinguished by Python and Owlready.
- `property_chain`: The property chains to which this property is equivalent.
- `class_property_type`: Indicating the type of restrictions created when this property is used as class properties. This attribute is a list; the allowed values are `["some"]`, `["only"]`, `["some", "only"]`, and `["relation"]` (see 6.3).

Operators and special syntax

- property.<annotation_property_name>: Returns the list of annotation values for the property.
- property.INDIRECT_<annotation_property_name>: Returns the list of annotation values for the property, including indirect values (due to annotation property inheritance).
- property[<entity>]: Returns the list of property values for the given entity. Always returns a list, even if the property is functional.
- annotation_property[<entity>, <property>, <value>]: Returns the list of annotation values for the given relation, expressed as an (entity, property, value) triple.

Methods

- ancestors(include_self = True): Returns the set of ancestor properties of the property (parent properties, grandparents, etc.). The parameter is:

  include_self: If this parameter is True, the property itself is included in the returned set.

- subclasses(only_loaded = False, world = None): Returns a generator for iterating over the child properties of the property. Parameters are:

  only_loaded: If this parameter is True, only properties already loaded in Python are considered.

  world: This parameter is used to indicate the world in which to look for subproperties; it is used only for the following properties: Property, ObjectProperty, DataProperty, and AnnotationProperty, when using a world other than default_world.

- `descendants(include_self = True, only_loaded = False, world = None)`: Returns the set of properties descending from the property (child properties, children of child properties, etc.). Parameters are:

  `include_self`: If this parameter is `True`, the property itself is included in the returned set.

  `only_loaded`: If this parameter is `True`, only properties already loaded in Python are considered.

  `world`: This parameter is used to indicate the world in which to look for descendant properties; it is used only for the following properties: `Property`, `ObjectProperty`, `DataProperty`, and `AnnotationProperty`, when using a world other than `default_world`.

- `disjoints()`: Returns a generator to iterate over disjoints that include the property.

- `some(Class)`: Creates an existential restriction on the property. The parameter is:

  `Class`: The class to which the restriction relates or None for an untyped existential restriction.

- `only(Class)`: Creates a universal restriction on the property. The parameter is:

  `Class`: The class to which the restriction relates.

- `value(value)`: Creates a value restriction on the property. The parameter is:

`value`: The value to which the restriction relates, which can be an individual or a datatype value.

- `exactly(nb, value = None)`: Creates an exact cardinality restriction on the property. Parameters are:

  `nb`: The cardinality.

  `value`: The value to which the restriction relates or `None` for an untyped restriction.

- `min(nb, value = None)`: Creates a minimum cardinality restriction on the property. Parameters are:

  `nb`: The cardinality.

  `value`: The value to which the restriction relates or `None` for an untyped restriction.

- `max(nb, value = None)`: Creates a maximum cardinality restriction on the property. Parameters are:

  `nb`: The cardinality.

  `value`: The value to which the restriction relates or `None` for an untyped restriction.

- `has_self(value = True)`: Creates a "has self" restriction on the property. The parameter is:

  `value`: `True` if the relationship with oneself is present (default value) or `False` otherwise.

C.6 Constructs (Contruct class and its descendants)

Methods

- subclasses(only_loaded = False): Returns the list of the constructor's child classes (the list also includes the classes declared as equivalent to the constructor). The parameter is:

  only_loaded: If this parameter is True, only constructors already loaded in Python are considered.

- destroy(): Destroys the constructor (usually automatically called by Owlready).

C.6.1 Restriction class

Attributes

- property: The property to which the restriction relates.
- type: The type of the restriction (a value among the following constants: SOME, ONLY, VALUE, MAX, MIN, EXACTLY, and HAS_SELF).
- value: The value to which the restriction relates (a class for restrictions of the type SOME, ONLY, MAX, MIN, and EXACTLY or an individual or a datatype value for VALUE restrictions, a Boolean for HAS_SELF restrictions).
- cardinality: The cardinality of the restriction (only available for MAX, MIN, and EXACTLY restrictions).

C.6.2 Intersection (And class)

Attributes

- `Classes`: The list of classes to which the intersection relates.

C.6.3 Union (Or class)

Attributes

- `Classes`: The list of classes to which the union relates.

C.6.4 Complement (Not class)

Attributes

- `Class`: The class to which the complement relates.

C.6.5 Property inverse (Inverse class)

Attributes

- `property`: The property that is inverted.

C.6.6 Individual set (OneOf class)

Attributes

- `instances`: The list of individuals involved.

C.7 SWRL rules

C.7.1 `Variable` class

Attributes

- `name`: The name of the variable (without the initial "?").
- `iri`: The IRI of the variable of the form "urn:swrl#<variable_name>".

C.7.2 Rules (`Imp` class)

Attributes

- `body`: The list of the rule conditions (implicitly linked by logical "and"). Corresponds to the "if" part of the rule.
- `head`: The list of the rule consequences. Corresponds to the "then" part of the rule.

Operators and special syntax

- `str(rule)`: Translates the rule into a rule language similar to that of Protégé, in a character string (e.g., "Woman(?X) -> Person(?X)").

Methods

- `set_as_rule(rule, namespaces = None)`: Defines the rule from a string in a rule language similar to that of Protégé. If the rule already had conditions or consequences, these are destroyed and replaced by the new rule. Parameters are:

  `rule`: The rule, expressed as a string.

`namespaces`: A list of namespaces (ontology or `Namespace`) in which entities (class, properties, etc.) are searched. By default, the ontology in which the rule is defined is used.

- `get_variable(name, create = True)`: Returns a variable defined in the rule ontology from its name. Parameters are:

  `name`: The name of the variable (starting by "?").

  `create`: If this parameter is `True`, and the requested variable does not exist yet, a new variable is created and returned.

C.7.3 Class assertion atom (`ClassAtom` class)

Attributes

- `class_predicate`: The OWL class.
- `arguments`: The list of arguments, comprising a single element—the variable or the individual belonging to the class.

Syntax in SWRL rule language

- ClassName(?variable)
- `http://server.org/full/iri/ontology.owl#ClassName(?variable)`

C.7.4 Datatype assertion atom (`DataRangeAtom` class)

Attributes

- `data_range`: The datatype (e.g., `int` or `float`).
- `arguments`: The list of arguments, comprising a single element—the variable belonging to the given datatype.

Syntax in SWRL rule language

- Datatype(?variable), for example: int(?x)

C.7.5 Object property value atom (`IndividualPropertyAtom` class)

Attributes

- `property_predicate`: The OWL object property.
- `arguments`: The argument list, consisting of two elements—the variable or individual and the property value for that variable/individual.

Syntax in SWRL rule language

- PropertyName(?variable, individual)
- PropertyName(individual, ?variable)
- PropertyName(?variable1, ?variable2)
- `http://server.org/full/iri/ontology.owl#PropertyName`(?variable, individual)

- http://server.org/full/iri/ontology.owl#PropertyName(individual, ?variable)
- http://server.org/full/iri/ontology.owl#PropertyName(?variable1, ?variable2)

C.7.6 Data property value atom (DatavaluedPropertyAtom class)

Attributes

- property_predicate: The OWL data property.
- arguments: The argument list, consisting of two elements—the variable or individual and the property value for that variable/individual.

Syntax in SWRL rule language

- PropertyName(?variable, value), examples of values are 1, 1.5, character string
- PropertyName(?variable1, ?variable2)
- http://server.org/full/iri/ontology.owl#PropertyName(?variable, value)
- http://server.org/full/iri/ontology.owl#PropertyName(?variable1, ?variable2)

C.7.7 Same individual atom (SameIndividualAtom class)

Attributes

- arguments: The list of arguments, comprising two elements, which can be variables or individuals.

Syntax in SWRL rule language

- SameAs(?variable1, ?variable2)

C.7.8 Distinct individual atom (`DifferentIndividualAtom` class)

Attributes

- `arguments`: The list of arguments, comprising two elements, which can be variables or individuals.

Syntax in SWRL rule language

- DifferentFrom(?variable1, ?variable2)

C.7.9 Built-in function atom (`BuiltinAtom` class)

Attributes

- `builtin`: The predefined function in the form of a character string, for example, "add" or "multiply".
- `arguments`: The list of arguments; the number of arguments depends on the chosen builtin function.

Syntax in SWRL rule language

- builtin(?argument1, ?argument2,...)

C.8 PyMedTermino2

C.8.1 Terminology class

Attributes

- `name`: The name of the terminology.
- `iri`: The full IRI of the terminology in PyMedTermino2.
- `children`: The list of the root concept in the hierarchy of the terminology.

Operators and special syntax

- `terminology[<code>]`: Returns the concept corresponding to the code passed as index or `None` if there is no corresponding concept in the terminology.

Methods

- `descendant_concepts(include_self = True, no_double = True)`: Returns the list of all the concepts in the terminology. The returned list is a "special list" which combines the advantages of a Python list with those of a generator: if this list is used in a loop, the concepts will be loaded as the iterations go. Parameters are:

  `include_self`: If this parameter is `True`, the terminology itself is included in the returned list.

  `no_double`: If this parameter is `True`, duplicates are eliminated (NB: this only has an impact for multiaxial terminologies, that is to say, using multiple inheritance, such as SNOMED CT but not CIM10).

- `search(keywords)`: Performs a full-text search in the labels and synonyms of the terminology. The parameter is:

  `keywords`: The keyword(s). Several keywords can be separated by spaces, and the character "*" can be used as a wildcard at the end of the word.

- `has_concept(code)`: Returns `True` if the given code corresponds to a concept in the terminology. The parameter is:

  `code`: The code to search for.

C.8.2 Concept in a terminology

Attributes

- `name`: The code of the concept.
- `iri`: The full IRI of the concept in PyMedTermino2.
- `terminology`: The terminology containing the concept.
- `parents`: The list of the parent concepts (NB: for monoaxial terminologies such as ICD10, the list has at most one element).
- `children`: The list of the child concepts.

Operators and special syntax

- `concept >> terminology`: Maps the concept to another terminology and returns a set of concepts belonging to this other terminology. The returned set can contain zero, one, or more concepts.

Methods

- `ancestor_concepts(include_self = True, no_double = True)`: Returns the list of the ancestor concepts of a concept (i.e., parent, grandparents, etc.). The returned list is a "special list" which combines the advantages of a Python list with those of a generator: if this list is used in a loop, the concepts will be loaded as the iterations go. Parameters are:

  `include_self`: If this parameter is `True`, the concept itself is included in the returned list.

  `no_double`: If this parameter is `True`, duplicates are eliminated (NB: this only has an impact for multiaxial terminologies, that is to say, using multiple inheritance, such as SNOMED CT, but not ICD10).

- `descendant_concepts(include_self = True, no_double = True)`: Returns the list of descendant concepts in the terminology (i.e., children, grandchildren, etc.). The returned list is a "special list" which combines the advantages of a Python list with those of a generator: if this list is used in a loop, the concepts will be loaded as the iterations go. Parameters are:

  `include_self`: If this parameter is `True`, the concept itself is included in the returned list.

  `no_double`: If this parameter is `True`, duplicates are eliminated (NB: this only has an impact for multiaxial terminologies, that is to say, using multiple inheritance, such as SNOMED CT, but not ICD10).

C.8.3 Set of concepts (`Concepts` class)

Operators and special syntax

- `concepts & concepts`: Performs the (standard, i.e., nonsemantic) intersection of two sets.
- `concepts | concepts`: Performs the (standard) union of two sets.
- `concepts - concepts`: Performs the (standard) difference of two sets.
- `concepts >> terminology`: Maps the set of concepts to another terminology and returns a set of concepts belonging to this other terminology. The returned set can contain zero, one, or more concepts.

Methods

- `add()`, `clear()`, `discard()`, `isdisjoint()`, `issubset()`, `issuperset()`, `intersection()`, `union()`, `difference()`, `symmetric_difference()`, `remove()`, `update()`, `copy()`: These methods are inherited from Python's set class and behave identically to standard Python sets.
- `find(parent_concept)`: Returns the first concept of the set which is the sought concept or one of its descendants. The parameter is:

  `parent_concept`: The concept to find in the set.
- `extract(parent_concept)`: Returns the subset of concepts in the set that descend from the given concept (including the given concept itself). This method is

similar to `find()`, but it returns all the concepts in the set matching the criterion, not only the first one encountered. The parameter is:

`parent_concept`: The concept to find from the set.

- `subtract(parent_concept)`: Returns a new set, containing all the concepts of the initial set, except those which descend from the concept passed as a parameter (including the concept itself). This method is similar to `extract()`, but it returns all the concepts in the set that do not match the criteria, not the ones that do. The parameter is:

  `parent_concept`: The concept to subtract from the set.

- `subtract_update(parent_concept)`: Removes from the set all the concepts which descend from the concept passed as a parameter (including the concept itself). This method is similar to `subtract()`, but it modifies the set in place instead of returning a new set. The parameter is:

  `parent_concept`: The concept to subtract from the set.

- `imply(other)`: Returns `True` if the set of concepts implies the other set passed as a parameter, that is, if all the concepts of the other set are descendants of at least one concept of the set. The parameter is:

  `other`: The other set for the comparison.

- `is_semantic_subset(other)`: Returns `True` if the set is a semantic subset of the other set passed as a parameter, that is, if all the concepts of the set are descendants from at least one concept of the other set. The parameter is:

  `other`: The other set for the comparison.

- `is_semantic_superset(other)`: Returns `True` if the set is a semantic superset of the other set passed as a parameter, that is, if all the concepts of the set are the ancestor of at least one concept of the other set. The parameter is:

  `other`: The other set for the comparison.

- `is_semantic_disjoint(other)`: Returns True if the set is semantically disjoint from the other set passed as a parameter, that is, if no concept of one of the sets is a descendant of a concept of the other set. Be careful, this method does not take into account the common descendants that the concepts may have: for example, the sets {cardiac disease} and {infection} will be considered as semantically disjoint even though there are infectious heart diseases. The parameter is:

  `other`: The other set for the comparison.

- `semantic_intersection(other)`: Returns the semantic intersection of two sets of concepts. This method takes into account the inheritance relations which may exist between the concepts of the two sets; on the other hand, it does not take into account the inheritance relations with other concepts absent from the two sets (e.g., the descendants common to several concepts of the two sets). The parameter is:

other: The other set for the comparison.

- keep_most_specific(more_specific_than = None): Keeps only the most specific concepts in the set and removes all concepts more general than another concept from the set (or from the set passed as a parameter, if it is not None). The parameter is:

  more_specific_than: If this parameter is present, it is the set of more general concepts to consider. If this parameter is absent, the set itself is used.

- keep_most_generic(more_generic_than = None): Keeps only the most general concepts in the set and removes all concepts more specific than another concept from the set (or from the set passed as a parameter, if it is not None). The parameter is:

  more_specific_than: If this parameter is present, it is the set of more specific concepts to consider. If this parameter is absent, the set itself is used.

- remove_entire_families(only_family_with_more_than_one_child = True): Removes all "entire families" from the set and replaces them with their parent concept. An entire family is a subset of concepts that make up all of the children of a parent concept. For example, if the concept "Digestive disease" has four child concepts "Mouth disease", "Esophageal disease", "Stomach disease", and "Bowel disease" (and no other child concepts), then the set {Mouth Disease,

Esophageal Disease, Stomach Disease and Bowel Disease} constitutes a complete family, which will be replaced by their common parent, Digestive Disease, by this method. The parameter is:

`only_family_with_more_than_one_child`: If this parameter is `True`, a family made of a single element will be ignored.

- `lowest_common_ancestors()`: Returns the set of the lowest common ancestors to the concepts of this set. This method makes it possible to "generalize" several concepts by one or more concepts of a higher level. For monoaxial terminologies (such as ICD10), the returned set contains a single concept.
- `all_subsets()`: Returns the list of all the subsets included in this set, that is, all the sets including part of the concepts of the set (including the empty set and the set itself).

C.9 Global functions

- `sync_reasoner(x = None, infer_property_values = False, debug = 1, keep_tmp_file = False)`: Executes the reasoner and applies the inferences to the quadstore. Parameters are:

  `x`: The object on which to reason. It can be a world or a list of ontologies. By default, `default_world` is used.

  `infer_property_values`: If this parameter is `True`, the values of the properties of individuals are also inferred.

debug: The level of verbosity (1 by default). The value 0 prevents any display.

keep_tmp_file: If this parameter is True, temporary files will not be deleted after reasoning. This option is useful for debugging if there is a problem with the reasoning.

- sync_reasoner_hermit(x = None, infer_property_values = False, debug = 1, keep_tmp_file = False): As before, but forces the use of the HermiT reasoner.
- sync_reasoner_pellet(x = None, infer_property_values = False, debug = 1, keep_tmp_file = False): As before, but forces the use of the Pellet reasoner.
- close_world(entity, Properties = None, close_instance_list = True, recursive = True): Automatically creates constructors and restrictions to consider the given entity in a closed world (and not in an open world as it is the default). Parameters are:

  entity: The entity to consider in a closed world. It can be an individual, a class, or an ontology.

  Properties: The list of properties to consider when closing. If the value is None (the default), all properties are taken into account.

  close_instance_list: If this parameter is True, the list of individuals in each class is restricted to the existing individuals.

`recursive`: If this parameter is `True` and the entity is a class, the `close_world()` function is called recursively on subclasses and individuals of the class.

- `set_render_func(func)`: Defines the function to use to render entities, that is, to transform them into strings for display.

  `func`: The render function. It must take an entity as a parameter and return a string.

- `set_datatype_iri(datatype, iri)`: Sets (or redefines) the default IRI associated with a standard Python datatype.

  `datatype`: The Python datatype (e.g., `int` or `float`).

  `iri`: The IRI to associate with this datatype.

- `declare_datatype(datatype, iri, parser, unparser)`: Declares a new Python datatype and associates it with an OWL datatype and IRI (see 11.6).

  `datatype`: The Python datatype (usually a user-defined Python class).

  `iri`: The IRI to associate with this datatype.

  `parser`: A function for parsing the new datatype from a string. This function must accept a string as a parameter and return the parsed datatype value.

  `unparser`: A function for serializing the new datatype to a string. This function must accept a datatype value as a parameter and return the corresponding string description.

Index

A, B

C

L. Jean-Baptiste, *Ontologies with Python*, https://doi.org/10.1007/978-1-4842-6552-9

R

S

T

U, V

W, X, Y, Z